COMPUTATIONAL THINKING EDUCATION IN K–12

COMPUTATIONAL THINKING EDUCATION IN K–12

ARTIFICIAL INTELLIGENCE LITERACY AND PHYSICAL COMPUTING

EDITED BY SIU-CHEUNG KONG AND HAROLD ABELSON

THE MIT PRESS   CAMBRIDGE, MASSACHUSETTS   LONDON, ENGLAND

The MIT Press would like to thank the anonymous peer reviewers who provided comments on drafts of this book. The generous work of academic experts is essential for establishing the authority and quality of our publications. We acknowledge with gratitude the contributions of these otherwise uncredited readers.

This book was set in Stone Serif and Avenir LT Std by Westchester Publishing Services. Printed and bound in the United States of America.

Library of Congress Cataloging-in-Publication Data

Names: Kong, Siu Cheung, editor. | Abelson, Harold, editor.
Title: Computational thinking education in K-12 : artificial intelligence
    literacy and physical computing / edited by Siu-Cheung Kong and Harold
    Abelson.
Description: Cambridge, Massachusetts ; London, England : The MIT Press,
    [2022] | Includes bibliographical references and index.
Identifiers: LCCN 2021035151 | ISBN 9780262543477 (Paperback)
Subjects: LCSH: Critical thinking—Study and teaching. | Computer
    literacy—Study and teaching. | Artificial intelligence—Educational
    applications.
Classification: LCC LB1590.3 .C655 2022 | DDC 371.33—dc23/eng/20211213
LC record available at https://lccn.loc.gov/2021035151

10 9 8 7 6 5 4 3 2 1

CONTENTS

INTRODUCTION TO COMPUTATIONAL THINKING EDUCATION IN K–12

Siu-Cheung Kong, Harold Abelson, and Wai-Ying Kwok

Computing has been an essential element in national economies and societal institutions since the 1960s. As such, it has been a major component of technical education. But only in the past decade have innovations such as social networks, online news, and internet commerce made information technology omnipresent in daily life for much of the world's population. This has driven the call for K–12 school education, even at levels as early as primary school, to include computing as an essential topic in preparing students for a world that is being increasingly shaped by information technology. In the words of the Computer Science Teachers Association (CSTA) in their 2017 K–12 computer science standards, "Computer science and the technologies it enables rest at the heart of our economy and the way we live our lives. To be well-educated citizens in a computing-intensive world and to be prepared for careers in the 21st century, our students must have a clear understanding of the principles and practices of computer science."

While these words, first written in 2011, highlight the principles of computer science for K–12, the emphasis in K–12 computing education continues to shift from computer science to a broader perspective of computational thinking (CT), which is viewed not so much as about technology but rather as a method of thought. As explained in a current handbook on educational technology, "CT is essentially a framework to describe a set of critical thinking and problem-solving skills, and it has gained significant traction as a viable and useful way of thinking about how to teach these skills in formal educational settings" (Hunsaker 2018).

The popularity of this view derives from a seminal article by Jeannette Wing. In it Wing (2006) emphasizes that CT involves "solving problems, designing systems, and understanding human behavior, by drawing on the concepts fundamental to computer science," and she argues that CT is "a fundamental skill for everyone, not just computer scientists" (33). These sentiments were quickly and enthusiastically echoed by computer science educators, but they initially did not receive much attention beyond that community. This has changed over the past decade, as people have come to increasingly experience the impact of computing at a personal level and to better appreciate the role of computing in society and in our institutions. Educational authorities around the world now share a consensus that timely and flexible policies should be adopted to foster broad exposure to computational thinking education (CTE) throughout the curriculum and for students to start their CTE journey in schooling life as early as middle school, possibly even earlier.

DESIRABLE ROLES FOR COMPUTATIONAL THINKING EDUCATION IN K–12

Advocates for CTE in K–12 generally cite two classes of reasons: (1) CTE as a tool to concretely realize "thinking education" for young people and (2) CTE as a route to empowering young people to participate in an information society.

COMPUTATIONAL THINKING EDUCATION FOR CONCRETELY REALIZING THINKING EDUCATION

Wing's articulation of CT as a tool for thinking traces to the work of Papert at MIT and the creation of the Logo computer language, the first programming language explicitly designed for children. Papert's first paper on Logo was called "Teaching Children Thinking," in which he argued that manipulating computing could give children a sense of applied knowledge and self-confidently realistic images of themselves as intellectual agents

(Papert 1971). The first use of the term "computational thinking" in the sense meant here is due to Papert (1980).[1]

Underlying this view is a theory of learning called *constructionism*. This was proposed by Papert as an elaboration of the *constructivist* theory of knowledge developed by the psychologist Jean Piaget, with whom Papert had worked before coming to MIT. Piaget's constructionism holds that learning occurs as an active process of organizing knowledge based on experience, rather than just through passive observation. Papert's constructionism extends this to the idea that learning is most effective when it is part of an activity that constructs a meaningful product (Papert 1987). For Papert, computers could be powerful "construction kits," with which children can construct their own knowledge.

Following Wing's article, there have been many proposed articulations of the competences and dimensions central to CT. Some stress creativity and general constructionist approaches to learning, while others adhere to the centrality of ideas from computer science. For example, one popular definition holds that "we consider computational thinking to be the thought processes involved in formulating problems so their solutions can be represented as computational steps and algorithms" (Aho 2011).

The range of opinions notwithstanding, there's general concurrence that CT is a thinking process—the ability to think like a computer scientist for solving real-world problems—and that people who possess CT are able to systematically identify real-life problems and formulate them for possible computational solutions. There's also shared recognition of some of the key concepts involved, such as abstraction and algorithmic thinking, whether or not these are expressed in a programming language. Yet despite an emerging consensus on *what* to teach in K–12 computing, advances in technology, together with a universe of new applications, have provided new options for *how* to teach about computing. This has stimulated a healthy diversity of approaches to CTE that occupies the first focus of this volume.

COMPUTATIONAL THINKING EDUCATION FOR EMPOWERMENT IN AN INFORMATION SOCIETY

Teaching thinking aside, it's inescapable that we live in a society increasingly shaped by information technology. Just as we want students to understand the natural world, we should want them to understand the digital world. As computer scientist Simon Peyton-Jones argues, "Why do we ask every child to learn science from primary school? . . . It's because science teaches us something about the world around us, and if we know nothing about the way the world around us works, we're disempowered citizens" (Peyton-Jones 2014).

This reference to understanding might evoke an image of passive observation, but the importance of CTE goes beyond understanding. K–12 students, even primary school students, are personally engaged with information technology, through online media, social networking, and electronic commerce. These applications are subjects of active current debate, in which young people should contribute a voice. Primary goals for CTE should therefore include empowering students to be "conscientious consumers" with the ability to participate in democratic discussions around the technology (see chapter 9 by DiPaola, Payne, and Breazeal). Students can also have the opportunity to apply CT to address real-world issues. CTE curricula could even start by having students work through real-world problems without using computation before returning to them to apply CT ideas and computational tools (Huang et al. 2021).

This emphasis on real-world applications and empowered understanding comes full-circle when students can create computational applications that improve on their lives, their families and their communities. Tissenbaum, Sheldon, and Abelson (2019) advocate moving from computational thinking to "computational action," arguing that even primary school students can achieve such an impact.

FOCUS AREAS FOR THIS VOLUME

The chapters in this volume are organized into three sections, each one highlighting an area where CT is rapidly evolving. "A Multiplicity of Computational Thinkings" reflects the profusion of educational options and concerns as CTE expands throughout K–12. "Computational Thinking and Artificial Intelligence Literacy in K–12" describes the challenges for CTE emerging in response to today's explosive progress in artificial intelligence. "Computational Thinking and Physical Computing Education in K–12" examines the impact on CTE of the increasing integration of computing into physical objects. These three themes are tightly intertwined.

Together they reflect the challenges to CTE arising from the increasing power of computing devices and the ongoing permeation of information technology through all aspects of life.

FOCUS AREA 1: A MULTIPLICITY OF COMPUTATIONAL THINKINGS

When Wing highlighted the idea of CT fifteen years ago, Facebook and Twitter had just been introduced, and the smartphone was still a year in the future. Computing was certainly important, but it did not figure in most people's personal experience. In that environment, CTE saw itself as an enterprise of engaging students with the "principles and practices of computer science," as expressed in the CSTA standards cited above.

This paradigm is starting to show its age.

CTE can still serve as an introduction for students to great ideas in computer science. But more and more, students need to learn about computing not only through the power of its ideas, but through its impact on the world around us, its impact on society, and its impact on our daily lives. For CT educators, this creates a wealth of options both in new content and new pedagogical approaches. It also prompts reexamining the reasons why CTE should be a subject for everyone in K–12, including many students whose style of learning might be a poor match to the abstract aspects of computer science.

One manifestation of this reexamination is to reconsider the role of programming in CTE, or at least the role of popular programming languages like Java and Python. The emergence of block-based programming languages like Scratch and App Inventor in the past decade has created opportunities for students to create original applications using graphical drag-and-drop interfaces that are accessible to those with little or no programming background. The consequence is the opportunity for students to exercise creativity and personal expression through computing even in primary school, and the centrality of programming in CTE is a current topic of debate among educators.

The six chapters in this section of the book show leaders in CTE practice and research confronting these new opportunities.

In "A Case for Why: Society, School, Self" Brennan takes a hard-headed look at the rationale for teaching CT, pointing out that before looking at *how* to teach CT, one must start with *why* teach it. The chapter examines three classes of reasons—society, school, and self—and describes the challenges with each of these. There is a strong constructionist perspective and an emphasis on programming as a vehicle for self-expression. Brennan discusses teachers' perspectives on the pedagogical concerns and challenges of implementing CTE in K–12 classrooms. She then shares and comments on the pedagogical designs favorable to the delivery of CTE to K–12 students. Last, she shares some practical considerations for deploying the creative approaches to the design of CTE activities in K–12 classrooms for fostering every young student to effectively develop CT.

The second chapter in this section—"Providing Students with Computational Literacy for Learning About Everything" by Guzdial—makes a strong case for teaching programming, both as a general problem-solving skill and as a tool for student understanding and empowerment in the world in which they live. This does not require learning a complete programming language like Python or Javascript. Rather it can be done through task-specific microworlds. As an example, the paper describes a microworld for constructing image filters using matrix transformations.

"Developing Computational Thinking Skills with Multiple Models and Representations" by Hoppe and Manske argues for the importance of using multiple models and representations in CT development through domain-specific learning. The authors reflect on the common use of visual block-based programming with imperative sequential models and then introduce and compare the use of "reactive rule-based programming" as an alternative computational representation for delivering CTE in K–12. They recommend and illustrate the mixed use of computational representations in CTE activities for effectively supporting young students to develop CT competence as well as domain-specific knowledge.

The fourth chapter in this section—"Toward a Theory (and Practice) of Multiple Computational Thinkings" by Román-González, Moreno-León, and Robles—argues that CT is best viewed through Gardner's theory of multiple intelligences, and that consequently there is not "computational thinking" but rather there are multiple computational *thinkings*. The chapter supports this claim through several examples that illustrate differences in CT assessment results that would seem contradictory in the light of measuring computational thinking if CT were unidimensional. It then gives examples of how CT could be taught in the context of eight different intelligences:

verbal-linguistic, logical-mathematical, musical, bodily-kinesthetic, visual-spatial, interpersonal, intrapersonal, and naturalistic. The chapter indicates ways in which this theory might be tested, pointing out that standard CT tests are not adequate for this task. If the theory is validated, it would indicate that CT curricula should be much more diverse, and more tolerant of multiple intelligences.

In "Learning Computational Thinking in Phenomena-Based Co-creation Projects—Perspectives from Finland," Silander, Riikonen, Seitamaa-Hakkarainen, and Hakkarainen describe "phenomenon-based learning," which is widely used in Finland, and advocate for this approach to CTE. With this method, one always starts from real-world phenomena so that learning is highly contextualized. It's not enough to just understand algorithms or CT: phenomena must be studied as complete entities from various points of view that cross boundaries between school subjects and integrate different themes. There is a strong emphasis on makerspaces and project-based learning and realization the CT is more than just programming.

The final chapter in this section, by Dindler, Iversen, Caspersen, and Smith shines a spotlight on "Computational Empowerment," a framework that grows out of the participatory design tradition common in Scandinavia. This framework reaches far beyond the issues addressed in typical CT instruction. The authors present three key pillars for computational empowerment: (1) students should engage critically and curiously with the design of technology; (2) they should analyze and reflect on how technology affects use as individuals and members of society; (3) they should be able to promote democratic practices in the design of technology. CT itself is only part of a curriculum that addresses computational empowerment. One should also address the need for students to make informed choices about the use of digital tools and to proactively engage in the digitization of society.

FOCUS AREA 2: COMPUTATIONAL THINKING AND ARTIFICIAL INTELLIGENCE LITERACY IN K–12

Computational thinking and artificial intelligence (AI) have a long history together. Papert was co-director with Marvin Minsky of the MIT Artificial Intelligence Laboratory, and many contributors to the MIT Logo project were also researchers in AI. There was a great interest in understanding the relation between machine intelligence and children's intellectual development. So it is understandable that the area to emerge from this work would be called computational *thinking*. More pointedly, the influence of AI on CT has now become transformative.

AI has been a solid branch of computer science since the 1960s, but over the past fifteen years, world attention to AI has exploded to the point where its potential for global economic impact on society is compared to the impact of the steam engine in the 1800s (Bughin et al. 2018). This excitement poses challenges to CTE. One is the sheer pace of innovation in AI. Educators who are barely assimilating the call to include CT in the K–12 curriculum are now being asked to address a new constellation of ideas, with breakthrough applications heralded every few months.

More significantly, today's AI draws on concepts that have until now received little attention in CTE curricular work. Abstraction and modularity remain fundamental, but algorithmic thinking concepts like sequencing and conditionals become less critical in light of increased emphasis on machine learning and statistical methods. For example, in understanding the outputs of systems that perform image classification or medical diagnosis, it can be more important for students to consider the effect of the training data, as opposed to the learning algorithms.

The most important implication of progress in AI for CTE is the need to pay attention to the societal impact of computing in primary school. AI researchers and developers are beginning to come to grips with their responsibility for the consequences of their work, especially in areas of safety and fairness. Many technology companies have adopted policies around "responsible AI," and university courses in AI increasingly include units on ethical design in their AI curricula. That same concern is moving into CTE, with K–12 education beginning to draw on ideas from ethics and sociology alongside traditional technical disciplines.

In "The Computational Thinking and Artificial Intelligence Duality," Heintz discusses and illustrates the duality of CT and AI. The essence of this duality is the main focus of traditional computer science: CT is based on algorithms and programs expressed as step-by-step instructions, whereas the main focus of modern AI is to develop algorithms and programs that learn from data even where the problem may not be well defined. Heintz describes the complementary thinking strengths of computers and humans. He elaborates the synergy between AI literacy and CT competence for the success in the AI economy and discusses the scope of AI literacy and CT competence that should be cultivated in K–12 students for leveraging the duality between CT and AI in daily problem-solving contexts.

The second chapter in this section—"Artificial Intelligence Thinking in K–12" by Touretzky and Gardner-McCune—discusses and illustrates the issue of AI thinking in AI education for CT development. The authors introduce the national guidelines under the AI4K12 Initiative for AI education in K–12 in the United States and then discuss the "five big ideas in AI": perception, representation and reasoning, learning, natural interaction, and societal impact.

"Preparing Children to be Conscientious Consumers and Designers of AI Technologies" by DiPaola, Payne, and Breazeal presents an extended rationale and standards for AI education in middle school, together with sample curriculum elements. The authors propose three key objectives for middle school AI: (1) students should shift from being just consumers of AI to become conscientious consumers of AI; (2) they should become ethical designers of AI; and (3) they should be able to participate in democratic discussions around AI. The chapter outlines a week-long workshop for middle school, which emphasizes for students that AI design reflects the values of the designers. It uses image classification as an example of how classifiers can be biased, and it includes a session in which students redesign YouTube with the aid of an "ethical matrix" tool that encourages students to consider the values of the system designers.

FOCUS AREA 3: COMPUTATIONAL THINKING AND PHYSICAL COMPUTING EDUCATION IN K–12

The third current of CTE change explored in this volume is the increasing influence of physical devices. Physical devices are hardly new territory for CTE in K–12. Indeed, some of the first work in schools by Papert's MIT Logo group involved middle-school students in 1968 programming a robot called the turtle, and "turtle" has been a persistent meme in educational computing ever since. Today there is a growing variety of inexpensive robotic toys that support computer controls and other digital interfaces, and this is prompting critical rethinking of key CTE approaches.

One line of rethinking emphasizes that these are physical devices in the real world. Bringing computing "off the screen" makes it concrete and tangible and makes CTE accessible even to students at pre-primary level. It also makes project work more readily sharable and social and is encouraging CTE theorists to look beyond only constructionism and draw upon Vygotsky's view of learning as a social process.

A second line of rethinking results from the fact that programming in the presence of sensors and actuators requires use of event-driven programs that can react to changes in the environment. This consequently decreases the centrality of the straight-line programs whose elements form the introductory material of much of CTE in K–12.

Three chapters in this volume explore these ideas from different perspectives.

In "Examining the Multidimensional Learning Affordances of Robotics for Computational Thinking and Science Inquiry," Sullivan shares and discusses experience in the U.S. on multi-dimensional learning for CT development afforded by robotics. She elaborates the nature of the interaction and the synergy among three fundamental problem spaces in robotics learning: the robotic device, the software program, and the actual physical environment for navigation by the robotic device. She illustrates the creation and deployment of robotics learning environments that meaningfully engage students in CT development along with the process of science inquiry. The chapter adopts a Vygotskyan perspective that emphasizes social interaction open-ended collaboration. It also describes how the work across three perspectives supports the principles of science literacy as described in the US Next Generation Science Standards (2013), including abstraction and making inferences from data.

The second chapter in this section—"Toward a Research Agenda for Developing Computational Thinking Skills by Sense-Reason-Act Programming with Robots" by Fanchamps, Specht, Slangen, and Hennissen—shares and discusses the experience in the Netherlands with CT development through Sense-Reason-Act programming with robots. The authors review the approach of Sense-Reason-Act programming in computer-related education in K–12 schools. They also present their pioneering work on the design of dynamic problem-solving environments for CT development, where the approach of Sense-Reason-Act programming with robots is used to support students in developing competences ranging from straight-line programming to dynamic problem-solving algorithms.

In "Computational Thinking in the Interdisciplinary Robotic Game: The CHARM of STEAM," Shih shares and discusses the experience in Taiwan with a robotic game for CT development, in which students in grades 4 through 8 control physical robots that move on a large map. This "Great Voyage Game" supports students in developing interdisciplinary knowledge about the history, geography, diplomacy, and economy of European countries in the Age of Discovery. The chapter includes a careful analysis of student skills correlated with STEM (science, technology, engineering, and math) topics and CT principles.

The goal of this edited collection is to advance a voice and substantially augment discussion and debate about CT in K–12. The chapters are organized into three sections to reflect the profusion of educational approaches as CTE expands throughout K–12; describe the evolving challenges for CTE in response to today's explosive progress in AI; and examine the impact on CTE of the increasing integration of computing into physical objects. Taken together, these themes add immediacy and vibrancy to a field that is already emerging as a key concern for educational research. A list of additional readings on CTE for K–12 is also provided in the bookend appendix for readers as an easy reference to the major keystone works in the field.

NOTE

1. The term "computational thinking" itself appeared as early as the nineteenth century to refer to the use of quantitative methods in science, and later to the emphasis on reasoning in teaching arithmetic. The modern association of the term with computers and education comes from Papert (1980), who also referred to this as "procedural thinking."

REFERENCES

Aho, Alfred. 2011. "Computation and Computational Thinking." *Ubiquity* 2011 (1). https://doi.org/10.1145/1922681.1922682.

Bughin, Jacques, Jeongmin Seong, James Manyika, Michael Chui, and Raoul Joshi. 2018. "Notes from the AI Frontier: Modeling the Impact of AI on the World Economy." https://www.mckinsey.com/featured-insights/artificial-intelligence/notes-from-the-ai-frontier-modeling-the-impact-of-ai-on-the-world-economy.

Computer Science Teachers Association (CSTA). 2017. "K–12 Computer Science Standards, Revised 2017." https://www.csteachers.org/page/standards.

Huang, Ronghuai, Junfeng Yang, Guangde Xiao, and Hui Zhang. 2021. "Computational Thinking and the New Curriculum Standards of Information Technology for Senior High Schools in China" (forthcoming).

Hunsaker, Enoch. 2018. "Computational Thinking." In *The K–12 Educational Technology Handbook*, edited by Anne Ottenbreit-Leftwich and Royce Kimmons. EdTech Books. https://edtechbooks.org/k12handbook/computational_thinking.

Next Generation Science Standards. 2013. *Next Generation Science Standards*. https://www.nextgenscience.org/search-standards.

Papert, Seymour. 1971. "Teaching Children Thinking." *MIT Artificial Intelligence Laboratory AI-247*. https://dspace.mit.edu/handle/1721.1/5835.

Papert, Seymour. 1980. *Mindstorms: Children, Computers, and Powerful Ideas*. New York: Basic Books.

Papert, Seymour. 1987. *Constructionism: A New Opportunity for Elementary Science Education*. Proposal to National Science Foundation Division for Research on Learning.

Peyton-Jones, Simon. 2014. "Teaching Creative Computer Science." TEDexExeter talk. Streamed live on April 29, 2014, YouTube video, 14:49. https://www.youtube.com/watch?v=Ia55clAtdMs.

Tissenbaum, Mike, Josh Sheldon, and Hal Abelson. 2019. "From Computational Thinking to Computational Action." *Communications of the ACM* 62 (3): 34–36.

Wing, Jeannette M. 2006. "Computational Thinking." *Communications of the ACM* 49 (3): 33–35.

I

A MULTIPLICITY OF COMPUTATIONAL THINKINGS

1

A CASE FOR WHY

SOCIETY, SCHOOL, SELF

Karen Brennan

ASKING WHY

At Harvard University, in the Graduate School of Education, I teach a large design class, in which students develop self-directed projects throughout the term. The course explores constructionist and constructivist theories of learning. As such, all of the projects inevitably connect to learning in some way: students designing for their own learning, students designing for others' learning, or some combination of both. Early on in the project development process, we engage in an exercise that unpacks the aspirations underlying their projects by iteratively asking one question five times: "And why is that important to you?" I love this exercise because it evaluates our designs according to purpose, peeling back layers of intentions. It quickly and sharply highlights contradictions and tensions between *how* we are actually doing things and *why* we wanted to do those things in the first place.

I have been thinking about this exercise in relation to the considerable attention that computational thinking (CT) is presently garnering in K–12 settings. With individual classroom designs, district mandates, statewide initiatives, and national-level activities, there is no shortage of efforts to make CT accessible to all learners. As increasing numbers of K–12 teachers are being asked to include CT as part of their pedagogical considerations, many teachers are reasonably asking, "Why should I teach computational thinking?"

Before exploring the *why* of CT, it is necessary to clarify *what* CT is. Although this term has a long history and there remains little consensus on the specifics, it is often defined broadly as what one learns through participation in the domain of computer science. Denning (2017) offered a helpful guided tour and critique of CT through the history of computer scientists' conceptions of the field's contributions—from Alan Perlis's early exhortations about algorithms to Seymour Papert's introduction of the term *computational thinking* in *Mindstorms* in 1980 to Jeannette Wing's popularization of CT to Al Aho's focus on abstractions and the more recent operationalization of CT for K–12 by organizations such as Computer Science Teachers Association (CSTA), Computing at School, and International Society for Technology in Education (ISTE).

I have been particularly interested in the extent to which programming is included—or not—as a necessary component of CT. I first encountered CT as a construct through Wing's renowned 2006 article, "Computational Thinking," in *Communications of the ACM*. At the time, my work was focused on young people's participation and learning with Scratch programming. CT seemed like an interesting, if underspecified, framework for thinking about what one may learn through programming. That curiosity about CT and young people programming with Scratch led to the development of a CT framework and set of assessment strategies, which I created in collaboration with Mitch Resnick at MIT and program evaluators at Educational Development Center (EDC) (Brennan and Resnick 2012). Our CT framework emphasizes programming as a way of developing as a computational thinker—that is, developing fluency with computational *concepts* (core conceptual knowledge required to construct programs, such as sequences, loops, and variables), *practices* (the practices or strategies one employs when putting that core conceptual knowledge into action in a computer program, such as being iterative and incremental, or employing abstraction and modularization), and *perspectives* (the evolving conceptions of self, others, and world that develop through the learner-directed creation of programs).

There are benefits and challenges to aligning one's commitments and work to a popular term, as I did with CT. One benefit is recognition:

even for a term as contested as *computational thinking*, others in research and practice can generally understand what is meant. Another benefit is that individuals can contribute to the framing and shaping of the term itself. My particular approach to CT foregrounds programming in a way that others do not and consequently influences the conversation about what CT is and how it may be supported. A central challenge, of course, is the inherent limits of language and our understanding of particular words. Some argue that "thinking" is too passive and too psychologically interior as a signifier, which has led to other framings—such as computational participation (Kafai 2016), critical computational literacy (Lee and Soep 2016), and computational action (Tissenbaum, Sheldon, and Abelson 2019)—that more explicitly signal the active and social qualities of this learning.

I am not unduly preoccupied with this critique of the passivity or introversion of thinking in CT. My approach to design and research is guided primarily by *constructionist* epistemological commitments. Constructionism, which builds on the learner-centered commitments of constructivism, articulates the profound and powerful interconnectedness of thinking as mental construction and making as physical construction (Kafai and Resnick 1996). The externalization of our thinking, such as by creating a computer program, creates opportunities for ourselves and for others to inspect, test, reflect on, and respond to our thinking. Owing to my constructionist commitments, then, I regard thinking as inherently active and social.

To be transparent about my conceptions and commitments, I mention my framing of CT as a set of concepts, practices, and perspectives developed through programming and my guiding learning theory as constructionism. These necessarily are the motivation behind and focus for the arguments I make in this chapter about *why* we should want to support CT in K–12. Although these positions are certainly not universal, I hope that, whether you think of CT differently (e.g., unplugged activities) or are guided by different learning theory (e.g., behaviorist, cognitivist, or constructivist), the arguments in this chapter will nonetheless be of value. With this framing in mind, let us turn our attention to the various conceptions of CT in K–12.

EXPLORING WHY

Over the past ten years, there have been a variety of efforts in academia to explore the *why* of CT. For example, in a 2010 National Research Council report about a workshop focused on defining CT, academic participants outlined a set of five justifications, including (1) "succeeding in a technological society," (2) "increasing interest in the information technology professions," (3) "maintaining and enhancing U.S. economic competitiveness," (4) "supporting inquiry in other disciplines," and (5) "enabling personal empowerment."

More recently, Vogel, Santo, and Ching (2017) engaged stakeholders in New York City in a participatory process to identify justifications for computer science education for all K–12 students. This process led to the development of seven justifications, including "(1) economic and workforce development impacts, (2) equity and social justice impacts, (3) competencies and literacies impacts, (4) citizenship and civic life impacts, (5) scientific, technological and social innovation impacts, (6) school improvement and reform impacts, and (7) fun, fulfillment and personal agency" (610). This list was then taken up and refined by Blikstein (2018) in a Google-funded report about the state of K–12 computing education. This list was presented as "four distinct positions," including (1) "the labor market rationale," (2) "the computational thinking rationale," (3) "the computational literacy rationale," and (4) "the equity of participation rationale" (8). Beyond academia, similar lists of justifications have been developed by practitioner-facing organizations, including CSTA, ISTE, Association for Computing Machinery (ACM), and Code.org.

As these three lists suggest, a wide variety of interconnected and overlapping justifications have been imagined for why CT may be helpful for students. Rather than presenting a laundry list of justifications in my conversations with K–12 teachers, I tend to group these various justifications into three broad categories: *society* (justifications that connect the learner to the broader world, such as expectations for technological literacy and workforce arguments), *school* (justifications that situate the learner in an academic context, such as general aspirations for thinking and means of learning about other subjects), and *self* (justifications that focus on learners' understandings of themselves, such as identity development and opportunities for cultivating creative agency).

Before exploring each of these categories, I note a few properties of the *society-school-self* categorization. All three categories focus on student benefits; they are framed as things that are good for learners, first and foremost, and, through a lens of diversity, equity, and inclusion, good for *all* learners, rather than only a select few. The categories are nonhierarchical; that is, there is not an implicit ranking of importance or value. (Although, as I discuss later, I do not personally prioritize them equally, which in turn informs my design decisions.) Relatedly, the categories are overlapping; for example, one can be committed to justifications that are related to society (e.g., preparing students for future work) *and* justifications related to school (e.g., understanding ways of thinking). A main difference among the categories and justifications, however, is the variation in time horizons. For a third grader (typically eight years old and in the fourth year of schooling), an argument about jobs likely has a different sense of urgency and relevance than for a twelfth grader (typically eighteen years old and in the thirteenth year of schooling), whereas an argument about creativity has immediate relevance, age notwithstanding. For each of the categories, I describe the essence of the narrative that motivates the category, including specific examples of justifications, as well as some considerations and cautions.

SOCIETY

The broad social impact of computing is undeniable; our personal, professional, and public lives have been dramatically reconfigured over the past twenty years by code—with no signs of abating, given ongoing discoveries and developments in artificial intelligence and automation. Accompanying this radical reconfiguration has been a set of arguments related to why young people need to learn to program in the service of their future participation in society. One common argument is that programming forms a necessary computational and technological literacy. From the early 1960s to present day, learning how to program has been argued to be a necessary critical skill for understanding our changing technological and social landscape (Lee and Soep 2016; Vee 2013). These arguments are frequently grounded in a desire to differentiate "use of" or "consumption of" from "making with" programmed artifacts (Rushkoff 2010) and to challenge simplistic narratives around children as "digital natives," which are often more reflective of adult aspirations than actual student actions or participation (Buckingham 2007).

Another common argument emphasizes programming as essential for future jobs and employment. As noted by Guzdial (2015), "most of the arguments . . . for computing in schools are based on jobs" (1). Although there is a sense of value in programming in the present moment (which I will explore shortly), in my conversations with K–12 teachers and their students, there has been a pervasive theme of "the future" around learning how to program, especially related to jobs and the workforce. Teachers and students have a sense that there will be future job opportunities that will be missed if they do not focus on learning to program in the present. There is also a more diffuse notion of innovation—that learning how to program will somehow position them, eventually, to shape or change the future.

Both of these justifications—about literacy more broadly and workforce preoccupations—are echoed in the literature about justifications for CT (Blikstein 2018; Flórez et al. 2017; Shein 2014; Vogel, Santo, and Ching 2017). Arguments about preparing students for the future are intuitively appealing; they are aligned with long-standing articulations of the main project of school, that is, preparing young people for future participation and success in the world they will eventually enter as adults (Bransford, Brown, and Cocking 2000; Graham 1984). However, it is worthwhile to problematize these future-oriented framings. Certainly it is our responsibility to prepare students for a world that will undoubtedly be different from the world as it is today. But are we designing learning experiences based on technologies that may cease to exist? And how do we prepare students to participate in a world in which programming may, at some point, become less essential because of automation of at least some aspects of programming? It is also our responsibility to prepare students to contribute to making the world different than it is today. How do we, for example, prepare students to avoid repeating the problematic computing workplace cultures of today, which are widely recognized as being grossly unsuccessful in addressing issues of diversity, equity, and inclusion? How do we help students bring focus and attention to the increasing numbers of ethical issues connecting computing and society?

SCHOOL

A more immediate set of justifications for CT focus on cognitive and academic benefits in the K–12 school context. For example, it is often argued that by engaging in the types of algorithmic thinking and problem-solving that accompany the design and debugging of computer programs, students are building capacity for logical thinking and problem-solving more generally. Relatedly, it is sometimes argued that CT (and, specifically, programming) can serve learning in other domains. In the early days of programming in schools, integration with mathematics was a focus, as popularized by the Logo programming language and by Papert's *Mindstorms*. In the current CT resurgence, Weintrop et al. (2016) offered three reasons why disciplinary integration is appealing in schools: (1) the potential for the development of CT and disciplinary knowledge to be mutually reinforcing; (2) the advancement of equity given that core subjects (like math and science) are required, and including CT and programming in them will reach all students rather than a limited number of students who engage in computing electives; and (3) the experience of authentic professional practice given the ascendant role of computing in many STEM (science, technology, engineering, and math) disciplines. Disciplinary integration is increasingly popular in research and practice in part because of current funding priorities: for example, the US National Science Foundation's large investments in STEM plus Computing (STEM+C) research as expanded or amplified by intersections with computing, computer science, and CT.

These arguments about the benefits of programming in K–12 for developing discipline-specific knowledge and for young people's thinking more broadly have long and contested histories, exemplified by the early days of Logo efforts, including public disagreements between Seymour Papert (1987) and Roy Pea (1987) about what young people are doing and learning. In spite of a sense that the types of thinking and learning opportunities that students have while programming seem different than other types of activities in which they may engage, it is reasonable to be cautious about overreach of claims. There is a lack of evidence that the problem-solving skills developed in programming can transfer to other problem-solving contexts, which is unsurprising given the thorniness of transfer in education more broadly (Denning 2017; Guzdial 2015). There are also questions about the unique contributions of programming and CT in contrast with other forms of domain thinking (e.g., computational thinking vs. mathematical thinking, historical thinking, scientific thinking, and so on) (Grover and Pea 2013). As a practical caution, this interest in programming across the curriculum is motivated, in no small part, by the bureaucratic challenge of determining where to include computer science in a K–12 curriculum that is already very full (Cooper et al. 2014). In other words, disciplinary integration is sometimes a strategy for addressing administrative concerns rather than benefiting student learning. Regardless of motivation, disciplinary integration is challenging, particularly given many teachers' time constraints and lack of disciplinary expertise (Fincher 2015) and as evidenced by the history and failures of experiences in teaching Logo programming in schools (Hickmott and Prieto-Rodriguez 2018).

SELF

As part of a fundraising event several years ago, my research team members and I interviewed 150 K–12 students from around the United States about their Scratch experiences, asking these young people, "What would you tell your friend about Scratch?" It was striking to me that, although students invoked some of the discourses I have mentioned thus far (e.g., workforce ambitions or general/disciplinary thinking), students from kindergarten through grade 12 overwhelmingly talked about the importance of *creativity and self-expression* and, relatedly, *empowerment and identity*. They talked about the power of taking their ideas and bringing them into the world and how those acts changed the ways in which they saw themselves as agents in the world.

The justifications of creativity and empowerment are recognized throughout the CT literature. Lee and Soep (2016) described the thinking associated with programming as "complex, circular, ambiguous, multiple, social, and rhizomatic" ways of thinking that centrally depend on "imagination and creativity" (484). Creativity and empowerment are also recognized in practice-focused writing. For example, the first "big idea" from the Advanced Placement Computer Science Principles course is that "[c]omputing is a creative activity" (College Board 2017, 1). Creative acts can contribute to self-perceptions of empowerment. As Cooper and Dann

(2015) shared about their own teaching practice, "In our classes, we see the joy when students complete their programming projects. The sense of empowerment, creativity, and independence that is generated by successfully creating a program to perform some task (however trivial) is almost tangible" (54). This connection between creativity and empowerment in programming and computing is not new: Guzdial (2015) observed that, in the early days of computing, "[R]esearchers and visionaries like Seymour Papert, Cynthia Solomon, Alan Kay, and Andrea diSessa saw the computer as a new medium for human expression and empowerment" (1).

While enthusiasm for creativity and empowerment is understandable given the potential benefits for student interest and motivation, it has been challenging to realize these benefits in K–12 schools. Even tools such as Scratch that have an expressed commitment to supporting student creativity are not necessarily used in ways that actually support creativity in classrooms (Yadav and Cooper 2017). Why? The culture of school is too often in tension with the culture of creativity (Resnick 2017). This mismatch between creative culture and school culture can be overwhelming for teachers, who find themselves negotiating limitations of class time, their own professional preparation, uncertainties about how to assess these learning aspirations (particularly students' evolving conceptions of self), and broader expectations about their roles in the classroom (Brennan 2015a; Brennan and Resnick 2012). Misalignment between creative culture and school culture can similarly be challenging for students, who may be unsettled by changes in what teachers expect of them and, in turn, resist those changes (Brennan 2015a; Holt 1972).

DESIGNING FOR WHY

Why have I belabored the *why* of CT in this chapter? As Guzdial (2015) asserted, "[A]s teachers and designers of education, the first question we should ask is, 'Why?'" (1). It is critical to foreground this question because the *why* informs the *how* of supporting access to CT; it serves as the foundation for subsequent design decisions about the instructional surround (Blikstein 2018). A lack of clarity about *why* can lead to misalignment between intentions and actions. How does one choose among curricula or decide when to introduce CT into an instructional sequence, for example, without understanding *why* these learning opportunities should be included in the first place? Although I am focusing on teachers and classroom practice here, these concerns are not restricted to the microcosms of individual classrooms; questions about purpose should be central no matter how one contributes to the educational enterprise—from classroom teachers, to parents, to administrators. Policy makers have an especially critical role, given that policy determines priorities (i.e., emphasizing a particular why) and shapes action (i.e., suggesting the how) (Coburn 2016; McDonnell 1995). Understanding the motivation is even more important with any initiative that is surrounded with considerable momentum or hype, where the intentions and objectives are obfuscated by the frenzy of trying to keep up with what everyone else seems to be doing, as well as attempts by corporate interests to influence the agenda for their own purposes. The history of education is littered with examples of these hype cycles—moments of great enthusiasm that are then followed by disappointment and abandonment of efforts (David and Cuban 2010; Graham 1984).

In my own research and design work, although I appreciate the *society*- and *school*-grounded justifications, I am guided primarily by *self*-oriented justifications, particularly justifications that foreground the creativity of young people. I appreciate this particular grounding for its immediacy, as expressed by the young people I have had the benefit of working with over the past decade, but also for its broader impacts. As recognized by educational philosophers from Friedrich Froebel to John Dewey to Paolo Freire to bell hooks, creativity is a central part of human development and experience, essential to learning as a lifelong endeavor.

Unfortunately, I frequently encounter examples of how intentions for creativity are unexpectedly subverted in classrooms, from having few opportunities for variation in student work to having little time for exploration or creation, to a lack of conceptual capacity-building that would enable greater creative fluency. So, in addition to offering a broad reminder to check one's actions against one's aspirations, I would like to offer more concrete guidance for the specific aspiration of fostering creativity. This is challenging, however, when there are so many different ways of supporting creativity. A list of actions to take or curriculum to follow would be woefully insufficient to represent the enormous opportunity we have collectively, in this moment, as designers committed to supporting CT for all K–12 students. So, inspired by Postman and Weingartner (1969), I will instead offer a set of questions. Questions are a delightfully effective way to identify disparities between action and intention; they are suggestive rather than directive, respectful both of variation in learning contexts and of teacher agency when designing learning experiences. The questions offered here are guided by my constructionist commitments to learning, which foreground learner agency and creativity. I articulate these commitments as opportunities for students to engage in *personalizing, making, sharing,* and *reflecting* (Brennan 2015b).

My questions about personalizing emphasize opportunities for learners to express their interests and exercise their agency. Who is deciding what is important to learn? Where do students connect their programming activities with what they are interested in and care about? How does the design of the learning experience recognize the variation within the group of learners? My questions about making focus on opportunities for learners to iteratively practice and develop their programming skills. In a given class period, how is student time allocated? Are they doing more listening or more creating? Are they following or are they exploring? My questions about sharing focus on opportunities for learners to learn with and from each other, in both a formative and summative manner, to receive feedback and to circulate existing expertise. At what moments do students share their work? How often do students get to see what their peers are doing—or what their near-peers have done? How are process and product shared? My questions about reflecting emphasize the importance of not just doing but also thinking about what one is doing, both in real time and after the fact, as a critical part of learning and development. What types of questions are students asked about their process and work by others? What types of questions do students ask themselves about their process and work? How do students document their progress and their learning?

I continually ask myself these questions when I am designing and researching learning experiences to support creativity in K–12 computing. They serve as guidelines to my work, reminding me when I am straying too far from my core commitments. These particular questions reflect my personal commitments; as such, your own questions may be different. But whether your work is designing classroom experiences, assessing the appropriateness of a K–12 CT intervention, appreciating the ambitions of individual students, or supporting some other dimension of CT for all learners, I hope that this exploration underscores the value of continually attending to the alignment between intention and action in our collective work as educators.

REFERENCES

Blikstein, Paulo. 2018. *Pre-college Computer Science Education: A Survey of the Field.* Mountain View, CA: Google LLC. https://goo.gl/gmS1Vm.

Bransford, John, Ann L. Brown, and Rodney R. Cocking. 2000. *How People Learn: Brain, Mind, Experience, and School.* Washington, DC: National Academy Press.

Brennan, Karen. 2015a. "Beyond Right or Wrong: Challenges of Including Creative Design Activities in the Classroom." *Journal of Technology and Teacher Education* 23 (3): 279–299.

Brennan, Karen. 2015b. "Beyond Technocentrism: Supporting Constructionism in the Classroom." *Constructivist Foundations* 10 (3): 289–296.

Brennan, Karen, and Mitchel Resnick. 2012. "Using Artifact-Based Interviews to Study the Development of Computational Thinking in Interactive Media Design." Paper presented at the American Educational Research Association meeting, Vancouver, BC, Canada.

Buckingham, David. 2007. *Beyond Technology: Children's Learning in the Age of Digital Culture.* Malden, MA: Polity Press.

Coburn, Cynthia E. 2016. "What's Policy Got to Do with It? How the Structure-Agency Debate can Illuminate Policy Implementation." *American Journal of Education* 122 (3): 465–475.

College Board. 2017. *AP Computer Science Principles Course Overview.* Last modified June 2017. https://apcentral.collegeboard.org/pdf/ap-computer-science-principles-course-overview.pdf.

Cooper, Stephen, and Wanda Dann. 2015. "Programming: A Key Component of Computational Thinking in CS Courses for Non-Majors." *ACM Inroads* 6 (1): 50–54.

Cooper, Steve, Shuchi Grover, Mark Guzdial, and Beth Simon. 2014. "A Future for Computing Education Research." *Communications of the ACM* 57 (11): 34–36.

David, Jane L., and Larry Cuban. 2010. *Cutting through the Hype: The Essential Guide to School Reform.* Cambridge, MA: Harvard Education Press.

Denning, Peter J. 2017. "Remaining Trouble Spots with Computational Thinking." *Communications of the ACM* 60 (6): 33–39.

Fincher, Sally. 2015. "What Are We Doing When We Teach Computing in Schools?" *Communications of the ACM* 58 (5): 24–26.

Flórez, Francisco Buitrago, Rubby Casallas, Marcela Hernández, Alejandro Reyes, Silvia Restrepo, and Giovanna Danies. 2017. "Changing a Generation's Way of Thinking: Teaching Computational Thinking Through Programming." *Review of Educational Research* 87 (4): 834–860.

Graham, Patricia Albjerg. 1984. "Schools: Cacophony about Practice, Silence about Purpose." *Daedalus* 113 (4): 29–57.

Grover, S., and R. Pea. 2013. "Computational Thinking in K–12: A Review of the State of the Field." *Educational Researcher* 42 (1): 38–43.

Guzdial, Mark. 2015. *Learner-Centered Design of Computing Education: Research on Computing for Everyone.* Synthesis Lectures on Human-Centered Informatics: Morgan & Claypool Publishers. https://doi.org/10.2200/S00684ED1V01Y201511HCI033.

Hickmott, Daniel, and Elena Prieto-Rodriguez. 2018. "To Assess or Not to Assess: Tensions Negotiated in Six Years of Teaching Teachers about Computational Thinking." *Informatics in Education* 17 (2): 229–244.

Holt, John Caldwell. 1972. *Freedom and Beyond.* New York: E. P. Dutton and Company.

Kafai, Yasmin B. 2016. "From Computational Thinking to Computational Participation in K–12 Education." *Communications of the ACM* 59 (8): 26–27.

Kafai, Yasmin, and Mitchel Resnick, eds. 1996. *Constructionism in Practice: Designing, Thinking, and Learning in a Digital World.* Hillsdale, NJ: Lawrence Erlbaum.

Lee, Clifford H., and Elizabeth Soep. 2016. "None but Ourselves Can Free Our Minds: Critical Computational Literacy as a Pedagogy of Resistance." *Equity & Excellence in Education* 49 (4): 480–492.

McDonnell, Lorraine M. 1995. "Opportunity to Learn as a Research Concept and a Policy Instrument." *Educational Evaluation and Policy Analysis* 17 (3): 305–322.

National Research Council (U.S.). 2010. *Report of a Workshop on the Scope and Nature of Computational Thinking.* Washington, DC: National Academies Press. https://www.nap.edu/catalog/12840/report-of-a-workshop-on-the-scope-and-nature-of-computational-thinking.

Papert, Seymour. 1980. *Mindstorms: Children, Computers, and Powerful Ideas.* New York: Basic Books.

Papert, Seymour. 1987. "Computer Criticism vs. Technocentric Thinking." *Educational Researcher* 16 (1): 22–30.

Pea, Roy D. 1987. "The Aims of Software Criticism: Reply to Professor Papert." *Educational Researcher* 16 (5): 4–8.

Postman, Neil, and Charles Weingartner. 1969. *Teaching as a Subversive Activity.* New York: Delta.

Resnick, Mitchel. 2017. *Lifelong Kindergarten: Cultivating Creativity Through Projects, Passion, Peers, and Play.* Cambridge, MA: MIT Press.

Rushkoff, Douglas. 2010. *Program or Be Programmed: Ten Commands for a Digital Age.* New York: OR Books.

Shein, Esther. 2014. "Should Everybody Learn to Code?" *Communications of the ACM* 57 (2): 16–18.

Tissenbaum, Mike, Josh Sheldon, and Hal Abelson. 2019. "From Computational Thinking to Computational Action." *Communications of the ACM* 62 (3): 34–36.

Vee, Annette. 2013. "Understanding Computer Programming as a Literacy." *Literacy in Composition Studies* 1 (2): 42–64.

Vogel, Sara, Rafi Santo, and Dixie Ching. 2017. "Visions of Computer Science Education: Unpacking Arguments for and Projected Impacts of CS4All Initiatives." In *Proceedings of the ACM SIGCSE Technical Symposium on Computer Science Education.* Seattle, WA, 609–614.

Weintrop, David, Elham Beheshti, Michael Horn, Kai Orton, Kemi Jona, Laura Trouille, and Uri Wilensky. 2016. "Defining Computational Thinking for Mathematics and Science Classrooms." *Journal of Science Education and Technology* 25 (1): 127–147.

Wing, Jeannette M. 2006. "Computational Thinking." *Communications of the ACM* 49 (3): 33–35.

Yadav, Aman, and Steve Cooper. 2017. "Fostering Creativity Through Computing." *Communications of the ACM* 60 (2): 31–33.

2

PROVIDING STUDENTS WITH COMPUTATIONAL LITERACY FOR LEARNING ABOUT EVERYTHING

Mark Guzdial

LEARNING ABOUT COMPUTING IS LEARNING ABOUT PROGRAMMING

Learning about computing almost always requires learning about programming. There have been some brilliant people, like Alan Turing and John von Neumann, who could think about computing without a language or notation, but those people are rare. It is analogous to learning mathematics, including addition, subtraction, and multiplication, without writing digits like "34.9" or symbols like "+."

Programming is defining a computation, something that a computer can do. A program describes a process. A program can be specified in any notation, so we should pick one that best suits the programmer and the domain. The most popular programming languages today are demanding, requiring students to use complex cognitive skills such as abstraction and decomposition of a problem into subcomponents. Programming does not have to be so complex and overwhelming. A simple programming language can still be effective for learning. Programming is a powerful tool for helping students learn in many different domains. I argue in this chapter that *providing students with the ability to program is providing them with a literacy that can be an advantage in learning about everything else.*

The term *computer science* first appeared in print in the *Journal of Engineering Education* in 1961 in an article by George Forsythe (Knuth 1972).

Forsythe described (in 1968) that he saw computation as a "general-purpose mental tool" that would "remain serviceable for a lifetime." Explicitly, *computer science* was defined as something that students could use to aid in their thinking and their learning, especially in STEM (science, technology, engineering, and mathematics) classes. In this chapter, I argue that the value of learning programming is even greater than what Forsythe described.

There are many possible benefits to students learning to program. The first section of the chapter lists many of these, ending with the most powerful—programming as a new kind of literacy. The next section explains why the computer can help with learning everything else, because it is the "master simulator." Finally, I argue that even a simple programming language can have enormous advantage in learning. We don't need all the power of C, Scheme, or Logo to learn with programming as a literacy.

WHY SHOULD STUDENTS LEARN TO PROGRAM?

Learning to program does not impart to the learner general problem-solving skills. There have been several studies looking for transfer from teaching programming to general problem-solving skills. Probably the first study investigating this claim was done by Roy Pea and Midian Kurland in 1984. David Palumbo completed a meta-review of the research relating learning programming and learning problem-solving (1990). Since then, the topic has been revisited, but I read Palumbo's results as painting a picture of programming as an opportunity to teach problem solving rather than an experience where problem-solving is learned automatically.

It is possible to teach problem-solving using programming, but problem-solving skills are not the automatic and direct result of learning to program (Grover and Pea 2013). Sharon Carver showed how to teach problem-solving with programming (Carver 1988). She wanted students to learn debugging skills, such as being able to take a map and a set of instructions and then figure out where the instructions are wrong. She taught those debugging skills by having students debug Logo programs. Students successfully transferred those debugging skills from Logo programming to the map task. That's significant from a cognitive and learning sciences perspective. But her students didn't learn much programming;

she didn't need much programming to teach that problem-solving skill. Other studies have found similar results (Grover, Pea, and Cooper 2015; Kalelioglu and Gülbahar 2014).

Fortunately, there are many other benefits of learning to program. These are described in the paragraphs that follow.

TO UNDERSTAND THE WORLD IN WHICH THEY LIVE

Simon Peyton Jones argued that computer science is a science like all the others (Peyton Jones 2013). We teach chemistry to students because they live in a world with chemical interactions. We teach biology because they live in a world full of living things. We teach physics because they live in a physical world. We should teach computer science because they live in a digital world.

Students live in a world where secret messages can be hidden inside of pictures and where machines can be infected with viruses. They live in a world where they own many computers, some of which do nothing more sophisticated than control their microwave oven. They do not need to know how all of this works at a level that they could build it (although they may want to). They do need to understand enough to troubleshoot the computing in their lives: for example, to know that it is unlikely for the internet to ever "break," but the router in their home can fail. They need to understand enough to protect themselves: for example, why running any arbitrary program downloaded from the internet may be dangerous for their security. They also need to understand that they can make their own apps and games and that anyone with any computer can invent something that is world changing. Students should know the basic principles of how their world works.

TO USE COMPUTERS MORE EFFECTIVELY

We all use computers ubiquitously, from the cellphones in our hands to the laptops on which we work. Does knowing how the computer works lead to more effective use of the computer? Are people who program less likely to make mistakes with software? Are they more resilient in bouncing back from errors? Can programmers solve computing problems (those that happen in applications or with hardware, even without programming) more easily?

I bet the answer is yes, but I am unaware of research results that support that argument. There are likely common elements to mental models that are used to understand the computational systems with which we interact. Some of those common elements may include the causal and repeatable nature of computers, which is unlike our everyday experience (e.g., your PowerPoint animations likely work exactly the same way every time). Programming may be a way to learn those common elements explicitly and efficiently.

TO INFLUENCE THEIR WORLD

The default behavior of users with computers is to consume. We consume books, videos, music, and commentary in an endless stream or scroll. The promise of programming is to turn digital consumers into digital producers who can use computing to have an effect on the world.

Yasmin Kafai calls this promise *computational participation* (Kafai 2016), and Tissenbaum, Sheldon, and Abelson (2019) call it *computational action*. The computer's connectivity, malleability, and representational power give students the ability to make digital products and share them widely. From YouTube videos to new apps, the computer provides a rich medium for creativity and a far-reaching distribution mechanism.

The question of the role of programming changes if we reframe programming. Imagine if programming was *not* a complex and hard-to-learn activity. What if learning to program was like learning to use a drawing app, a photo editing tool, or a video editor. If we think of programming as defining a process for someone else to use, then teaching students to program is giving them another way that they can create digital artifacts (i.e., stored and executable process) and share them with the world.

TO STUDY AND UNDERSTAND PROCESSES

Alan Perlis (first Association for Computing Machinery [ACM] Turing Award laureate) argued in 1962 that everyone on every campus should learn to program (Perlis 1962). He said that computer science is the study of *process*. He contrasted learning computer science with learning calculus.

Calculus is the study of *rates*, which is important for many disciplines. Perlis argued that *all* students need to learn about process, from managers who work on logistics to scientists who try to understand molecular or biological processes. Programming automates process, which creates opportunities to simulate, model, and test theories about processes at scale. Abelson, Sussman, and Sussman (1996) stated that mathematics is about formalizing declarative knowledge ("what is"), while programming is about formalizing imperative knowledge ("how to").

Perlis was prescient in predicting computational science and engineering. Today, people play "what-if" games with spreadsheets daily. We use computing to track our weather and our packages. Most professionals use a computer to explore models. The ability to construct models and test hypotheses by executing those models is one of the most powerful abilities that a computer can provide us. It is especially powerful because it extends a basic human capability—to imagine a possible future world. The computer can allow us to realize this world (at a level of fidelity that makes sense for our needs) and test it in simulation. Testing our imagined worlds is difficult to do at the level of precision that a computer affords.

TO HAVE A NEW WAY TO LEARN SCIENCE AND MATHEMATICS

Mathematics places a critical role in understanding our world. The power of mathematics in science is obvious, but the adoption of mathematics in society may be even more influenced by its importance for business. Without a doubt, the world runs on numbers.

Our notation for mathematics is mostly static equations representing models about the world. Increasingly, we are finding that representing code is different and gives us new insights. This is what Andy diSessa has been saying in his calls for computational literacy (2001). Bruce Sherin (2001), Idit Harel (1990), Yasmin Kafai (2014), Uri Wilensky (2016), and many others have shown us how code gives us a powerful new way to learn science and mathematics. Bootstrap:Algebra (Schanzer et al. 2015) teaches algebra with computing. Every student of mathematics should also be a student of programming, because it provides a different, dynamic notation for understanding mathematical ideas. When the programming context is tied to a real application (from image manipulation to video games), the computation can help to concretize the mathematical concepts (Wilensky 1991), which can make them more engaging and easier to learn.

TO BE ABLE TO ASK QUESTIONS ABOUT THE TECHNOLOGICAL INFLUENCES ON THEIR LIVES

C. P. Snow (1962) also argued for everyone to learn computing in 1962, but with more foreboding. He correctly predicted that computers and computing algorithms were going to control important aspects of our lives. He said, "I am asking whether we are now running into a position where only those who are concerned with the computer, who are formulating its decision rules, are going to be knowledgeable about the decision," and "It is not only that I am afraid of misjudgments by persons armed with computing instruments; it is also that I am afraid of the rest of society's contracting out, feeling that they no part in what is of vital concern to them because it is happening altogether incomprehensibly and over their heads." Snow would likely have agreed with Cathy O'Neil's premise in *Weapons of Math Destruction* (2016), that computer algorithms are not inherently objective and that programmers' biases may influence their judgments.

If we don't know about computing, we have "contracted out," in Snow's terms. We don't even know what to ask about the algorithms that are controlling our lives. It shouldn't be magic. Even if you're not building these algorithms, simply knowing about them gives you power. C. P. Snow argues that you need that power.

AS A JOB SKILL

The most common argument for teaching computer science in the United States is as a job skill. The original Code.org video (2013) argued that everyone should learn programming because we have a shortage of programmers. While the need for more programmers is important for supporting our technological society, that is not a good enough reason to put programming in front of every student. Moreover, that's not a reason to bear the enormous cost to change our school systems so that we have enough teachers to teach all those students. Not everyone is going to become a software developer, and it does not make any sense to train everyone for a job that only some will do.

But if you think about computing as a literacy, and not as a career, it becomes more clear that computing will be an important *component* job skill for many. Some fifteen years ago, we could already see that the ratio of professional software developers to people who program just as *part* of their job was somewhere between 1:4 and 1:9 (Scaffidi et al. 2005). A more recent analysis shows that, for the same job category, workers (who are not software developers) who program make higher wages than those comparable workers (in the same job category) who do not (Scaffidi 2017). Learning to program gives students new skills that have value in the economy.

Today, not everyone has access to computing education. It tends to be centralized in more urban/suburban and more affluent schools. Even when it's available, it is mostly White and Asian males taking the class (Margolis et al., 2017; Parker and Guzdial 2019). It is a social justice issue if we do not make this economic opportunity available to everyone.

TO DEVELOP A NEW LITERACY

Alan Kay and Adele Goldberg made the argument in the 1970s that computing is a whole new medium. In fact, it is humans' first meta-medium—it can be all other media, and it includes interactivity so that the medium can respond to the reader/user/viewer (Kay and Goldberg 1977). Computing gives us a new way to express ideas, to communicate to others, and to explore ideas. Everyone should have access to this new medium.

Kay (1977) described what the experience of using the computer as a literacy should be like: "Computer literacy is a contact with the activity deep enough to make the computational equivalent of reading and writing fluent and enjoyable.'" We can use Kay's perspective to contrast programming and textual literacy. We can and do study reading and writing for their own sake: for example, we read classics of literature and learn to compose our own essays. For most of us, the greatest power of reading and writing is that *every day* it enables us to express ideas, to communicate with others, and to understand our world. Literacy supports and affects how we learn. Programming can be studied for itself, and there are obviously full-time, professional programmers—just as there are full-time, professional writers. But programming can also be an everyday skill that can inform the way we think and communicate.

The computer's great power as a form of literacy is that it doesn't have to look like a computer. Kay (1995) pointed out that the computer as meta-medium could be anything else: "The computer is the greatest 'piano' ever invented, for is it the master carrier of representations of every kind. The heart of computing is building a dynamic model of an idea through simulation." The computer can be anything, which makes it a powerful tool for learning about everything. The most powerful aspect of the computer is the ability to encode models and execute them as simulations.

As Sherin (2001) demonstrated when he taught physics with Boxer, the computer provides a modeling capability different than equations. Algebraic equations are useful for describing *balance*. Given all but one of the variables in the equation, we can manipulate the equation to compute that last variable. Computer programs typically do not work the same way. Rather, computer programs can represent *causality*. Students learning a programming model of physics learn about how acceleration influences velocity and velocity influences position (Guzdial 1995)—a causal chain that is not obvious in kinematics equations.

THE COMPUTER AS A TOOL FOR LEARNING EVERYTHING

When computers were first being developed as tools for learning, the goal wasn't learning computer science. From Kemeny and Kurtz developing Basic, to Papert, Solomon, Feurzeig, and Bobrow developing Logo, the goal was using the computer to learn about *something else* (Guzdial and du Boulay 2019). Kemeny and Kurtz wanted everyone on campus to be able to use computing in their work. Papert and the Logo developers wanted students to learn about poetry, mathematics, and artificial intelligence.

In their seminal work "Personal Dynamic Media," Kay and Goldberg showed their new Smalltalk system being used in a wide variety of disciplines, with representations that matched the discipline. They used the new graphical user interfaces to represent circuit diagrams, music, art, animations, and a simulation of a hospital. Today, we recognize that each discipline has its own representations and ways of communicating, which is called *disciplinary literacy* (Moje 2015). The computer is powerful for teaching in all disciplines, in part, because it can support disciplinary literacy.

The interface and language of the computer doesn't have to look the way that computer scientists want it to look. We can adapt the language and interface to use the representations and abstractions of the domain. We want students to learn abstractions that are powerful and generalize, but these need not be abstractions that are native to the computer. There is nothing sacred about FOR loops, bits and bytes, or arrays and linked lists. Many domains have powerful abstractions. We can use the computer to teach any of those, to adapt to any of those abstractions, and to represent them in an authentic way.

HOW MUCH PROGRAMMING DOES A STUDENT NEED FOR LITERACY?

Programming languages are growing in size and complexity. The definition of equality (==) in JavaScript is a list of twenty-two dense rules (ECMA 2011), and that is one of the most basic operators. The number of primitives and the sizes of the libraries grow with every new release of a language. To "learn Python" is a significant challenge, one that can take years to achieve. Certainly, we cannot expect students to learn *all* of *any* language to be literate. So, how much programming does a student really need to be expressive and to learn?

Scratch is likely the most successful programming environment ever developed for children (Maloney et al. 2008, 2010), with tens of millions of users around the world. Empirical studies of students using the block-based programming language show that most students use very few of the capabilities of the language (Fields, Kafai, and Giang 2017). Most loops are simply forever loops. Few students use any Boolean expressions at all. Students don't need to know and use much programming to find Scratch compelling. Even a small bit of programming has expressive power that draws in tens of millions of students. What is likely more important than the Scratch programming language are the environment and community in which it is embedded.

Bootstrap:Algebra is a powerful way to teach algebra through programming (Schanzer et al. 2015). Students build video games by writing equations that describe the current frame of the video in terms of the previous frame, then translate those equations into code. The analysis process that students are taught in Bootstrap:Algebra helps them in solving word problems in algebra (Schanzer et al. 2018). But students don't actually use much programming when building their video games. There is no explicit repetition (iteration or recursion). Students can improve their learning of algebra without learning everything that is in a modern programming language. Even a small bit of programming has power in enabling powerful learning outside of computing.

Of course, there is a purpose for all those other programming language features that aren't used in Scratch or aren't taught in Bootstrap:Algebra. The programming needs are dependent on the students' goals. The important point is that students do not need to know *everything* in order to learn enough to gain benefits of computational literacy.

Consider a comparison with textual literacy. There are professionals who write for a living: for example, those who produce news stories or novels. Most people find value in writing even if they do not write for newspapers or publishers. Every day, people find value in writing letters and grocery lists with less sophisticated words or grammatical constructs. When people are learning a foreign language, they can often achieve basic communication with a limited vocabulary and few verb tenses. Similarly, there is value in even a small bit of programming.

WHY AREN'T WE THERE YET?

Over the last decade, the United States has made dramatic progress in increasing access to computing education. For example, in Georgia, 43 percent of high schools offer computer science classes (Parker and Guzdial 2019). However, only 1 percent of Georgia high school students take any of those computer science classes. In Indiana, 33 percent of schools offer computer science, but only about 2.5 percent of students ever take a computer science class (Guzdial 2019; Guzdial and Arquilla 2019; Parker and Guzdial 2019).

The reasons are complicated why students are still avoiding computer science, even when they have access to computing education. Certainly, one of the explanations is that not all computing education experiences are high quality. Some afterschool programs and internships dissuade students from continuing in computing (Weston et al. 2019). A more compelling explanation is that students do not see that computing is a pathway to achieving their goals (Lewis et al. 2019). Students who leave computing have a very different perception of the field than those who stay in computer science (Biggers et al. 2008).

One solution to give more students access to computing education is to find new ways to integrate computing across the curriculum. The idea is to follow the lead of Bootstrap:Algebra to find ways that programming can enhance learning in other subjects. If we can't convince students to come to programming and computational literacy, maybe we can bring programming to them and provide computational literacy to support the learning that students *are* interested in.

REDESIGNING PROGRAMMING FOR MICROWORLDS: TASK-SPECIFIC PROGRAMMING

Microworlds are one of the great inventions for using programming to teach a wide range of subjects. The idea of microworlds is to provide a limited subset of the programming environment with tailored operations that match the domain of the microworld. Seymour Papert (1980) first defined microworlds as a "subset of reality or a constructed reality whose structure matches that of a given cognitive mechanism so as to provide an environment where the latter can operate effectively. The concept leads to the project of inventing microworlds so structured as to allow a human learner to exercise particular powerful ideas or intellectual skills." Andrea diSessa (with Hal Abelson) built on this idea in Boxer (diSessa and Abelson 1986) and said in his book *Changing Minds* (diSessa, 2001): "A microworld is a type of computational document aimed at embedding important ideas in a form that students can readily explore. The best microworlds have an easy-to-understand set of operations that students can use to engage tasks of value to them, and in doing so, they come to understanding powerful underlying principles. You might come to understand ecology, for example, by building your own little creatures that compete with and are dependent on each other."

Typically, a microworld is built on top of a general-purpose language: for example, Papert used Logo and diSessa used Boxer. Thus, the designer of the microworld could assume familiarity with the syntax and semantics of the programming language and perhaps some general programming concepts like mutable variables and control structures. The problem here is that with Logo and Boxer, like any general-purpose programming language, it takes time to develop proficiency. They are large and complex things to learn, and learning those can get in the way of the powerful ideas or intellectual skills that Papert and diSessa are interested in.

Task-specific programming (TSP) aims to provide the same easy-to-understand operations for a microworld, but with a language and environment designed for a particular purpose. The task-specific programming language (TSPL) is purposefully limited in the abstractions and concepts needed for the tasks or explorations in the microworld so that programming becomes much easier to learn than a complete programming language. Some task-specific programming languages have been usable in only five to ten minutes (Chasins et al. 2018). The ease of use makes it possible to think about learning different concepts with different microworlds, that is, different task-specific programming languages. Perhaps an elementary or secondary school student might encounter several different TSPLs in a single year.

AN EXAMPLE TASK-SPECIFIC PROGRAMMING ENVIRONMENT

The domain for the following example task-specific programming environment is precalculus. The operations in this prototype environment are the simple matrix transformations taught in many precalculus curricula—matrix addition and subtraction and scalar multiplication. The concrete purpose in this microworld is the creation of image filters. The point of this prototype is to engage students in practicing the intellectual skills of matrix manipulation by engaging them in developing image filters. Image filters become the concrete purpose for learning the abstraction of matrix manipulation.

Figure 2.1 is the main screen for the prototype. Students see a picture (*left-hand side*) that is decomposed into matrices representing the red channel of the pixels in the picture (*bottom left*), and the green and blue channel matrices next to that. A set of matrix transformations is listed at the top left—this is the *program* that, applied to the input picture (*on left*), produces the output picture (*on right*). The Change Picture button changes the input picture so that the students can apply the operations to different pictures to see that the program processes an arbitrary picture to generate a similar image effect on all pictures.

The matrix transformations listed in figure 2.1 are a program, but the language is not typed (as in a textual programming language) nor assembled like a jigsaw puzzle (as in a block-based programming language). Instead, the statements are constructed with a purpose-built editor that is grounded in the disciplinary literacy of precalculus. Each matrix transformation is created and edited on a screen like in figure 2.2.

There are two possible transformations, which are selected by radio button:

- The red, green, or blue matrices can be redefined ("set") as the sum or difference between four matrices: red, green, blue, or a matrix where every value is 255. The matrices and operation (plus or minus) are selected with pull-down menus. In the example, figure 2.2, the red matrix (*top left*) is set to the difference of the green matrix and the blue matrix (*top middle*). The matrices are presented, using the notation

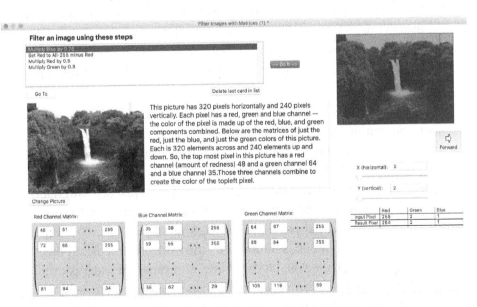

2.1 Defining an image filter as a sequence of matrix transformations.

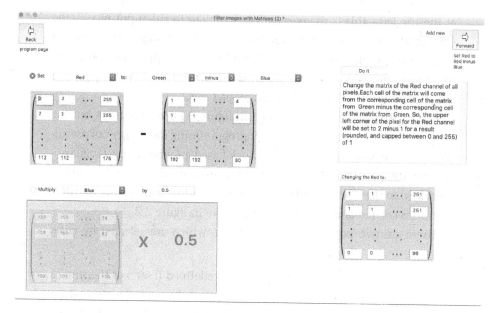

2.2 Defining one matrix transformation.

commonly appearing in precalculus texts, with the output matrix (the new red matrix) appearing on the right. The *all-255* matrix can be used to compute the inverse of an image, by setting the red, green, and blue matrices to 255 minus the current value in the matrix.

- Alternatively, one of the matrices (red, green, or blue) can be multiplied by a scalar. The matrix can be selected by pull-down menu, and the scalar value is typed into a text area.

The image filter language is simple and grounded in the concepts and notation of precalculus. The image filter prototype is an example of task-specific programming to support learning matrix transformations for precalculus. Students may use this tool to meet a challenge (e.g., to generate a particular image manipulation effect) or to practice with tracing and using matrix arithmetic (e.g., in this given effect, what happens to pixels in the original picture whose RGB values are [128, 104, 12]). Our approach to adoption is informed by the work on SimCalc. In their scaling-up paper, Tatar et al. (2008) wrote: "Conversely, a wider path to adoption exists if one can engineer materials to support short-term use without extensive professional development and with a wide variety of pedagogical styles. In the short term, innovators may be able to make an earlier, more immediate impact on a wide audience and set a credible base of authentic improvement that can then serve longer term growth." This is exactly our approach. While task-specific programing tools may fit into project-based activities (Blumenfeld et al. 1991, 1994; Krajcik and Blumenfeld 2006), the goal is to be usable in a variety of activities.

We use our prototypes in participatory design sessions with teachers (DiSalvo 2016; Wilensky and Stroup, 1999). Our goal is to develop task-specific programming that teachers would find useful and would integrate into their classes, so we ask them to try it in the context of what students find challenging about precalculus. The prototype is an artifact to think with. Precalculus teachers learn and use it and then tell us what would *really* be useful to them. We then iterate on the design.

Sessions with precalculus teachers support our hypothesis that they can start using it in less than ten minutes. The general response from precalculus teachers has been guardedly positive. The teachers see that the microworlds aim to take an abstract concept in precalculus and ground it in a concrete application. They appreciate our attention to disciplinary literacy and to the learning outcomes for precalculus. Several of our informants saw the benefits of connecting precalculus to contexts that students found personally meaningful, like Instagram or Snapchat photo filters.

However, the teachers tell us that we are solving the wrong problems. While some students struggle with matrix notation and element-by-element operations, most do not. The hard parts of matrices in precalculus are matrix multiplication and determinants, and even convolution. Those parts are so difficult for students that matrices are often left out of a school's precalculus curriculum, which puts students at a disadvantage when they face linear algebra in undergraduate courses. We are currently iterating on this design.

A task-specific programming environment is unlikely to achieve all the goals described at the beginning of this chapter. Rather, task-specific programming may be an easier-to-use and easier-to-adopt programming experience than textual or block-base languages. Students will not use task-specific programming environments alone as a notational tool for computational literacy, but use of such tools may help students to gain understanding about the nature of programs, programming, and debugging. Task-specific programming may help students develop the first competencies on trajectories to learn programming (Rich et al. 2017, 2019).

CONCLUSION: FINDING PATHWAYS TO COMPUTATIONAL LITERACY

There are many reasons for students to learn programming, from understanding the digital world in which they live, to developing computational participation and action skills, to developing a new way to understand the world in which they live. Programming offers a powerful notation for learning and thinking that is unlike mathematical equations. The computer is the master simulator—it can look like any domain. Learning programming can be about learning domains that students are already interested in. Learning to program is not just about learning to become a software developer.

Achieving that vision may require us to rethink our programming environments. Languages developed for professional programmers, or developed for children in an earlier age with fewer computational end-interface skills, are unlikely to provide the affordances for learning that we can design in purpose-built environments. Task-specific programming is an approach for providing a pathway to computational literacy.

REFERENCES

Abelson, Harold, Gerald Jay Sussman, and Julie Sussman. 1996. *Structure and Interpretation of Computer Programs.* 2nd ed. Cambridge, MA: MIT Press.

Biggers, Maureen, Anne Brauer, and Tuba Yilmaz. 2008. "Student Perceptions of Computer Science: A Retention Study Comparing Graduating Seniors vs. CS Leavers." In *SIGCSE '08: Proceedings of the 39th SIGCSE Technical Symposium on Computer Science Education.* 402–406. https://doi.org/10.1145/1352135.1352274.

Blumenfeld, Phyllis C., Joseph S. Krajcik, Ronald W. Marx, and Elliot Soloway. 1994. "Lessons Learned: A Collaborative Model for Helping Teachers Learn Project-based Instruction." *Elementary School Journal* 94 (5): 539–551.

Blumenfeld, Phyllis C., Elliot Soloway, Ronald W. Marx, Joseph S. Krajcik, Mark Guzdial, and Annemarie Palincsar. 1991. "Motivating Project-Based Learning: Sustaining the Doing, Supporting the Learning." *Educational Psychologist* 26 (3 & 4): 369–398.

Carver, Sharon M. 1988. "Learning and Transfer of Debugging Skills: Applying Task Analysis to Curriculum Design and Assessment." In *Teaching and Learning Computer Programming: Multiple Research Perspectives*, edited by Richard E. Mayer, 259–297. Hillsdale, NJ: Lawrence Erlbaum Associates.

Chasins, Sarah E., Maria Mueller, and Rastislav Bodik. 2018. "Rousillon: Scraping Distributed Hierarchical Web Data." In *Proceedings of the 31st Annual ACM Symposium on User Interface Software and Technology, UIST '18*. New York, 963–975.

Code.org. "What Most Schools Don't Teach." Streamed live on February 26, 2013, YouTube video, 5:43. https://youtu.be/nKIu9yen5nc.

DiSalvo, Betsy. 2016. "Participatory Design through a Learning Science Lens." In *Proceedings of the 2016 CHI Conference on Human Factors in Computing Systems*. New York, 4459–4463.

diSessa, Andrea A. 2001. *Changing Minds*. Cambridge, MA: MIT Press.

diSessa, Andrea A., and Harold Abelson. 1986. "Boxer: A Recon-structible Computational Medium." *Communications of the ACM* 29 (9): 859–868.

ECMA International. 2011. *Ecma-262 Edition 5.1, The ECMAScript Language Specification*. https://262.ecma-international.org/5.1/#sec-11.9.3.

Fields, Deborah A., Yasmin Bettina Kafai, and Michael T. Giang. 2017. "Youth Computational Participation in the Wild: Understanding Experience and Equity in Participating and Programming in the Online Scratch Community." *ACM Transactions on Computing Education* 17 (3): 15:1–15:22.

Grover, Shuchi, and Roy Pea. 2013. "Computational Thinking in K–12: A Review of the State of the Field." *Educational Researcher*, 42 (1): 38–43.

Grover, Shuchi, Roy Pea, and Stephen Cooper. 2015. "Designing for Deeper Learning in a Blended Computer Science Course for Middle School Students." *Computer Science Education*, 25 (2): 199–237.

Guzdial, Mark. 1995. "Software-Realized Scaffolding to Facilitate Programming for Science Learning." *Interactive Learning Environments* 4 (1): 1–44.

Guzdial, Mark. 2019. "Computing Education as a Foundation for 21st Century Literacy." In *Proceedings of the 50th ACM Technical Symposium on Computer Science Education, SIGCSE '19*. New York, 502–503.

Guzdial, Mark, and John Arquilla. 2019. "Is CS Really for All, and Defending Democracy in Cyberspace." *Communications of the ACM*, 62 (6): 8–9.

Guzdial, Mark, and Benedict du Boulay. 2019. "History of computing education research." In *The Cambridge Handbook of Computing Education Research*, edited by Sally A. Fincher and Anthony V. Robins, 11–39. Cambridge: Cambridge University Press.

Harel, Idit, and Seymour Papert. 1990. "Software Design as a Learning Environment." *Interactive Learning Environments* 1 (1): 1–32.

Kafai, Yasmin Bettina. 2016. "From Computational Thinking to Computational Participation in K–12 Education." *Communications of the ACM* 59 (8): 26–27.

Kafai, Yasmin Bettina, Quinn Burke, and Mitchel Resnick. 2014. *Connected Code: Why Children Need to Learn Programming*. Cambridge, MA: MIT Press.

Kalelioglu, Filiz, and Yasemin Gülbahar. 2014. "The Effects of Teaching Programming via Scratch on Problem Solving Skills: A Discussion from Learners' Perspective." *Informatics in Education* 13 (1): 33–50.

Kay, Alan C. 1977. "Microelectronics and the Personal Computer." *Scientific American* 237 (3): 230–245.

Kay, Alan C. 1995. "Computers, Networks and Education." *Scientific American* 272 (3): 148–155.

Kay, Alan C., and Adele Goldberg. 1977. "Personal Dynamic Media." *IEEE Computer* 10 (3): 31–41.

Knuth, Donald E. 1972. "George Forsythe and the Development of Computer Science." *Communications of the ACM* 15 (8): 721–726.

Krajcik, Joseph S., and Phyllis C. Blumenfeld. 2006. "Project-based Learning." In *The Cambridge Handbook of the Learning Sciences*, edited by R. Keith Sawyer, 317–333. Cambridge: Cambridge University Press.

Lewis, Colleen, Paul Bruno, Jonathan Raygoza, and Julia Wang. 2019. "Alignment of Goals and Perceptions of Computing Predicts Students' Sense of Belonging in Computing." In *Proceedings of the 14th International Conference on Computing Education Research, ICER '19*. New York, 11–9.

Maloney, John, Mitchel Resnick, Natalie Rusk, Brian Silverman, and Evelyn Eastmond. 2010. "The Scratch Programming Language and Environment." *ACM Transactions on Computing Education* 10 (4): 16:1–16:15.

Maloney, John H., Kylie A. Peppler, Yasmin Bettina Kafai, Mitchel Resnick, and Natalie Rusk. 2008. "Programming by Choice: Urban Youth Learning Programming with Scratch." In *SIGCSE '08: Proceedings of the 39th SIGCSE Technical Symposium on Computer Science Education*. New York, 367–371.

Margolis, J., R. Estrella, J. Goode, J. J. Holme, and K. Nao. 2017. *Stuck in the Shallow End: Education, Race, and Computing*. Cambridge, MA: MIT Press.

Moje, Elizabeth B. 2015. "Doing and Teaching Disciplinary Literacy with Adolescent Learners: A Social and Cultural Enterprise." *Harvard Educational Review* 85 (2): 254–278.

O'Neil, Cathy. 2016. *Weapons of Math Destruction: How Big Data Increases Inequality and Threatens Democracy*. New York: Crown.

Palumbo, David B. 1990. "Programming Language/Problem-Solving Research: A Review of Relevant Issues." *Review of Educational Research* 60 (1): 65–89.

Papert, Seymour. 1980. *Mindstorms: Children, Computers, and Powerful Ideas*. Sussex, UK: Basic Books.

Parker, Miranda C., and Mark Guzdial. 2019. "A Statewide Quantitative Analysis of Computer Science: What Predicts CS in Georgia Public High School?" In *Proceedings of* the 2019 ACM Conference on International Computing Education Research, ICER '19. New York, 317.

Pea, Roy D., and D. Midian Kurland. 1984. "On The Cognitive Effects of Learning Computer Programming." *New Ideas in Psychology* 2 (2): 137–168.

Perlis, Alan J. 1962. "The Computer in the University." In *Computers and the World of the Future*, edited by Martin Greenberger, 180–217. Cambridge, MA: MIT Press.

Peyton Jones, Simon. 2013, September. "Computer Science as a School Subject." In *Proceedings of the 18th ACM SIGPLAN International Conference on Functional Programming*. Seattle, 159–160.

Rich, Kathryn M., Carla Strickland, T. Andrew Binkowski, and Diana Franklin. 2019. "A K-8 Debugging Learning Trajectory Derived from Research Literature." In *Proceedings of the 50th ACM Technical Symposium on Computer Science Education, SIGCSE '19*. New York, 745–751.

Rich, Kathryn M., Carla Strickland, T. Andrew Binkowski, Cheryl Moran, and Diana Franklin. 2017. "K-8 Learning Trajectories Derived from Research Literature: Sequence, Repetition, Conditionals." In *Proceedings of the 2017 ACM Conference on International Computing Education Research, ICER '17*. New York, 182–190.

Scaffidi, Christopher. 2017. "Workers Who Use Spreadsheets and Who Program Earn More than Similar Workers Who Do Neither." In *2017 IEEE Symposium on Visual Languages and Human-Centric Computing (VL/HCC)*. Raleigh, NC, 233–237.

Scaffidi, Christopher, Mary Shaw, and Brad A. Myers. 2005. "An Approach for Categorizing End User Programmers to Guide Software Engineering Research." *ACM SIGSOFT Software Engineering Notes* 30 (4): 1–5.

Schanzer, Emmanuel, Kathi D. Fisler, and Shriram Krishnamurthi. 2018. "Assessing Bootstrap: Algebra Students on Scaffolded and Unscaffolded Word Problems." In *SIGCSE '18: Proceedings of the 49th ACM Technical Symposium on Computer Science Education*. New York, 8–13.

Schanzer, Emmanuel, Kathi D. Fisler, Shriram Krishnamurthi, and Matthias Felleisen. 2015. "Transferring Skills at Solving Word Problems from Computing to Algebra through Bootstrap." In *Proceedings of the 46th ACM Technical Symposium on Computer Science Education*. New York, 616–621.

Sherin, Bruce L. 2001. "A Comparison of Programming Languages and Algebraic Notation as Expressive Languages for Physics." *International Journal of Computers for Mathematical Learning* 6: 1–61.

Snow, Charles Percy. 1962. "Scientists and Decision Making." In *Computers and the World of the Future*, edited by Martin Greenberger. Cambridge, MA: MIT Press.

Tatar, Deborah, Jeremy Roschelle, Jennifer Knudsen, Nicole Shechtman, Jim Kaput, and Bill Hopkins. 2008. "Scaling Up Innovative Technology-Based Mathematics." *Journal of the Learning Sciences* 17 (2): 248–286.

Tissenbaum, Mike, Josh Sheldon, and Hal Abelson. 2019. "From Computational Thinking to Computational Action." *Communications of the ACM* 62 (3): 34–36.

Weston, Timothy J., Wendy M. Dubow, and Alexis Kaminsky. 2019. "Predicting Women's Persistence in Computer Science- and Technology-Related Majors from High School to College." *ACM Transactions on Computing Education* 20 (1): 1:1–1:16.

Wilensky, Uri. 1991. "Abstract Meditations on the Concrete and Concrete Implications for Mathematics Education." In *Constructionism*, edited by Idit Harel and Seymour Papert, 193–203. Norwood, NJ: Ablex.

Wilensky, U., K. Orton, D. Weintrop, E. Beheshti, M. Horn, and K. Jona. 2016. "Bringing Computational Thinking into High School Mathematics and Science Classrooms." In *Transforming Learning, Empowering Learners: The International Conference of the Learning Sciences (ICLS)* , Vol. 2, edited by C. K. Looi, J. L. Polman, U. Cress, and P. Reimann. Singapore: International Society of the Learning Sciences.

Wilensky, Uri, and Walter Stroup. 1999. "Learning through Participatory Simulations: Network-Based Design for Systems Learning in Classrooms." In *Proceedings of the 1999 Conference on Computer Support for Collaborative Learning.* Stanford, CA: International Society of the Learning Sciences, 80.

3

DEVELOPING COMPUTATIONAL THINKING SKILLS WITH MULTIPLE MODELS AND REPRESENTATIONS

H. Ulrich Hoppe and Sven Manske

INTRODUCTION

According to Hoppe and Werneburg (2019), the "essence of Computational Thinking (CT) lies in the creation of 'logical artifacts' that externalize and reify human ideas in a form that can be interpreted and 'run' on computers." These logical artifacts can be the results of programming activities, which link CT to programming as a medium. Although the term *computational thinking* has gained popularity more recently, especially through Jeannette Wing's formative paper (2006), Seymour Papert (1996) earlier described the idea and used the term in conjunction with the development of the Logo language as medium for learning mathematics.

Wing (2008, 2017) emphasizes the importance of abstraction in CT. In contrast to the general common-sense notion of abstraction, in computer science it is common to speak of "abstractions" (plural) as constructs, not as a general notion of thinking process in which details of concrete examples are factored out. We can refer to Wing (2008) for a characterization: "The essence of computational thinking is abstraction. . . . In working with layers of abstraction, we necessarily keep in mind the relationship between each pair of layers, be it defined via an abstraction function, a simulation relation, a transformation or a more general kind of mapping. . . . And so the nuts and bolts in computational thinking are defining abstractions, working with multiple layers of abstraction and understanding the relationships among the different layers. Abstractions are the 'mental' tools of computing."

Following Wing, we see abstractions as mental constructs that can be operationalized in different ways to make them executable using abstract machines or different types of programming languages. Aho (2012) uses the term *models of computation* to address the operationalization of constructive abstractions. Variations of such mappings are found between different classes of programming languages (e.g., imperative versus declarative languages) but also comprise "abstract machines" such as automata or grammars. It is important to realize that CT can build on different, even competing, abstractions. We will use the term *representational flexibility* here to denote the characteristic of a CT environment supporting different models of computation.

The idea of abstractions as mental and formal-operational constructs relying on "models of computation" is still not too prominent in the discussions around CT and CT education. The term *computational models* is more commonly used to characterize the computational artifacts that result from or are manipulated in CT activities. From a computer science perspective it is also important to discuss how certain classes of computational models depend on abstract machines or computational paradigms. Computational models have always also been a central ingredient of approaches for learning about STEM (science, technology, engineering, and math) through modeling and simulation. There is a spectrum of activities using such simulations that range from setting up input parameters to modifying or defining the behavior of the simulation through programming. This spectrum of activities includes CT skills (Sengupta et al. 2013). However, in such environments the basic computational "ingredients," namely the underlying data structures and a basic processing model, are usually predefined and fixed. In a computer science perspective on CT, it is desirable to enable that the learners actively experience different computational approaches and paradigms.

The study described in this chapter combines two different models of computation applied to a specific problem and investigates sequencing effects depending on the order of the learning experiences with the one and the other model. The two different computational approaches are applied to the same problem, namely enabling a programmable agent to escape from a maze. In this context, successful problem-solving requires understanding and skills on two levels. On one level, we have the problem of finding a maze strategy, as discussed in the context of *Turtle Geometry* (Abelson and diSessa, 1981). Programming is one way of expressing such strategies that allows for testing and improvement. In this perspective, programming would be instrumental to solving the maze problem in the sense of "learning through programming." In the CT perspective, the maze problem could be used as a challenge to develop certain programming skills in the sense of "learning to program." The co-existence of these two orientations frequently is found in programming-based microworlds (cf. diSessa 2000).

The aim of our study is to investigate the influence of "representational flexibility" in terms of multiple models of computation on both problem understanding and the development of programming skills.

REPRESENTATIONAL FLEXIBILITY

When it comes to an operationalization of CT as a thought process to be carried out, the task of formulating problems and solutions in a way that they can be carried out by computers unveils many degrees of freedom. This flexibility manifests in a variety of aspects when dealing with computational constructs and representations. We attribute "representational flexibility" to a learning environment that preserves and supports alternatives regarding the constructs and representations. This would even allow for asking students to explicitly choose a certain representation as part of a creative CT activity.

Choosing the right representation has had a huge impact both on the individual process and on the development of scientific computation (Tedre and Denning 2016). It led to an entry of computational methods into different science disciplines advancing the computational sciences. Tedre and Denning (2016) argue, "Computer simulation became the main engine of progress across sciences and engineering fields, and computational thinking was its mental toolbox." However, this certain wave in the history of CT was not driven by computer science but was inspired mainly by highly specific application domains. On an individual level, the choice of the appropriate representation or programming tool becomes relevant as the thought processes require learners to think at multiple levels of abstraction. According to Dijkstra (1974), the cognitive skills involved in programming can be described as a mental zoom lens, when the programmer "switches back and forth between various semantic levels, between global and local considerations, between macroscopic and microscopic concerns." In the following, we address different dimensions in which representational flexibility can manifest.

MODELS OF COMPUTATION AND PROGRAMMING TOOLS

The creation of logical, computational artifacts relies on a certain model of computation as an abstract engine. They can be categorized into sequential models (e.g., finite state machines or Turing machines), functional models (e.g., lambda calculus), or concurrent models (e.g., Petri nets). Although the direct use of computational models apart from automata is underrepresented in K–12 education, there are a few examples of environments that make use of such models. For example, the CardBoard (later: FreeStyler) environment supported modeling and running Petri nets in an educational setting (Pinkwart, Hoppe, and Gaßner 2001).

The grounding of computation on such abstract engines, and accordingly the choice of such foundations, is not very much in the focus of the current, more educationally inspired CT discourse. It may seem that these choices have little to do with CT practice. However, there are relevant examples that explicitly address the choice of basic "models of computation" or representations:

- The "Kara" microworld (Hartmann, Nievergelt, and Reichert 2001) uses a programmable ladybug to introduce concepts of computer science and programming. It comes with different versions based on different abstract engines. The original version was based on finite state machines, but later versions based on programming languages (JavaKara, RubyKara) were added. The microworld of Kara allows for solving the same or similar problems based on different "models of computation" in the sense of Aho. The FSM version allows for linking the Kara experience to automata theory in general, whereas the Java and Ruby versions may be used as introductions to programming.

- Kafura and Tatar (2011) report on a Computational Thinking Course for computer science students in which different abstract formalisms or engines (including Petri nets, BNF grammars, lambda expressions) with corresponding tools were employed to construct computational models in response to various problems. This example shows that relying on abstract models of computation can be an alternative to using programming in the construction of computational artifacts.
- Curzon and McOwan (2016) describe computational modeling as a part of algorithmic thinking. The algorithm simulates the transformation of an idea in a virtual world; it is possible that these ideas can be things from the real world like laws of physics but also a fantasy world, which is modeled as a game.

The growing interest in teaching and learning programming during the last decade has predominantly led to using visual block-based programming interfaces in combination with imperative/procedural programming languages. Scratch (Resnick et al. 2009) is a prominent example of this type. Although it has been criticized for supporting or allowing bad programming habits (Meerbaum-Salant, Armoni, and Ben-Ari 2011), it is a de facto standard for exploratory programming in current CT education. However, visual programming environments are not necessarily bound to the imperative paradigm. Although very similar to Scratch in its visual appearance, the Snap! environment also provides elements of functional programming such as anonymous and higher-order functions in a visual block-based style (Harvey and Mönig 2015).

Although common programming languages do not show fundamental differences in their models of computation, there is still a big difference across the various programming paradigms and in the levels of abstraction as part of the mental models and thought processes involved in the programming. A purely functional language such as Haskell offers higher abstractions from mathematical thinking than writing assembler code that is closer to the set of operations provided by a concrete machine. Because of the set of computational constructs and paradigms that underlie the specific programming tool, novices may expect difficulties when they anticipate a certain behavior from their mental models (Rogalski and Samurçay 1990). One example is using the equal operator for assignment in several imperative programming languages, in contrast to algebra, where the operator is an assertion of equality.

In summary, there is a tension between models of computation and learners' cognitive models in programming. The choice of the right programming tools is important on different levels. Therefore, it is desirable to support a representational flexibility in the CT environment and activity. Representational flexibility in this aspect means that the user in such a CT environment has the ability to switch between different models of computation, programming tools, problem representations, or levels of abstraction.

This flexibility is not limited to the choice of a concrete programming tool, paradigm, or language: it can be extended to the particular application domain and the corresponding problem space as part of problem-solving in CT activities. In the tradition of Logo and turtle graphics, labyrinths are good examples for representational flexibility in this context. On the one hand, the algorithmic specification of maze strategies can be situated in the geometry of the microworld (turtle geometry) and solved with procedural programs using actions in the concrete environment. Alternatively, the labyrinth may be represented as an abstract graph, and the solution to the labyrinth may be based on general graph search. This can have implications on which programming tool is suited best for the domain-specific solution. It is plausible for many applications that domain-specific languages (see the next subsection) are the appropriate ways to address problem-formulating and problem-solving processes.

MICROWORLDS AND DOMAIN-SPECIFIC LANGUAGES

Andi diSessa's notion of "computational literacies" (diSessa 2000) presupposes the availability and accessibility of computational media as a basis for creative invention and computational representation. The computational medium would include a "model of computation" in Aho's sense but would also provide more or less easy access to different types of abstractions. The medium may be a programming language, but as we have seen before, it can also be an "abstract engine" or even a physical model in the "unplugged" sense. For programming languages, it is well known that they resonate with computational abstractions (as constructs) in specific ways. For example, the concept of a variable as a storage or memory location is typical for imperative languages. This implies that variables can have mutable values, which is different from the concept of variables in pure functional or logical languages. Computational media for creative and constructive learning are often combined with concrete application domains (corresponding also to learning domains) for which the medium and its representational primitives are particularly designed. This is captured in the notion of a "microworld":

A microworld is a type of computational document aimed at embedding important ideas in a form that students can readily explore. The best microworlds have an easy-to-understand set of operations that students can use to engage tasks of value to them, and in doing so, they come to understanding powerful underlying principles. You might come to understand ecology, for example, by building your own little creatures that compete with and are dependent on each other. (diSessa 2000)

The educational affordances and usage patterns that originate from microworlds are immense and have been widely discussed from an educational technology point of view (e.g., Rieber 1996). From a computer science perspective, microworlds in the sense described by diSessa can be conceived as *domain-specific languages* designed to facilitate constructive learning in certain domains. Compare the general characterization given by van Deursen, Klint, and Visser (2000): "A domain-specific language (DSL) is a programming language or executable specification language that offers, through appropriate notations and abstractions, expressive power focused on, and usually restricted to, a particular problem domain." This suggests that the principles of designing and implementing DSLs should be considered when we develop microworlds as computational media for learning.

Regarding the structuring of learning processes and the enrichment of such processes with computational media, inquiry learning in science and CT education are closely related. However, a discourse that is primarily driven by pedagogical inspirations and interest tends to neglect the importance of genuine computer science concepts and their role in shaping CT. The understanding of the computational principles underlying and constituting such logical artifacts, including "models of computation" in the sense of Aho as well as specific "abstractions as constructs," are of central importance for CT. In contrast, in general scientific inquiry learning, computational models are instrumental for the understanding the domain of interest (e.g., the functioning of ecosystems or certain chemical reactions). Usually, the computational media used in general inquiry learning contexts are of limited "representational flexibility" regarding the choice of data structures and abstract operational mechanisms.

THE EFFECT OF PROGRAMMING PARADIGMS ON PROBLEM-SOLVING

Visual block-based programming (VBBP) can be seen as the current standard for introductory programming in K–12 education with Scratch as the most prominent facilitator (Resnick et al. 2009). There is evidence that VBBP, with a well-defined semantics including a concrete environment inspired by turtle geometry, can facilitate a smooth start of learning programming and avoid issues of programming syntax as in textual languages. Overall, it provides a rich and stimulating learning environment (Grover and Pea 2013). However, it is also reported that students perceive that these tools are less powerful, cumbersome to use for larger projects, and inauthentic if compared to conventional text-based programming tools (DiSalvo 2014; Weintrop and Wilensky 2015). Although Scratch is mostly characterized through the imperative programming paradigm, it promotes the creation of interactive programs through a rich event-based programming interface. However, the mechanisms provided tend to encourage learners to misuse the constructs "broadcast" and "wait," which is sometimes perceived as a bad practice (Aivaloglou and Hermans 2016). This deficit is compensated for in the App Inventor (Wolber et al. 2011), which follows a similar visual approach but focuses on the development of mobile applications, which are "native" to events. In contrast to proposing a one-size-fits-all solution for introductory programming, we advocate the use of different programming paradigms and representations in such environments.

A CT environment can be characterized as holding representational flexibility if it provides the learners or users with a certain choice regarding programming tools, paradigms, abstractions, and other aspects that have been discussed in the previous section. However, little evidence exists in research on CT regarding sequencing effects when switching between different representations and programming tools. In this section, we present ctMazeStudio, which is a virtual learning environment that has been developed to explore the effects and implications of representational flexibility on CT.

CTMAZESTUDIO: A MULTI-PARADIGMATIC ENVIRONMENT

The *ctMazeStudio* system facilitates the definition of agent behavior in a maze environment with different difficulty levels through two different programming paradigms. The goal is to define a strategy that lets the agent find a way out of any maze of the given level. In the overall learning process, the learners will formulate strategies of more and more general nature, ending up with a correct implementation of "wall following."

The reactive rule-based approach facilitates the formulation of strategies in a bottom-up and "situated" fashion: In a given situation (i.e., with the agent in a certain position in a certain maze), the learner is provided with a "localized" rule that reflects the concrete situation in the neighborhood of the agent in its pre-instantiated conditions (IF-part) and still empty actions (THEN-part). Now, the learner has to fill in a corresponding action or action sequence made up of 90-degree turns or stepwise movements forward. These rules will be "memorized" by the agent and will be re-applied under the same conditions. This approach was inspired by the kind of visual agent programming introduced in "KidSim" (Smith, Cypher, and Spohrer 1994).

To support this kind of learning and problem-solving activity, ctMazeStudio contains three components: the rule editor, the behavior stage, and a rule library (figure 3.1). The rule editor (figure 3.2) provides the actual "local" programming interface, which is invoked when a new situation is encountered. The editor shows a condition component (IF-part) and an action component (THEN-part). For the given conditions, the students select desired actions to define a situated rule of "reactive" behavior. The user can also delete conditions, which implies that the corresponding rule will be applied in situations more general than the given one, disregarding one of the premises (as a generalization mechanism).

As can be seen in figure 3.3, the current situation implicitly specifies the conditions from which the rule-building starts. If there is no existing rule that matches the current premises, the system requests the student to define actions for the given situation. Afterward, the newly defined rule will be applied to all situations matching the same condition.

The architecture of the rule-based subsystem of ctMazeStudio is shown in figure 3.4. In the graphical user interface, the user can create a new rule or modify an existing rule in the rule editor. Each created rule is listed in

Behavior Stage

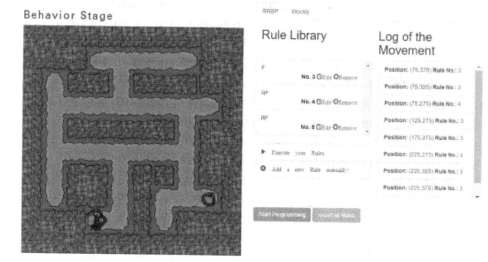

3.1 ctMazeStudio with rule library.

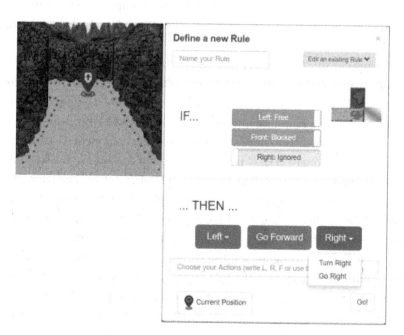

3.2 ctMazeStudio's "situated" rule editor.

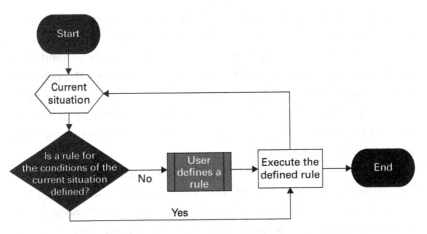

3.3 Flow diagram for reactive rule-based programming (RRBP).

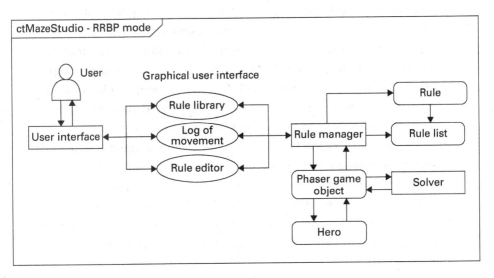

3.4 Architecture of the rule-based system.

the rule library, initially in the order of creation. The ordering of the rules determines the order of the matching and ensuing execution, which is relevant if the rule conditions are not disjoint. The rule manager combines the library of rules with the interpretation of the rules and renders the result through a game engine. Depending on the success of the rule execution in the solver, the rule is transformed into code to trigger the movement of the agent ("hero") in the game engine, which causes it to proceed.

The rule library shown in figure 3.1 allows for managing the collection of all previously defined rules. The learners can edit or delete already defined rules, directly enter new rules, and change the order (and thus priority) of the rules to be checked. In the behavior stage, the behavior of the agent is visualized. Depending on the entries in the rule library, the corresponding actions are executed, and the specific entry in the rule library is highlighted. The execution will stop if no more applicable rules are found or the goal is reached.

On the higher levels, learners must apply different strategies to improve their programming code (i.e., the rule set). When they develop and test their rule sets, they may revise formerly defined rule sets through generalization (dropping of conditions) or reordering. The challenge is to create a maximally powerful rule set with a minimum number of rules. This requires a level of understanding that allows for predicting global behavior based on locally specified rules. In the maze example, a small set of rules (minimally three) will be created to implement a wall-following strategy. A correct algorithmic solution has to ensure that the wall is always kept either on the right or on the left hand. This strategy works with any kind of maze that has no cycles or "islands." Beyond the predefined levels, this strategy can still be refined to avoid circling around islands.

A specific characteristic of this approach to programming is that the learner is confronted with concrete situations and "forced" to decide what should happen. Afterward the learner sees the cascading effect of this decision and can rethink or refine it. Many individual decisions combine to an overall picture of reactions that solves the entire task. When applying the rule library to other mazes, learners can evaluate and generalize the rules.

In addition to the reactive rule-based mode, the ctMazeStudio environment can also be programmed through a visual block-structured interface (figure 3.5). The visual programming component for this variant of ctMazeStudio has been implemented based on *Google Blockly*. Conceptually, it requires a top-down imperative programming approach with conditionals and loops as control structures. ctMazeStudio therefore supports a specific type of "representational flexibility" with the combination of reactive rule-based programming (RRBP) and visual block-based programming (VBBP).

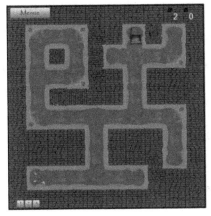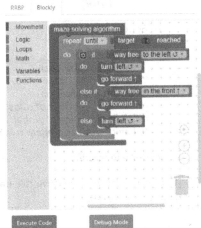

3.5 Block-structured programming interface.

RRBP and VBBP are not only different on a representational or coding level; they also stand for different ways of tackling the maze challenge. These differences include the aspect of control: RRBP is based on an agent model with an implicit mechanisms of rule selection and execution (i.e., a predefined, local control model), whereas the VBBP require to define a global control regime as part of the code. The analysis of cases in terms of conditions comes as a follow-up activity in RRBP starting from given situation patterns, whereas it is a primary modeling step in VBBP. The basic differences related to the two programming approaches are summarized in figure 3.6.

HYPOTHESES AND STUDY DESIGN

The principal of supporting multiple computational approaches when teaching CT is based on the rationale that we should not restrict CT to one specific model of computation but convey the richness of different types of computational models. Learning environments based on one specific computational approach will support a learning progression within this approach. However, in our maze environment, we can also examine the impact of the different computational representations and approaches on the understanding of the problem domain. This problem understanding, in turn, is related to algorithmic thinking (in the way of thinking about labyrinth algorithms).

RRBP	**_VBBP_**
▶ Bottom-up strategy	▶ Top-down strategy
▶ Local control, "situational" approach	▶ Explicit global control and case distinction
▶ Ex-post generalization *(minimizing number of rules requires inference of global behavior from aggregate rules)*	▶ Higher threshold (less specific support)
▶ Domain-specific	▶ More general

3.6 Comparison between reactive rule-based programming (RRBP) and visual block-based programming (VBBP).

The main higher-level learning goal is the understanding of wall-following as a general strategy. This understanding is induced by a level structure, which adds new facets of labyrinths (e.g., circles, islands) stepwise to the environment. During the study, the learners were asked to solve the levels and to create such an algorithm to solve all labyrinths.

Based on these premises, we have studied the effect of sequencing the usage of RRBP and of VBBP. Our central hypothesis was, *"(H1) The understanding and active mastery of wall-following will be better supported by RRBP."* Our two experimental conditions were RRBP first, followed by VBBP second (group A) and vice versa for group B. Accordingly, we would expect the learning gain (related to the maze strategy) to be higher for group A than for group B after the first trial. We would expect group B to "catch up" after the second round. Additional observations were made regarding the problem-specific and general coding abilities in the VBBP approach. Specifically, we would expect the following: *"(H2) Prior experience with RRBP will lead to better solutions in the VBBP modality in terms of finding and implementing correct strategies."*

Figure 3.7 represents the overall experimental procedure.

The tests of algorithmic understanding were related to the maze problem and operationalized through specific questions, involving also paper and pencil solutions with given labyrinths. CT competencies were tested through questions inspired by the CTt questionnaire proposed by González (2015) and the instruments used for the assessment by Grover and Basu

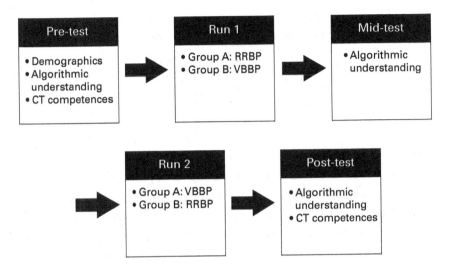

3.7 Experimental procedure.

(2017) have been adapted to the specific application domain and programming tools. Among others, this involves tasks about code comprehension, interpretation of statement sequences, and the formulation of algorithms in a Scratch-like representation that uses natural language. During a mid-test, learners were asked to describe the algorithm they had used to solve the labyrinth of the main level. These descriptions were evaluated manually to assess algorithmic thinking with respect to the learning goal of creating a wall-following strategy.

The study was conducted in a public German high school ("Gymnasium") with a group of thirty-one grade-nine students participating in an elective computer science course. Two were female and twenty-nine were male,[1] and all were between fourteen and sixteen years old (M = 14.87). The average self-assessment of programming skills was 2.77 on a five-point Likert scale. Group A had fifteen, and group B had sixteen participants. The duration of the test was ninety minutes.

EXPERIMENTAL RESULTS

Table 3.1 below captures the distribution of successful completions of level 8 (corresponding to wall following) for all groups and conditions.

Table 3.1 Success (completion of level 8)
per group and programming modality

	RRBP	VBBP
Group A	6	8
Group B	5	2

For both groups, the rate of success increased from trial 1 to trial 2 (A: 6 to 8; B: 2 to 5). The overall success was higher in group A.

The outcome for group A indicates that the correct problem understanding developed in the RRBP condition could be transferred to the second phase and allowed for a re-coding in the other modality (VBBP). In contrast, starting with VBBP did not facilitate success in solving the problem.

Although the results for RRBP look positive, there was a specific problem that often created a learning obstacle: The rule editor allowed for entering an unlimited sequence of actions so that a specific solution for the given maze could be specified at a single blow. However, such solutions would not be transferable to other mazes (not even of the same level). To avoid this problem, the number of actions in one rule can now be limited in the current version of ctMazeStudio. The maximally needed number of actions would be two to be able to combine a forward step with a turn.

Figure 3.8 shows the quantified results of the "algorithmic understanding" test applied after Run 1 (T1) and after Run 2 (T2). The questions were designed in such a way as to distinguish procedural and declarative knowledge related to this problem, and the diagram shows the results with this distinction. First, we compared the different measurements for each of the groups (A and B) separately using the non-parametric Wilcoxon signed-rank test. For both groups, the difference (increase) in procedural knowledge was not significant. However, group B showed a significant increase in declarative knowledge between T1 and T2 ($Z = 19.5$, $p = 0.026$). The corresponding difference (slight decrease) of declarative knowledge in group A was not significant.

Second, we used the Mann-Whitney U test to compare the declarative understanding between groups A and B. We found a significant difference for the measurements at time point T1 ($U = 68.5$, $p = 0.20$), but no

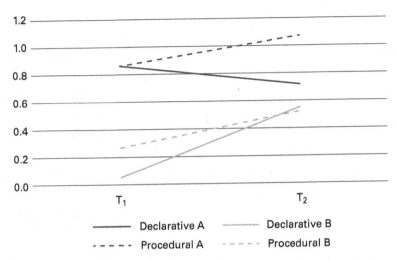

3.8 Algorithmic understanding: declarative and procedural knowledge of groups A and B, measured at T_1 and T_2.

significant difference at T2 (U = 105.5, p = 0.286). This corroborates our central hypothesis (H1): The RRBP experience is essential for a better (declarative) understanding of the maze strategy in both groups. The essential knowledge gain comes from the exposition to RRBP.

The second hypotheses (H2) is plausibly backed by the comparison of success figures in table 3.1: Success in the VBBP condition is four times higher if this modality is preceded by RRBP. However, an analysis of "productivity" in terms of number of trials did not show a difference between groups A and B in the VBBP condition.

DISCUSSION

This study investigated the differences in CT "induced" by different computational approaches or paradigms used in a maze problem-solving task. The differences were reflected and measured in terms of the understanding of the problem-related strategies as an effect of "learning through programming."

The RRBP approach favors a bottom-up and "situated" type of reasoning and is certainly more specifically adapted to the problem than VBBP. Accordingly, it provides an easier start. On the other hand, RRBP comes with the challenge of inferring the global behavior of the agent from a collection of locally defined rules. A correct implementation of the wall-following strategy requires the generalization of rules and typically also a reduction of the accumulated rule set. We demonstrated that the prior experience (of RRBP) supports the declarative understanding of the problem better than VBBP and leads to higher success rates in the VBBP condition, which is characterized by a top-down and imperative model of computation. In this sense, RRBP can "feed into" VBBP as a more general approach. Our findings suggest that we should exploit more variations in basic computational approaches ("representational flexibility") to support the development of CT conceived as a rich collection of cognitive skills.

CONSEQUENCES FOR CURRICULUM DESIGN AND ORCHESTRATING COMPUTATIONAL THINKING

Our study shows that models of computation or programming paradigms do not just represent different flavors of building and understanding concrete computational models to solve given problems. The choice of a paradigm can have an important impact on the students' ability to solve the problems at hand and may also influence the overall learning progression.

The provision to make a choice regarding the programming tool, paradigm, abstractions, or data structures enables learners to better express themselves through programming. Programming is a constructive activity that requires both creativity and formal rigor. Special languages and interfaces have been developed to make it more novice friendly and accessible; Scratch is one of the most prominent examples. However, based on the work reported here, we argue that there are conditions, in which other paradigms and approaches are more suited for a specific problem type and activity. To optimally facilitate CT skills, learners need to accommodate to choose their own representations carefully with respect to a given problem and to adapt it to their personal cognitive tools.

This has two main implications on the design of the curriculum or the orchestration of CT. The existence of one general programming tool may lead to a higher threshold in problem-solving for learners. This has been presented in this chapter in the domain of maze algorithms, where problem-solving strategies can be better applied and illustrated using reactive rules in a bottom-up approach. In the visual block-based approach, learners need to write their algorithms in advance and thus must perform bigger steps to see and evaluate results. Supporting the evaluation of pieces of code is often characterized as an important aspect in CT activities. However, representational flexibility should not be simplified nor be limited to the programming tool itself, the used paradigm, or the examples from this article.

The predominance of imperative programming in visual approaches can be traced back to the popularity of imperative programming languages at the time these approaches have been developed. Therefore, other approaches may be more supportive or helpful in the acquisition of CT skills. In his remarks on CT, Aho (2012) underlines the importance of clarifying the representational-operational basis of CT in terms of an underlying "model of computation" with well-defined operational semantics. Imperative programming in von Neumann architecture is a legitimate model of computation in this sense. However, there is a wide spectrum of other potential models of computation. The example of the Kara environment (Hartmann, Nievergelt, and Reichert 2001) shows that finite-state machines can be used as an alternative to Java programming in controlling a robot in microworld. We have also seen Petri nets being used to model the interaction in board games. The empirical evidence gathered with ctMazeStudio is certainly limited regarding the specificity of the task and the models of computation. Yet, it allowed us to demonstrate that there are benefits in providing learners with alternative models of computation to support computational problem-solving.

NOTE

1. The quantitative dominance of male participants is typical for elective (choice-based) computer science courses in German high schools. Given this sample, we have not been able to analyze gender effects.

REFERENCES

Abelson, Harold, and Andrea diSessa. 1981. *Turtle Geometry*. Cambridge, MA: MIT Press.

Aho, Alfred V. 2012. "Computation and Computational Thinking." *The Computer Journal* 55 (7): 832–835.

Aivaloglou, Efthimia, and F. Felienne Hermans. 2016. "How Kids Code and How We Know: An Exploratory Study on the Scratch Repository." In *Proceedings of the 2016 ACM Conference on International Computing Education Research*. New York, 53–61.

Curzon, Paul, and Peter W. McOwan. 2016. *The Power of Computational Thinking: Games, Magic and Puzzles to Help You Become a Computational Thinker*. London: World Scientific.

Dijkstra, Edsger W. 1974. "Programming as a Discipline of Mathematical Nature." *The American Mathematical Monthly* 81 (6): 608–612.

DiSalvo, Betsy. (2014). "Graphical Qualities of Educational Technology: Using Drag-and-Drop and Text-Based Programs for Introductory Computer Science." *IEEE Computer Graphics and Applications* 34 (6): 12–15.

diSessa, Andrea A. 2000. *Changing Minds: Computers, Learning and Literacy*. Cambridge, MA: MIT Press.

Giere, R. 1988. "Laws, Theories, and Generalizations." In *The Limits of Deductivism*, edited by Adolf Grunbaum and Wesley Salmon, 37–46. Berkeley: University of California Press.

González, Marcos Roman. 2015. "Computational Thinking Test: Design Guidelines and Content Validation." In *Proceedings of the EDULEARN15 Conference*. Barcelona, 2436–2444.

Google Blockly. Accessed December 19, 2019. https://developers.google.com/blockly.

Grover, Shuchi, and Satabdi Basu. 2017. "Measuring Student Learning in Introductory Block-Based Programming: Examining Misconceptions of Loops, Variables, and Boolean Logic." In *Proceedings of the 2017 ACM SIGCSE Technical Symposium on Computer Science Education*. New York, 267–272.

Grover, Shuchi, and Roy Pea. 2013. "Computational Thinking in K–12." *Educational Researcher* 42 (1): 38–43. https://doi.org/10.3102/0013189X12463051.

Hartmann, W., J. Nievergelt, and R. Reichert. 2001. "Kara, Finite State Machines, and the Case for Programming as Part of General Education." In *Proceedings IEEE Symposia on Human-Centric Computing Languages and Environments*. Washington, DC, 135–141.

Harvey, Brian, and Jens Mönig. 2015. "Lambda in Blocks Languages: Lessons Learned." In *2015 IEEE Blocks and Beyond Workshop (Blocks and Beyond)*, 35–38. Washington, DC: IEEE.

Hoppe, Heinz Ulrich, and Sören Werneburg. 2019. "Computational Thinking—More Than a Variant of Scientific Inquiry!" In *Computational Thinking Education*, edited by Siu Cheung Kong and Harold Abelson, 13–30. Singapore: SpringerOpen.

Kafura, Dennis, and Deborah Tatar. 2011. "Initial Experience with a Computational Thinking Course for Computer Science Students." In *Proceedings of the 42nd ACM Technical Symposium on Computer Science Education*. New York, 251–256.

Meerbaum-Salant, Orni, Michal Armoni, and Mordechai Ben-Ari. 2011. "Habits of Programming in Scratch." In *Proceedings of the 16th Annual Joint Conference on Innovation and Technology in Computer Science Education.* New York, 168–172.

Papert, Seymour. 1996. "An Exploration in the Space of Mathematics Educations." *International Journal of Computers for Mathematical Learning* 1 (1): 95–123.

Pinkwart, Niels, Ulrich Hoppe, and Katrin Gaßner. (2001, September). "Integration of Domain-Specific Elements into Visual Language Based Collaborative Environments." In *Proceedings Seventh International Workshop on Groupware, CRIWG 2001.* Washington, DC, 142–147.

Resnick, Mitchel, John Maloney, Andrés Monroy-Hernández, Natalie Rusk, Evelyn Eastmond, Karen Brennan, Amon Millner, Eric Rosenbaum, Jay Saul Silver, Brian Silverman, and Yasmin Kafai. 2009. Scratch: Programming for All. *Communications of the ACM* 52 (11): 60–67.

Rieber, Lloyd P. 1996. Microworlds. *Handbook of Research for Educational Communications and Technology,* 2, 583–603.

Rogalski, Janine, and Renan Samurçay. 1990. "Acquisition of Programming Knowledge and Skills." In *Psychology of Programming,* edited by J-M. Hoc, T. R. G. Green, D. J. Gilmore and R. Samurçay, 157–174. London: Academic Press.

Sengupta, Pratim, John S. Kinnebrew, Satabdi Basu, Gautam Biswas, and Douglas Clark. 2013. "Integrating Computational Thinking with K–12 Science Education Using Agent-Based Computation: A Theoretical Framework." *Education and Information Technologies* 18 (2): 351–380.

Smith, David Canfield, Allen Cypher, and Jim Spohrer. 1994. "KidSim: Programming Agents without a Programming Language." *Communications of the ACM* 37 (7): 54–67.

Tedre, Matti, and Peter J. Denning. 2016. "The Long Quest for Computational Thinking." In *Proceedings of the 16th Koli Calling International Conference on Computing Education Research.* New York, 120–129.

van Deursen, Arie, Paul Klint, and Joost Visser. 2000. "Domain-Specific Languages: An Annotated Bibliography." *ACM Sigplan Notices* 35 (6): 26–36.

Weintrop, David, and Uri Wilensky. 2015. "To Block or Not to Block, That Is the Question: Students' Perceptions of Blocks-Based Programming." In *Proceedings of the 14th International Conference on Interaction Design and Children,* 199–208. https://doi .org/10.1145/2771839.2771860.

Wing, Jeannette M. 2006. "Computational Thinking." *Communications of the ACM* 49 (3): 33–35.

Wing, Jeannette M. 2008. "Computational Thinking and Thinking About Computing." *Philosophical Transactions of the Royal Society of London A: Mathematical, Physical and Engineering Sciences* 366 (1881): 3717–3725.

Wing, Jeannette M. 2017. "Computational Thinking's Influence on Research and Education for All." *Italian Journal of Educational Technology* 25 (2): 7–14.

Wolber, David, Harold Abelson, Ellen Spertus, and Liz Looney. 2011. *App Inventor*. Sebastopol, CA: O'Reilly Media, Inc.

4

TOWARD A THEORY (AND PRACTICE) OF MULTIPLE COMPUTATIONAL THINKINGS

Marcos Román-González, Jesús Moreno-León, and Gregorio Robles

INTRODUCTION

New theories often emerge from seemingly contradictory evidence. When conflicting empirical results are found, a way forward is to enunciate new and broader theories that can accommodate those contradictions within a more comprehensive framework. That is the rationale for the present chapter.

In this vein, recent computational thinking (CT) studies in K–12 have yielded conflicting results depending on whether the computational concepts involved were used to solve a specific type-modality of problem or another. Thus, in a study by Román-González, Pérez-González, and Jiménez-Fernández (2017), participants from ten to sixteen years old were asked to use computational concepts, such as sequences, loops, conditionals, and functions to solve visuospatial problems, such as mazes or graphic designs, on a digital canvas (figure 4.1). On the other hand, in a study by Howland and Good (2015), participants from twelve to thirteen years old were asked to use similar computational concepts to solve linguistic-narrative problems (figure 4.2). To this end, children were taught to use Flip, "a programming language that aims to help 11–15 year olds develop computational skills through creating their own 3D role-playing games [i.e., interactive storytelling]" (Howland and Good, 224).

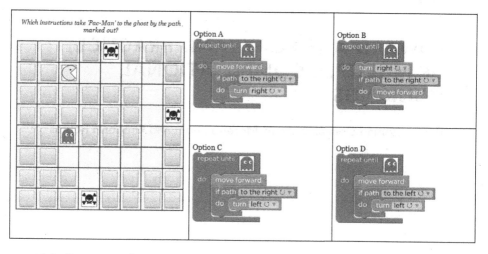

4.1 Computational concepts to solve a visuospatial problem (Román-González, Pérez-González, and Jiménez-Fernández 2017).

Flip has a unique feature that consists of combining a block-based programming language and a dynamically updating natural language version of the script under creation on the same interface (figure 4.3).

The former study (Román-González, Pérez-González, and Jiménez-Fernández 2017), which was fully conducted in pure pre-test condition (i.e., participants without any prior formal experience in computer programming), showed significant differences in favor of the boys and throughout all the school grades involved (figure 4.4, *left*). In contrast, the latter research (Howland and Good 2015) yielded conflictive results in favor of the girls, both in pre-test and post-test conditions (figure 4.4, *right*). How can it be possible if both studies measured the same psychological construct (i.e., CT) in participants with a similar age range?

Nevertheless, these aforementioned results are just seemingly contradictory since they reveal some alternative explanations:

- First, results summarized in figure 4.4 are consistent with classical and relevant literature on gender differences. Thus, several meta-analyses demonstrate higher male spatial ability, especially in tasks that involve mental rotation of figures (e.g., Linn and Petersen 1985; Voyer, Voyer, and Bryden 1995), which could explain differences in favor of boys in the study by Román-González, Pérez-González, and Jiménez-Fernández

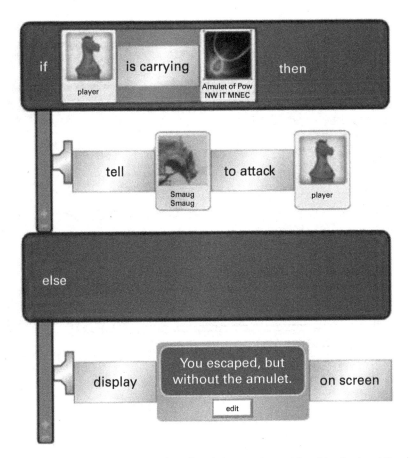

4.2 Computational concepts to solve a linguistic-narrative problem (Howland and Good 2015).

(2017). Analogously, some other meta-analyses show female superiority in tasks involving verbal-linguistic ability (e.g., Hyde and Linn 1988; Lewin, Wolgers, and Herlitz 2001), which could explain differences in favor of girls in the study by Howland and Good (2015).

- Moreover, there is a great deal of empirical evidence that demonstrates that CT is mainly a problem-solving ability linked with fluid intelligence (e.g., Boom et al. 2018; Román-González, Pérez-González, and Jiménez-Fernández 2017), which is characterized by adapting to the context demands. In other words, if we assume that CT is a fluid cognitive ability, then its concrete expression and behavior (i.e., its

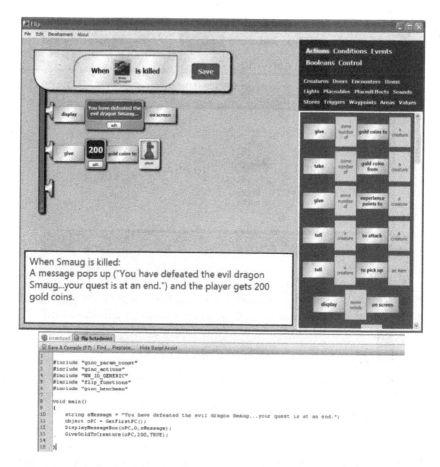

4.3 Interface of Flip, which blends block-based programming-language and natural language.

crystallization) may vary, depending on the type-modality of problems on which such ability is projected. The same applies to a fluid, such as water, that takes the shape of its container.

Therefore, all of the above suggests that CT could be manifested in multiple and different ways, depending on the type-modality of problems to be solved. In other words, it is plausible to hypothesize the existence not of a single, but of multiple, computational thinkings. This statement clearly resonates with the Theory of Multiple Intelligences (TMI) postulated by Howard Gardner (1983, 1999), in which the author claimed the

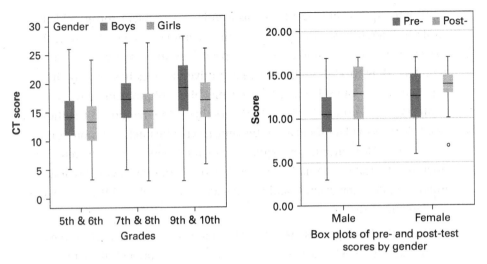

4.4 Gender differences in CT performance over visuospatial problems (*left*; Román-González, Pérez-González, and Jiménez-Fernández 2017) and linguistic-narrative problems (*right*; Howland and Good 2015).

existence not of a single, but of multiple, intelligences. Since we are going to intersect CT and TMI, let's clarify each of these terms.

From our point of view, CT can be defined as a human-cognitive ability that consists of formulating and representing problems so that they can be subsequently solved using computational concepts (e.g., sequences, loops, events, parallelism, conditionals, operators) and practices (e.g., experimenting and iterating, testing and debugging, reusing and remixing, abstracting and modularizing) (Moreno-León et al. 2019). Furthermore, we consider that computer programming is the fundamental way that enables CT to come alive (Lye and Koh 2014), although CT can be projected on different kinds of problems that may not involve directly programming tasks. In other words, *"Just like we distinguish* [for example] *between verbal aptitude (which is in the order of human cognitive abilities, with an important innate base) and literacy skill(s)* [i.e. reading and writing] *(which is an instrumental competence that requires a relatively formal teaching and learning process); we could similarly establish a distinction between CT (human cognitive ability) and programming skills (instrumental competence)"* (Moreno-León et al. 2019, 32).

On the other hand, TMI is a modular theory of intelligence. This means that, instead of considering the human mind as a single and general information-processing agent (i.e., as a universal problem solver, which works indifferently regardless the content or context of the problem), TMI perceives the human mind as a set of separate cognitive modules or faculties. According to TMI, each of these cognitive modules has very specific capabilities (i.e., can solve specific types-modalities of problems, always in context), and Gardner (1983, 1999) names these aforementioned faculties as *intelligences* to place them all at the same level of hierarchy. In more concrete terms, TMI currently recognizes eight intelligences, namely verbal-linguistic, logical-mathematical, musical, bodily-kinesthetic, visual-spatial, interpersonal, intrapersonal, and naturalistic. Additionally, TMI states two fundamental principles:

- The eight intelligences are relatively independent of each other (i.e., the subject's level in a given intelligence does not predict his/her level in another).
- A same intelligence may be needed to excel in different tasks or human activity fields (e.g., visual-spatial intelligence is needed to orient yourself in a city and to master graphic design tasks). In addition, to excel in some human activity fields may require a high level in more than one intelligence (e.g., being an excellent orchestra conductor probably demands high levels in musical, bodily-kinesthetic, and interpersonal intelligences).

Hence, in the following sections we intend to intertwine CT and TMI. In other words, we will try to reinterpret Gardner's theory in computational terms. This goal fully aligns with the initial premise of TMI: to be intelligent is to solve problems within a given context and to create products that are valuable within a given culture-society. Since our present context is mainly digital, given that our present culture-society relies on digital artifacts and products, then it seems necessary to revisit Gardner's intelligences from a computational approach. To some extent, Gardner himself has assumed this possibility since he has recently redefined *an intelligence* as "a capacity to compute using a particular type of information in service to a particular role" (Moran and Gardner 2018, 25).

Before continuing, readers should be aware that this chapter is speculative; that is, it aims to generate and stimulate discussion and to open new lines of research, not to establish a definitive and binding CT framework.

GROUNDING THE THEORY OF MULTIPLE COMPUTATIONAL THINKINGS

In this section, we will try to ground our theory through a (nonexhaustive) review of K–12 educational interventions, along which CT has been used and developed, mostly by means of computer programming, to solve different kinds of problems: verbal-linguistic, logical-mathematical, musical, bodily-kinesthetic, visual-spatial, interpersonal, intrapersonal, and naturalistic.

COMPUTATIONAL THINKING IN VERBAL-LINGUISTIC PROBLEMS

Verbal-linguistic intelligence involves a special sensitivity toward language, both spoken and written, an outstanding ability to learn (new/ foreign) languages, and the ability to use language to achieve certain objectives. Among the people with high verbal-linguistic intelligence are lawyers, speakers, writers, and poets. In other words, linguistic intelligence is needed to deal with problems that are formulated or represented in a verbal way (Gardner 1983, 1999).

We find several examples in the literature in which CT has been applied to verbal-linguistic contexts. In this regard, we highlight the pioneering studies of Quinn Burke, who almost one decade ago started to introduce basic computational concepts to middle school students within the context of the writing classroom and by means of Scratch (a block-based programming language) (Burke 2012; Burke and Kafai 2012). Other experiences and studies have infused CT into K–12 schools through digital (Campos, Signoretti, and Rodrigues 2017) or unplugged (Curzon et al. 2014) storytelling activities. Campos, Signoretti, and Rodrigues (2017) is a clear example of how a computational concept (e.g., conditional logic) can be embedded in a verbal-linguistic product (figure 4.5, *top*). In another vein, computational practices such as modeling have been used to support language learning in several areas (Sabitzer et al. 2018): reading comprehension, vocabulary acquirement, or grammar rules/structures visualization (figure 4.5, *bottom*). In reverse, some computational tools have been designed in which natural language supports and scaffolds the learning of a programming language (e.g., Howland and Good 2015; Proctor and Blikstein 2017). Finally, empirical evidence exists regarding the effectiveness of narrative and storytelling

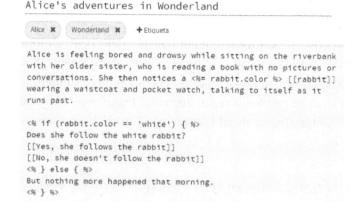

Alice's adventures in Wonderland

```
Alice ✕   Wonderland ✕   + Etiqueta

Alice is feeling bored and drowsy while sitting on the riverbank
with her older sister, who is reading a book with no pictures or
conversations. She then notices a <%= rabbit.color %> [[rabbit]]
wearing a waistcoat and pocket watch, talking to itself as it
runs past.

<% if (rabbit.color == 'white') { %>
Does she follow the white rabbit?
[[Yes, she follows the rabbit]]
[[No, she doesn't follow the rabbit]]
<% } else { %>
But nothing more happened that morning.
<% } %>
```

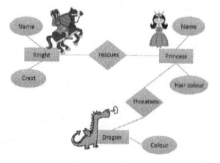

4.5 Conditional logic embedded in a linguistic-verbal context (*top*; Campos, Signoretti, and Rodrigues 2017), and modeling as a computational practice to support language learning (*bottom*; Sabitzer et al. 2018).

activities to encourage and promote CT in girls at K–12 levels (e.g., Kelleher, Pausch, and Kiesler 2007), consistently with Howland and Good (2015) (figure 4.4, *right*).

COMPUTATIONAL THINKING IN LOGICAL-MATHEMATICAL PROBLEMS

Logical-mathematical intelligence involves the ability to analyze problems logically, to carry out mathematical operations, and to conduct research with a scientific approach. Mathematicians, logicians, and scientists, among other occupations, employ logical-mathematical intelligence (Gardner 1983, 1999). At first glance, the close relationship between CT and mathematical intelligence seems evident, since they both share being mostly based on algorithmic thinking (Lockwood et al. 2016). In fact, some relevant CT definitions point out its algorithmic foundations. For example, Aho (2012) defines CT as "the thought process involved in formulating problems so their solutions can be represented as computational steps and algorithms" (Aho 2012, 832). Meanwhile, much of mathematical thinking consists of rules and procedures to reach a solution based on initial data (i.e., of applying algorithmic thinking on numerical information).

Furthermore, several authors have highlighted different points in common between CT and mathematical thinking, such as "conditional logic" (Morais, Basso, and Fagundes 2017), "reflective abstraction" (Cetin and Dubinsky 2017), or "modeling" (Sanford and Naidu 2017). From a more comprehensive perspective, Gadanidis (2017) has proposed "Five Affordances of Computational Thinking to support Elementary Mathematics Education": namely "agency," "access," "abstraction," "automation," and "audience."

Focusing on concrete experiences in K–12, which are aimed at fostering mathematics education through CT and computer programming, we consider that ScratchMaths project (https://www.ucl.ac.uk/ioe/research/projects/scratchmaths) is the most relevant and promising example (Benton et al. 2017, 2018). As can be seen in figure 4.6, ScratchMaths addresses several mathematical concepts, such as symmetry, polygons, place value, proportionality, or coordinates, by means of computational concepts and practices that are implemented in Scratch block-based programming language (Resnick et al. 2009).

All the mathematical concepts cited in the previous paragraph are part of the traditional mathematics curriculum. According to Olabe et al. (2014), this traditional curriculum is full of Type A problems, which "are deterministic in their solution (the solution is known and unique); and they are deterministic in process (the path to the solution is known and unique too)" (76). Nevertheless, an emerging stream of authors and research argues that computational tools, concepts, and practices are even more useful and powerful with Type B problems (i.e., nondeterministic in their solution and in their process). In addition, Type B problems are iterative in their nature, and they require experimentation for their resolution (e.g., Olabe et al. 2014; Sengupta et al. 2013; Weintrop et al. 2016). These authors also claim

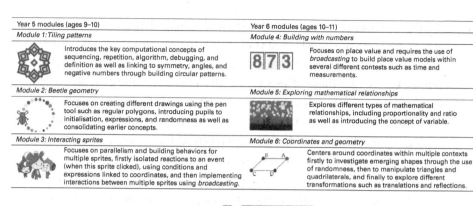

Year 5 modules (ages 9–10)	Year 6 modules (ages 10–11)
Module 1: Tiling patterns	*Module 4: Building with numbers*
Introduces the key computational concepts of sequencing, repetition, algorithm, debugging, and definition as well as linking to symmetry, angles, and negative numbers through building circular patterns.	Focuses on place value and requires the use of *broadcasting* to build place value models within several different contests such as time and measurements.
Module 2: Beetle geometry	*Module 5: Exploring mathematical relationships*
Focuses on creating different drawings using the pen tool such as regular polygons, introducing pupils to initialisation, expressions, and randomness as well as consolidating earlier concepts.	Explores different types of mathematical relationships, including proportionality and ratio as well as introducing the concept of variable.
Module 3: Interacting sprites	*Module 6: Coordinates and geometry*
Focuses on parallelism and building behaviors for multiple sprites, firstly isolated reactions to an event (when this sprite clicked), using conditions and expressions linked to coordinates, and then implementing interactions between multiple sprites using *broadcasting*.	Centers around coordinates within multiple contexts firstly to investigate emerging shapes through the use of randomness, then to manipulate triangles and quadrilaterals, and finally to explore different transformations such as translations and reflections.

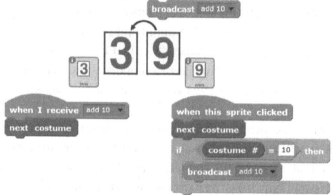

4.6 Overview of ScratchMaths modules and topics (*top*), and the Scratch program, which implements the mathematical concept of place value (*bottom*) (Benton et al. 2018).

that many more Type B problems should be included in the mathematics curriculum and within the broader framework of STEM education, in which physical and biologic complex systems (i.e., typical Type B problems) are frequently studied. In this regard, we find significant experiences that integrate CT and STEM education through modeling and simulation practices and by means of multi-agent–based computational tools (Sengupta et al. 2013; Weintrop et al. 2016).

COMPUTATIONAL THINKING IN MUSICAL PROBLEMS

Musical intelligence is defined as the ability to interpret, compose, and appreciate musical patterns (Gardner 1983, 1999). Composing music implies a series of knowledges and actions that align with several computational concepts and practices. Thus, music is a controlled sequence of notes, analogous to the commands that are sequenced under flow control structures in programming languages (e.g., repetition structures such as loops, see figure 4.7). Moreover, musical pieces combine and reuse smaller fragments of sounds, which is analogous to the practice of modularizing through functions in computer programming. In addition, within a musical piece, the different instruments must be synchronized, analogous to the computational concept of synchronization through events in programming. Finally, the sound has a series of parameters that can be digitized and represented by variables when programming music.

Since the foundational article of Michael Edwards in 2011, entitled "Algorithmic Composition: Computational Thinking in Music," many papers have been published on how music can motivate and promote CT development, and vice versa. For example, we find experiences in primary and secondary schools using block-based programming languages such as Blockly (Baratè et al. 2017), AgentCubes (Hug et al. 2017), TunePad (Gorson et al. 2017), or Scratch (Ruthmann et al. 2010) to compose music. From a different approach and aimed at high school students, Atherton

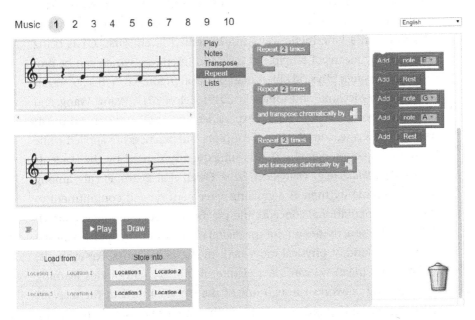

4.7 Flow control through repetition structures for composing music (Baratè et al. 2017).

and Blikstein (2017) present Sonification Blocks, "a programming language for data sonification, the process of creating audio algorithms and controlling them with streams of data" (733). At last, other authors propose to enrich musical CT with tangible devices/interfaces that must be physically manipulated by the kids, for example, LEGO bricks (Baratè, Ludovico, and Malchiodi 2017) or *Algo.Rhythm*, a tangible computational drum kit with programmable behaviors (Peng 2012), which borders on the next intelligence (bodily-kinesthetic).

COMPUTATIONAL THINKING IN BODILY-KINESTHETIC PROBLEMS

Bodily-kinesthetic intelligence involves the ability to use parts of the body, or its totality, to solve problems or create products. It is evident that dancers, actors, or athletes stand out for their high body-kinesthetic intelligence. Nevertheless, this type of intelligence also excels in artisans, surgeons, laboratory technicians, mechanics, and other technical professions (Gardner 1983, 1999).

Somehow, when developing CT in a kinesthetic manner, we assume the fundamentals of so-called "embodied cognition" theory (Shapiro 2019), which states that cognitive processes are shaped and enhanced by body activity and movement. We find in literature three main approaches to address CT in a kinesthetic way at K–12 school levels. First, CT is being developed by means of tangible devices and interfaces, which can be programmed through physical object manipulation (figure 4.8, *left*) (e.g., Aggarwal, Gardner-McCune, and Touretzky 2017; Melcer 2017; Wang, Wang, and Liu 2014). Second, we find several experiences where CT is fostered through dance. In this case, computational concepts and practices are applied while programming choreography that is subsequently danced by the students (figure 4.8, *middle*) (e.g., Daily et al. 2014; Owen et al. 2016). Finally, among the CT community there is a growing agreement on and commitment to teaching computational concepts and practices through unplugged activities (UA). These activities do not use digital devices and, therefore, typically imply some kind of physical movement in the participants. For example, in figure 4.8 (*right*) we can see a picture of primary school kids learning about sorting networks through one of the UA published in the relevant site (https://csunplugged.org/). It is worth noting that there is increasing

4.8 Examples of "embodied CT": Tangible devices (*left*), dancing and programming (*middle*), and learning about sorting networks by means of an unplugged activity (*right*).

empirical evidence on the effectiveness of the unplugged approach to develop CT in K–12 (e.g., Brackmann et al. 2017; Rodriguez et al. 2017).

COMPUTATIONAL THINKING IN VISUAL-SPATIAL PROBLEMS

Visual-spatial intelligence is defined as the ability to recognize and manipulate spatial patterns, either in large spaces (e.g., as pilots or navigators do) or in small spaces (e.g., as sculptors, chess players, graphic designers, or architects do). Therefore, visual-spatial intelligence is used to solve problems such as navigation and map usage, visualization of objects seen from different angles, or distribution of objects in a given space, among others (Gardner 1983, 1999).

Visual elements have played an essential role within the recent spread of CT and computer programming across K–12 education. On the one hand, block-based languages such as Blockly or Scratch provide visual elements/clues that scaffold children's learning of programming since early ages (even before learning to read or write, in the case of ScratchJr); these visual elements are fundamental to characterize the aforementioned languages as "low floor" (Weintrop and Wilensky 2017). On the other hand, many platforms and applications for kids aimed at teaching/learning to code pose visual puzzles in this regard, such as mazes or graphic/geometric patterns to be drawn (e.g., Kodable, LightBot, Code.org) (Kalelioğlu 2015). An example of a visual language used for solving a visual problem can be seen in figure 4.9. Finally, some authors report how visual thinking and visual techniques, such as mind maps or diagrams, can support CT development (e.g., Fronza, El Ioini, and Corral 2016; Jamil 2017).

In another vein, we find two main ways in which CT has been projected to face visual-spatial problems. First, within the context of algorithmic art (i.e., graphic design through computer algorithms; see Orr 2009). Second, CT and computer programming have been used in K–12 schools to create 3-D models, scenarios, and architectures (figure 4.10), often within the context of game-design (e.g., Bauer, Butler, and Popović 2017; Pinto-Llorente et al. 2018; Repenning et al. 2014).

COMPUTATIONAL THINKING IN INTERPERSONAL PROBLEMS

Interpersonal intelligence refers to the ability of people to understand and interpret the intentions, motivations, and desires of others and consequently to their ability to work effectively with other people. Therefore, interpersonal intelligence is built on the nuclear ability to discriminate differences between others (in particular, to feel contrasts in their moods,

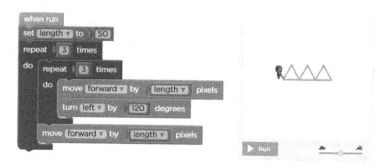

4.9 Visual language for solving a visual problem (https://studio.code.org/s/express-2019/stage/19/puzzle/6).

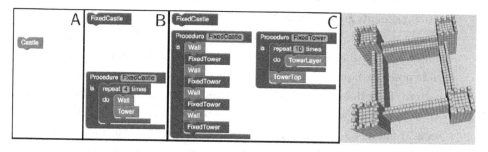

4.10 Architectural design by means of computer programming (Bauer, Butler, and Popović 2017).

temperaments, motivations, and intentions). At its highest level, this intelligence allows the individual to capture the intentions and desires of others, even if those have been hidden. Interpersonal intelligence manifests in an outstanding and sophisticated way in political and religious leaders, in teachers, in doctors and therapists, or in sellers and traders, among other occupations (Gardner 1983, 1999).

Computational concepts and practices are being applied within interpersonal problems and contexts, mainly by means of programming conversational interfaces, such as chatbots (Klopfenstein et al. 2017). Focusing on K–12, some experiences are found in this regard. For example, Benotti, Martnez, and Schapachnik (2018) have recently presented Chatbot (figure 4.11), a platform "designed to introduce high school students to Computer Science (CS) concepts in an innovative way: by programming chatbots. A chatbot is a bot that can be programmed to have a conversation with a human or robotic partner in some natural language such as English or Spanish. While programming their chatbots, students use fundamental CS constructs such as variables, conditionals and finite state automata, among others" (Benotti, Martnez, and Schapachnik 2018, 179). These authors also report that girls' engagement with Chatbot was higher than boys' for most indicators, which is consistent with the textual-linguistic features of its interface.

For a conversational interface to be fully functional within an interpersonal context (i.e., to be "interpersonally intelligent"), it must recognize (or even infer) and adaptively react to a wide range not only of cognitive states of the interlocutor (i.e., intentions, expectations, desires) but also of emotional states (Zhou et al. 2018). To address that challenge, classic rule-based programming (i.e., top-bottom approach) is inefficient and definitely not enough. Instead, bottom-up approaches, such as building models from data through machine learning (ML) techniques, are much more powerful and promising for this type of problem. In this vein, we have recently published several experiences in primary and secondary schools (Rodríguez-García et al. 2019), in which a text recognition model is built and trained with sample data through ML techniques (using the tool Machine Learning For Kids [ML4K], available at https://machinelearningforkids.co.uk/) and subsequently implemented as a virtual home assistant in Scratch (figure 4.12). It is worth noting that ML4K

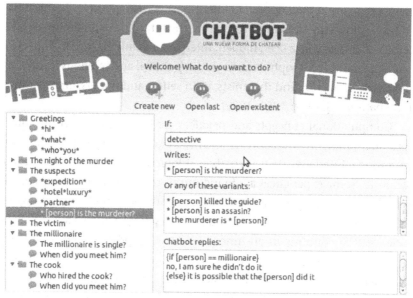

4.11 Chatbot (Benotti, Martnez, and Schapachnik 2018): K–12 students learn conditionals and variables (*top*), among other computational concepts, while programming a conversational interface (*bottom*).

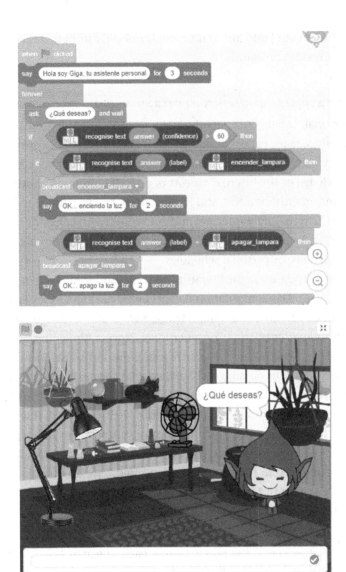

4.12 Virtual home assistant built with ML techniques and implemented in Scratch (Rodríguez-García et al. 2019).

allows students to build and train models not only from textual data but also from images or sounds.

COMPUTATIONAL THINKING IN INTRAPERSONAL PROBLEMS

Intrapersonal intelligence involves the ability to understand oneself (one's desires, fears, expectations, abilities) and to use this information to effectively regulate one's life. Thus, intrapersonal intelligence consists in the knowledge of the internal aspects of oneself (emotions, motivations, cognitions, or expectations) and in the ability to label and discriminate between them to finally interpret and guide one's own behavior (Gardner 1983, 1999). Typical products derived from intrapersonal intelligence are diaries, agendas, or personal schedules.

Looking inside scientific literature, we only find some tangential publications that relate computational concepts or practices to solving problems of one's life. (For example, Gärling, Kwan, and Golledge published in 1994 a paper entitled, "Computational-Process Modelling of Household Activity Scheduling.") Nevertheless, common sense and informal observation lead us to suggest that nowadays more and more people organize their own lives in computational or algorithmic terms ("*la vie algorithmique*" in French terms of Éric Sadin [2015]). Indeed, if we have a look inside grey literature, some relevant testimonials in this regard are found. For example, the computational visionary Stephen Wolfram has recently published in his blog the post entitled, "Seeking the Productive Life: Some Details of My Personal Infrastructure" (Wolfram, February 21, 2019), in which he says:

I'm a person who's only satisfied if I feel I'm being productive. I like figuring things out. I like making things. And I want to do as much of that as I can. And part of being able to do that is to have the best personal infrastructure I can. Over the years I've been steadily accumulating and implementing "personal infrastructure hacks" for myself. Some of them are, yes, quite nerdy. But they certainly help me be productive. And maybe in time more and more of them will become mainstream, as a few already have (. . .) At an intellectual level, the key to building this infrastructure is to structure, streamline and automate everything as much as possible—while recognizing both what's realistic with current technology, and what fits with me personally. In many ways, it's a good, practical exercise in computational thinking, and, yes, it's a good application of some of the tools and ideas that I've spent so long building.

In any case, it is essential that the new generations learn how to orga-nize their own lives in computational terms (i.e., to use the currently ubiquitous and pervasive algorithms for taking better personal decisions). Otherwise, there is a serious risk regarding how these algorithms can con-trol people's lives without their consent or awareness. In terms of Douglas Rushkoff (2010), it is a matter of "programming or being programmed." This motto could be the synthesis of the present subsection, expressed in sociocritical terms.

From a different and emerging cognitive perspective, CT can finally be linked to intrapersonal intelligence through so-called "executive func-tions" (EF). Following Robertson et al. (2020, 36), "EF is an umbrella term for higher order cognitive functions linked with the frontal lobes of the human brain and include abilities such as inhibiting impulsive responses, the ability to hold and simultaneously manipulate information in mind (known as working memory), attention shifting (or cognitive flexibility), planning and risk taking." On the one hand, we find recent exploratory studies in which CT correlates with EF (Robertson et al. 2020) and some other experimental research that demonstrates positive effects of coding on primary children's EF, specifically on planning and response inhibition skills (Arfé et al. 2019; Arfé, Vardanega, and Ronconi 2020). On the other hand, Gardner himself has also recognized *"the connection of EF strategies to intrapersonal intelligence, which processes information relative to the self"* (Moran and Gardner 2018, 25). The conclusion seems evident: CT can be developed mainly by means of coding tasks, which may enhance EF that could subsequently serve to better regulate one's cognition and behavior, that is, to be more "intrapersonally intelligent."

COMPUTATIONAL THINKING IN NATURALISTIC PROBLEMS
Naturalistic intelligence refers to the ability to recognize and classify the different natural species (Gardner 1999), either animal or plant species. One clear example of mastery within this intelligence was Carl Linnaeus, pioneer and father of biological taxonomies. From another perspective, naturalistic intelligence involves the ability to describe and understand the structure and evolution of biological systems (i.e., living being systems); for example, to understand what factors (and how) affect the evolution

of a given population of animals in a particular ecosystem. One essential characteristic of biological ecosystems is that they are complex (i.e., non-linear and dynamic), so they require multilevel explanations (Wilensky and Reisman 2006).

In this vein, Rubinstein and Chor (2014) have presented an excellent and comprehensive proposal on how to integrate CT in life science education. Moreover, focusing on K–12, we find several experiences in which the biological core concept of "natural selection" has been addressed in computational terms. In the first experience, Dickes and Sengupta (2013) "investigate how elementary school students develop multi-level explanations of population dynamics in a simple predator–prey ecosystem, through scaffolded interactions with a multi-agent-based computational model (MABM)" (921), by means of computer programming and modeling with the tool NetLogo (figure 4.13). In another experience, secondary students used computational concepts and practices to build algorithmic explanations of the natural selection process through several unplugged activities (Peel, Sadler, and Friedrichsen 2018). At a higher level of complexity and aimed at high school students, Wilensky and

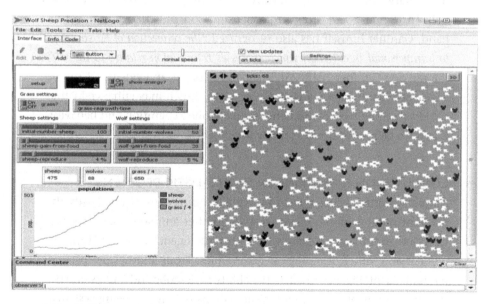

4.13 Wolf-Sheep predation model in NetLogo (Dickes and Sengupta 2013, Wilensky and Reisman 2006).

Reisman (2006) describe a "computation-based approach that enables students to investigate the connections between different biological levels. Using agent-based, embodied modeling tools ('NetLogo'), students model the microrules underlying a biological phenomenon and observe the resultant aggregate dynamics" (Wilensky and Reisman 2006, 171) (figure 4.13).

COMPUTATIONAL THINKING ASSESSMENT BATTERY (CTA*B*): A PROOF-OF-CONCEPT

In the previous section, we have reported a sufficient number of studies, experiences, and testimonials that show how CT can be used to address each. and every one of the types of problems stated by Howard Gardner (1983, 1999). That is, we have gathered enough preliminary hints and traces to ground our Theory of Multiple Computational Thinkings. At this point, the next step is to wonder and to anticipate how to empirically contrast the aforementioned theory. A way to confirm it could be to conduct empirical CT assessments/measurements on representative and large enough samples, whose results should reflect the hypothesized multifactorial structure of the construct (i.e., of CT).

To date, one of the most relevant assessment tools to measure CT at K–12 school levels is the Computational Thinking Test (CT*t*). The CT*t* is a multiple-choice test of 28 items, which has been designed from a psychometric approach and has been demonstrated to be reliable for kids between ten and sixteen years old. Furthermore, there is a great deal of evidence regarding the content (Román-González 2015), criterion (Román-González, Pérez-González, and Jiménez-Fernández 2017; Román-González et al. 2018a), predictive (Román-González et al. 2018b), and instructional (e.g., Brackmann et al. 2017; Rose, Habgood, and Jay 2019; Zhao and Shute 2019) validities of the CT*t*, which is currently available in Spanish, English, French, Portuguese, and German. Nevertheless, and regarding its structural/factorial validity, results coming from different and independent studies show that the CT*t* is unidimensional (e.g., Guggemos, Seufert, and Román-González 2021[1]; Román-González 2016; Wiebe et al. 2019). We consider the following arguments to explain this unidimensionality of the CT*t*:

- Following the psychometric notion of Fischer (1973), the items of a unidimensional construct may be linearly decomposed into problem-solving steps. Precisely, the items of the CT*t* can be linearly broken down into a series of computational concepts that are progressively incorporated and nested along the test (sequences, "repeat times" loops, "repeat until" loops, "if-then" conditionals, "if-then-else" conditionals, "while" conditionals, and simple functions).

- All the items of the CT*t* demand the subject to solve visual-spatial problems, such as mazes or graphic designs (figures 4.1 and 4.14). That is, the CT*t* only presents a single type-modality of problems (i.e., visual-spatial), among the eight proposed by Gardner. Then, the CT*t* may be unidimensional because of its single/exclusive visuospatial conception and design.

Consequently, the CT*t* seems to be insufficient and biased to empirically contrast our Theory of Multiple Computational Thinkings. An exclusive assessment instrument cannot be used to confirm an inclusive theory. Therefore, the CT*t* should be extended to a Computational Thinking Assessment Battery (CT*ab*) of tests, which should address the same aforementioned computational concepts but through an inclusive set of items that comprises the eight types of problems stated by the theory. Then, the

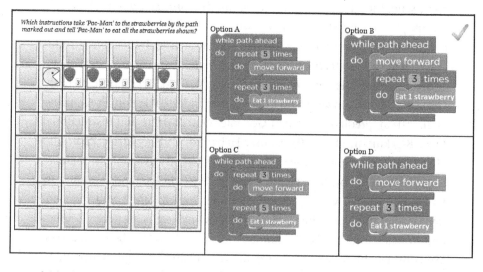

4.14 A visuospatial item for the upcoming CT*ab*.

CTab could be an adequate instrument to verify the hypothesized multi-dimensionality of CT.

A proof-of-concept (and very preliminary) design of a couple of items for the CTab can be seen in the next two figures. Figure 4.14 shows item 22 from the original CTt, which addresses a visual-spatial problem through "repeat" loops and "while" conditionals. Meanwhile, figure 4.15 translates and extrapolates that problem to a verbal-linguistic modality. To fully design the CTab, the same should be done with all the computational concepts involved and throughout all the types-modalities of problems.

DISCUSSION AND IMPLICATIONS

Here we discuss several implications of validating the multifactorial structure of the CTab and, consequently, of confirming our Theory of Multiple Computational Thinkings.

First, if the CTab were validated, then it would be possible to establish a personalized CT profile for any assessed person. Given that each of the multiple computational thinkings is supposed to be relatively independent of the others, it would be relevant to determine, for all students, in which modality of CT they are most capable and then to design a personalized

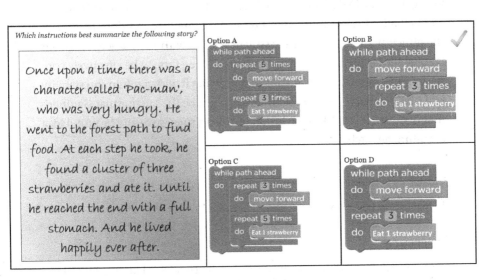

4.15 A verbal-linguistic item for the upcoming CTab.

CT educational intervention taking into account their strengths in this regard.

Second, if the theory is not only empirically confirmed but also accepted by the community of researchers, practitioners, and policy-makers, then the subsequent CT curricula and interventions would probably become more diverse and inclusive. CT education will be more equitable if a more diverse set of problems to be computationally solved are offered within K–12 scenarios.

Finally, confirming our Theory of Multiple Computational Thinkings could also reinforce Gardner's TMI. Throughout the last decades, TMI has been often harshly criticized because of its insufficient and inadequate empirical supporting evidence (e.g., Visser, Ashton, and Vernon 2006a, 2006b; Waterhouse 2006). In this vein, Visser, Ashton, and Vernon (2006a, 2006b) reported that administering their battery of tests, which supposedly encompassed the eight intelligences of Gardner, resulted in a large common factor (general or "g" factor) that clearly contradicted and discarded TMI principles. Gardner (2006) replied that most of the tests used in Visser's battery were heavily and exclusively loaded with verbal and logical information and were presented through typical school-like tasks, all of which derived in obtaining that single "g" factor. In other words, Gardner claims that TMI requires to be fairly contrasted with a more diverse and contextualized set of tests/tasks, but at the same time Gardner recognizes the difficulty of building an assessment battery with such a heterogeneous set of abilities/intelligences to be measured. Therefore, to be effectively contrasted, TMI could lack an anchor that provides it with a minimum stability and homogeneity. We consider that CT might be the anchor that Gardner's theory needs. It is a risky conclusion but also a suggestive and beautiful idea for future research.

NOTE

1. Manuscript under review.

REFERENCES

Aggarwal, Ashish, Christina Gardner-McCune, and David S. Touretzky. 2017. "Evaluating the Effect of Using Physical Manipulatives to Foster Computational Thinking in Elementary School." In *Proceedings of the 2017 ACM SIGCSE Technical Symposium on Computer Science Education (SIGCSE '17)*. Seattle, 9–14. https://doi.org/10.1145/3017680.3017791.

Aho, Alfred V. 2012. "Computation and Computational Thinking." *The Computer Journal* 55 (7): 832–835. https://doi.org/10.1093/comjnl/bxs074.

Arfé, Barbara, Tullio Vardanega, Chiara Montuori, and Marta Lavanga. 2019. "Coding in Primary Grades Boosts Children's Executive Functions." *Frontiers in Psychology* 10: 2713. https://doi.org/10.3389/fpsyg.2019.02713.

Arfé, Barbara, Tullio Vardanega, and Lucia Ronconi. 2020. "The Effects of Coding on Children's Planning and Inhibition Skills." *Computers & Education* 148: 1–16. https://doi.org/10.1016/j.compedu.2020.103807.

Atherton, Jack, and Paulo Blikstein. 2017. "Sonification Blocks: A Block-Based Programming Environment for Embodied Data Sonification." In *Proceedings of the 2017 Conference on Interaction Design and Children (IDC '17)*. Stanford, CA, 733–736. https://doi.org/10.1145/3078072.3091992.

Baratè, Adriano, Andrea Formica, Luca A. Ludovico, and Dario Malchiodi. 2017. "Fostering Computational Thinking in Secondary School through Music—An Educational Experience based on Google Blockly." In *Proceedings of the 9th International Conference on Computer Supported Education*. Vila Nova de Gaia, Portugal, 117–124. http://dx.doi.org/10.5220/0006313001170124.

Baratè, Adriano, Luca A. Ludovico, and Dario Malchiodi. 2017. "Fostering Computational Thinking in Primary School through a LEGO®-based Music Notation." *Procedia Computer Science* 112: 1334–1344. https://doi.org/10.1016/j.procs.2017.08.018.

Bauer, Aaron, Eric Butler, and Zoran Popović. 2017. "Dragon Architect: Open Design Problems for Guided Learning in a Creative Computational Thinking Sandbox Game." In *Proceedings of the 12th International Conference on the Foundations of Digital Games (FDG '17)*. Hyannis, MA, 1–6. https://doi.org/10.1145/3102071.3102106.

Benotti, Luciana, Mara Cecilia Martnez, and Fernando Schapachnik. 2018. "A Tool for Introducing Computer Science with Automatic Formative Assessment." *IEEE Transactions on Learning Technologies* 11 (2): 179–192. https://doi.org/10.1109/TLT.2017.2682084.

Benton, Laura, Celia Hoyles, Ivan Kalas, and Richard Noss. 2017. "Bridging Primary Programming and Mathematics: Some Findings of Design Research in England." *Digital Experiences in Mathematics Education* 3: 115–138. https://doi.org/10.1007/s40751-017-0028-x.

Benton, Laura, Piers Saunders, Ivan Kalas, Celia Hoyles, and Richard Noss. 2018. "Designing for Learning Mathematics through Programming: A Case Study of Pupils Engaging with Place Value." *International Journal of Child-Computer Interaction* 16: 68–76. https://doi.org/10.1016/j.ijcci.2017.12.004.

Boom, Kay-Dennis, Matt Bower, Amaël Arguel, Jens Siemon, and Antonia Scholk-mann. 2018. "Relationship between Computational Thinking and a Measure of Intelligence as a General Problem-Solving Ability." In *Proceedings of the 23rd Annual ACM Conference on Innovation and Technology in Computer Science Education (ITiCSE 2018)*. Larnaca, Cyprus, 206–211. https://doi.org/10.1145/3197091.3197104.

Brackmann, Christian P., Marcos Román-González, Gregorio Robles, Jesús Moreno-León, Ana Casali, and Dante Barone. 2017. "Development of Computational Think-ing Skills through Unplugged Activities in Primary School." In *Proceedings of the 12th Workshop on Primary and Secondary Computing Education (WiPSCE '17)*. Toronto, 65–72. https://doi.org/10.1145/3137065.3137069.

Burke, Quinn. 2012. "The Markings of a New Pencil: Introducing Programming-as-Writing in the Middle School Classroom." *Journal of Media Literacy Education* 4 (2): 121–135.

Burke, Quinn, and Yasmin B. Kafai. 2012. "The Writers' Workshop for Youth Pro-grammers: Digital Storytelling with Scratch in Middle School Classrooms." In *Pro-ceedings of the 43rd ACM Technical Symposium on Computer Science Education (SIGCSE '12)*. Raleigh, NC, 433–438. https://doi.org/10.1145/2157136.2157264.

Campos, André, Alberto Signoretti, and Mário Rodrigues. 2017. "An Interactive Book Authoring Tool to Introduce Programming Logic in Schools." In *Proceedings of the 9th International Conference on Computer Supported Education*. Porto, Portugal, 140–148. http://dx.doi.org/10.5220/0006333501400148.

Cetin, Ibrahim, and Ed Dubinsky. 2017. "Reflective Abstraction in Computational Thinking." *The Journal of Mathematical Behavior* 47: 70–80. https://doi.org/10.1016/j.jmathb.2017.06.004.

Curzon, Paul, Peter William McOwan, Nicola Plant, and Laura R. Meagher. 2014. "Introducing Teachers to Computational Thinking Using Unplugged Storytelling." In *Proceedings of the 9th Workshop in Primary and Secondary Computing Education (WiPSCE '14)*. Berlin, 89–92. https://doi.org/10.1145/2670757.2670767.

Daily, Shaundra Bryant, Alison E. Leonard, Sophie Jörg, Sabarish Babu, and Kara Gunder-sen. 2014. "Dancing Alice: Exploring Embodied Pedagogical Strategies for Learning Com-putational Thinking." In *Proceedings of the 45th ACM Technical Symposium on Computer Science Education (SIGCSE '14)*. Atlanta, 91–96. https://doi.org/10.1145/2538862.2538917.

Dickes, Amanda Catherine, and Pratim Sengupta. 2013. "Learning Natural Selection in 4th Grade with Multi-Agent-Based Computational Models." *Research in Science Education* 43 (3): 921–953. https://doi.org/10.1007/s11165-012-9293-2.

Edwards, Michael. 2011. "Algorithmic Composition: Computational Thinking in Music." *Communications of the ACM* 54 (7): 58–67. https://doi.org/10.1145/1965724.1965742.

Fischer, Gerhard H. 1973. "The Linear Logistic Test Model as an Instrument in Edu-cational Research." *Acta Psychologica* 37 (6): 359–374. https://doi.org/10.1016/0001-6918(73)90003-6.

Fronza, Ilenia, Nabil El Ioini, and Luis Corral. 2016. "Teaching Software Design Engineering across the K–12 Curriculum: Using Visual Thinking and Computational Thinking." In *Proceedings of the 17th Annual Conference on Information Technology Education*. Boston, 97–101. http://dx.doi.org/10.1145/2978192.2978220.

Gadanidis, George. 2017. "Five Affordances of Computational Thinking to support Elementary Mathematics Education." *Journal of Computers in Mathematics and Science Teaching* 36 (2): 143–151. https://www.learntechlib.org/primary/p/174346/.

Gardner, Howard. 1983. *Frames of Mind: The Theory of Multiple Intelligences*. New York: Basic Books.

Gardner, Howard. 1999. *Intelligence Reframed*. New York: Basic Books.

Gardner, Howard. 2006. "On Failing to Grasp the Core of MI Theory: A Response to Visser et al." *Intelligence* 34 (5): 503–505. https://doi.org/10.1016/j.intell.2006.04.002.

Gärling, Tommy, Mei-Po Kwan, and Reginald G. Golledge. 1994. "Computational-process Modelling of Household Activity Scheduling." *Transportation Research Part B: Methodological* 28 (5): 355–364. https://doi.org/10.1016/0191-2615(94)90034-5.

Gorson, Jamie, Nikita Patel, Elham Beheshti, Brian Magerko, and Michael Horn. 2017. "TunePad: Computational Thinking through Sound Composition." In *Proceedings of the 2017 Conference on Interaction Design and Children (IDC '17)*. Stanford, CA, 484–489. https://doi.org/10.1145/3078072.3084313.

Guggemos, Josef, Sabine Seufert, and Marcos Román-González. (2021). "Assessing Computational Thinking—A Person-Centered Approach." *Technology, Knowledge and Learning* (forthcoming).

Howland, Kate, and Judith Good. 2015. "Learning to Communicate Computationally with Flip: A Bi-modal Programming Language for Game Creation." *Computers & Education* 80: 224–240. https://doi.org/10.1016/j.compedu.2014.08.014.

Hug, Daniel, Serge Petralito, Sarah Hauser, Anna Lamprou, Alexander Repenning, Didier Bertschinger, Nadine Stüber, and Markus Cslovjecsek. 2017. "Exploring Computational Music Thinking in a Workshop Setting with Primary and Secondary School Children." In *Proceedings of the 12th International Audio Mostly Conference on Augmented and Participatory Sound and Music Experiences (AM '17)*. London, 1–8. https://doi.org/10.1145/3123514.3123515.

Hyde, Janet S., and Marcia C. Linn. 1988. "Gender Differences in Verbal Ability: A Meta-Analysis." *Psychological Bulletin* 104 (1): 53–69. https://doi.org/10.1037/0033-2909.104.1.53.

Jamil, Hasan M. 2017. "Visual Computational Thinking Using *Patch*." In *Advances in Web-Based Learning—ICWL 2017*, edited by Haoran Xie, Elvira Popescu, Gerhard Hancke, and Baltasar Fernández Manjón, 208–214. Cham: Springer. https://doi.org/10.1007/978-3-319-66733-1_23.

Kalelioğlu, Filiz. 2015. "A New Way of Teaching Programming Skills to K–12 Students: Code.org." *Computers in Human Behavior* 52: 200–210. https://doi.org/10.1016/j.chb.2015.05.047.

Kelleher, Caitlin, Randy F. Pausch, and Sara Kiesler. 2007. "Storytelling Alice Motivates Middle School Girls to Learn Computer Programming." In *Proceedings of the SIGCHI Conference on Human Factors in Computing Systems (CHI 2007)*. San Jose, CA, 1455–1464. https://doi.org/10.1145/1240624.1240844.

Klopfenstein, Lorenz Cuno, Saverio Delpriori, Silvia Malatini, and Alessandro Bogliolo. 2017. "The Rise of Bots: A Survey of Conversational Interfaces, Patterns, and Paradigms." In *Proceedings of the 2017 Conference on Designing Interactive Systems (DIS '17)*. Edinburgh, 555–565. https://doi.org/10.1145/3064663.3064672.

Lewin, Catharina, Gerhard Wolgers, and Agneta Herlitz. 2001. "Sex Differences Favoring Women in Verbal But Not in Visuospatial Episodic Memory." *Neuropsychology* 1 5(2): 165–173. https://doi.org/10.1037/0894-4105.15.2.165.

Linn, Marcia C., and Anne C. Petersen. 1985. "Emergence and Characterization of Sex Differences in Spatial Ability: A Meta-Analysis." *Child Development* 56 (6): 1479–1498. http://dx.doi.org/10.2307/1130467.

Lockwood, Elise, Autumn Asay, Anna F. DeJarnette, and Matthew Thomas. 2016. "Algorithmic Thinking: An Initial Characterization of Computational Thinking in Mathematics." In *Proceedings of the 38th Annual Meeting of the North American Chapter of the International Group for the Psychology of Mathematics Education*. Tucson, 1588–1595. https://files.eric.ed.gov/fulltext/ED583797.pdf.

Lye, Sze Yee, and Joyce Hwee Ling Koh. 2014. "Review on Teaching and Learning of Computational Thinking through Programming: What is Next for K–12?" *Computers in Human Behavior* 41: 51–61. http://dx.doi.org/10.1016/j.chb.2014.09.012.

Melcer, Edward. 2017. "Moving to Learn: Exploring the Impact of Physical Embodiment in Educational Programming Games." In *Proceedings of the 2017 CHI Conference Extended Abstracts on Human Factors in Computing Systems (CHI EA '17)*. Denver, 301–306. https://doi.org/10.1145/3027063.3027129.

Morais, Anuar Daian, Marcus Vinicius de Azevedo Basso, and Léa da Cruz Fagundes. 2017. "Educação Matemática & Ciência da Computação na escola: aprender a programar fomenta a aprendizagem de matemática? [Mathematics Education and Computer Science in school: does learning to code foster the learning of Mathematics?]." *Ciência & Educação (Bauru)* 23 (2): 455–473. https://dx.doi.org/10.1590/1516-731320170020011.

Moran, Seana, and Howard Gardner. 2018. "Hill, Skill, and Will: Executive Function from a Multiple-Intelligences Perspective." In *Executive Function in Education: From Theory to Practice*, edited by Lynn Meltzer, 25–56. New York: The Guilford Press.

Moreno-León, Jesús, Gregorio Robles, Marcos Román-González, and Juan David Rodríguez. 2019. "Not the Same: A Text Network Analysis on Computational Thinking Definitions to Study Its Relationship with Computer Programming." *RIITE*.

Revista Interuniversitaria de Investigación en Tecnología Educativa 7: 26–35. http://dx
.doi.org/10.6018/riite.397151.

Olabe, Juan Carlos, Xabier Basogain, Miguel Ángel Olabe, Inmaculada Maíz, and
Carlos Castaño. 2014. "Solving Math and Science Problems in the Real World with a
Computational Mind." *Journal of New Approaches in Educational Research* 3 (2): 75–82.
http://dx.doi.org/10.7821/naer.3.2.75-82.

Orr, Genevieve. 2009. "Computational Thinking through Programming and Algorithmic Art." In *SIGGRAPH 2009: Talks (SIGGRAPH '09)*. New Orleans. https://doi
.org/10.1145/1597990.1598021.

Owen, Charles B., Laura K. Dillon, Alison Dobbins, Noah Keppers, Madeline Levin-
son, and Matthew Rhodes. 2016. "Dancing Computer: Computer Literacy though
Dance." In *Proceedings of the 14th International Conference on Advances in Mobile
Computing and Multi Media (MoMM '16)*. Singapore, 174–180. https://doi.org/10.1145
/3007120.3007131.

Peel, Amanda, Troy D. Sadler, and Patricia Friedrichsen. 2019. "Learning Natural
Selection through Computational Thinking: Unplugged Design of Algorithmic
Explanations." *Journal of Research in Science Teaching* 56 (7): 983–1007. https://doi
.org/10.1002/tea.21545.

Peng, Huaishu. 2012. "Algo.Rhythm: Computational Thinking through Tangible
Music Device." In *Proceedings of the Sixth International Conference on Tangible, Embedded and Embodied Interaction (TEI '12)*. Kingston, Ontario, Canada, 401–402. https://
doi.org/10.1145/2148131.2148234.

Pinto-Llorente, Ana M., Sonia Casillas-Martín, Marcos Cabezas-González, and Francisco José García-Peñalvo. 2018. "Building, Coding and Programming 3D Models via
a Visual Programming Environment." *Quality & Quantity* 52: 2455–2468. https://doi
.org/10.1007/s11135-017-0509-4.

Proctor, Chris, and Paulo Blikstein. 2017. "Interactive Fiction: Weaving Together Literacies of Text and Code." In *Proceedings of the 2017 Conference on Interaction Design and
Children (IDC '17)*. Stanford, CA, 555–60. https://doi.org/10.1145/3078072.3084324.

Repenning, Alexander, David C. Webb, Catharine Brand, Fred Gluck, Ryan Grover,
Susan Miller, Hilarie Nickerson, and Muyang Song. 2014. "Beyond Minecraft: Facil-
itating Computational Thinking through Modeling and Programming in 3D." *IEEE
Computer Graphics and Applications* 34 (3): 68–71. https://doi.org/10.1109/MCG
.2014.46.

Resnick, Mitchel, John Harold Maloney, Andrés Monroy-Hernández, Natalie Rusk,
Evelyn Eastmond, Karen A. Brennan, Amon Millner, Eric Rosenbaum, and Jay Saul
Silver. 2009. "Scratch: Programming for All." *Communications of the ACM* 52 (11):
60–67. https://doi.org/10.1145/1592761.1592779.

Robertson, Judy, Stuart Gray, Toye Martin, and Josephine Boot. 2020. "The relationship between Executive Functions and Computational Thinking." *International*

Journal of Computer Science Education in Schools 3 (4): 35–49. https://doi.org/10.21585/ijcses.v3i4.76.

Rodriguez, Brandon, Stephen Kennicutt, Cyndi Rader, and Tracy Camp. 2017. "Assessing Computational Thinking in CS Unplugged Activities." In *Proceedings of the 2017 ACM SIGCSE Technical Symposium on Computer Science Education (SIGCSE '17)*. Seattle, 501–506. https://doi.org/10.1145/3017680.3017779.

Rodríguez-García, Juan David, Jesús Moreno-León, Marcos Román-González, and Gregorio Robles. 2019. "Developing Computational Thinking at School with Machine Learning: An Exploration." In *Proceedings of the 2019 International Symposium on Computers in Education (SIIE 2019)*. Tomar, Portugal, 49–54.

Román-González, Marcos. 2015. "Computational Thinking Test: Design Guidelines and Content Validation." In *Proceedings of the 7th International Conference on Education and New Learning Technologies (EDULEARN 2015)*. Barcelona, 2436–2444.

Román-González, Marcos. 2016. "Codigoalfabetización y pensamiento computacional en Educación Primaria y Secundaria: validación de un instrumento y evaluación de programas [Code literacy and computational thinking in primary and secondary education: Validation of an instrument and evaluation of programs]." PhD diss., Madrid: UNED.

Román-González, Marcos, Juan-Carlos Pérez-González, and Carmen Jiménez-Fernández. 2017. "Which Cognitive Abilities Underlie Computational Thinking? Criterion Validity of the Computational Thinking Test." *Computers in Human Behavior* 72: 678–691. https://doi.org/10.1016/j.chb.2016.08.047.

Román-González, Marcos, Juan-Carlos Pérez-González, Jesús Moreno-León, and Gregorio Robles. 2018a. "Extending the Nomological Network of Computational Thinking with Non-Cognitive Factors." *Computers in Human Behavior* 80: 441–459. https://doi.org/10.1016/j.chb.2017.09.030.

Román-González, Marcos, Juan-Carlos Pérez-González, Jesús Moreno-León, and Gregorio Robles. 2018b. "Can Computational Talent be Detected? Predictive Validity of the Computational Thinking Test." *International Journal of Child-Computer Interaction* 18: 47–58. https://doi.org/10.1016/j.ijcci.2018.06.004.

Rose, Simon P., M. P. Jacob Habgood, and Tim Jay. 2019. "Using Pirate Plunder to Develop Children's Abstraction Skills in Scratch." In *Extended Abstracts of the 2019 CHI Conference on Human Factors in Computing Systems (CHI EA '19)*. Glasgow, 1–6. https://doi.org/10.1145/3290607.3312871.

Rubinstein, Amir, and Benny Chor. 2014. "Computational Thinking in Life Science Education." *PLOS Computational Biology* 10 (11): 1–5. https://doi.org/10.1371/journal.pcbi.1003897.

Rushkoff, Douglas. 2010. *Program or Be Programmed*. New York: OR Books.

Ruthmann, Alex, Jesse M. Heines, Gena R. Greher, Paul Laidler, and Charles Saulters. 2010. "Teaching Computational Thinking through Musical Live Coding in Scratch."

In *Proceedings of the 41st ACM Technical Symposium on Computer Science Education (SIGCSE '10)*. Milwaukee, 351–355. https://doi.org/10.1145/1734263.1734384.

Sabitzer, Heike Demarle-Meusel, and Maria Jarnig. 2018. "Computational Thinking through Modeling in Language Lessons." In *Proceedings of the 2018 IEEE Global Engineering Education Conference (EDUCON)*. Santa Cruz de Tenerife, Canary Islands, 1913–1919. https://doi.org/10.1109/EDUCON.2018.8363469.

Sadin, Éric. 2015. *La vie algorithmique: critique de la raison numérique [The Algorithmic Life: A Critique of Digital Rationality]*. Paris: L'Echappée.

Sanford, John F., and Jaideep T. Naidu. 2017. "Mathematical Modeling and Computational Thinking." *Contemporary Issues in Education Research* 10 (2): 159–168. Retrieved from https://files.eric.ed.gov/fulltext/EJ1137705.pdf.

Sengupta, Pratim, John S. Kinnebrew, Satabdi Basu, Gautam Biswas, and Douglas Clark. 2013. "Integrating Computational Thinking with K–12 Science Education Using Agent-Based Computation: A Theoretical Framework." *Education and Information Technologies* 18: 351–380. https://doi.org/10.1007/s10639-012-9240-x.

Shapiro, Lawrence. 2019. *Embodied Cognition*. London: Routledge.

Visser, Beth A., Michael C. Ashton, and Philip A. Vernon. 2006a. "Beyond *g*: Putting Multiple Intelligences Theory to the Test." *Intelligence* 34 (5): 487–502. https://doi.org/10.1016/j.intell.2006.02.004.

Visser, Beth A., Michael C. Ashton, and Philip A. Vernon. 2006b. "*g* and the Measurement of Multiple Intelligences: A Response to Gardner." *Intelligence* 34 (5): 507–510. https://doi.org/10.1016/j.intell.2006.04.006.

Voyer, Daniel, Susan Voyer, and M. Philip Bryden. 1995. "Magnitude of Sex Differences in Spatial Abilities: A Meta-Analysis and Consideration of Critical Variables." *Psychological Bulletin* 117 (2): 250–270. https://doi.org/10.1037/0033-2909.117.2.250.

Wang, Danli, Tingting Wang, and Zhen Liu. 2014. "A Tangible Programming Tool for Children to Cultivate Computational Thinking." *Scientific World Journal*. https://doi.org/10.1155/2014/428080.

Waterhouse, Lynn. 2006. "Inadequate Evidence for Multiple Intelligences, Mozart Effect, and Emotional Intelligence Theories." *Educational Psychologist* 41 (4): 247–255. https://doi.org/10.1207/s15326985ep4104_5.

Weintrop, David, Elham Beheshti, Michael Horn, Kai Orton, Kemi Jona, Laura Trouille, and Uri Wilensky. 2016. "Defining Computational Thinking for Mathematics and Science Classrooms." *Journal of Science Education and Technology* 25 (1): 127–147. https://doi.org/10.1007/s10956-015-9581-5.

Weintrop, David, and Uri Wilensky. 2017. "How Block-Based Languages Support Novices: A Framework For Categorizing Block-Based Affordances." *Journal of Visual Languages and Sentient Systems* 3: 92–100.

Wiebe, Eric, Jennifer E. London, Osman Aksit, Bradford W. Mott, Kristy Elizabeth Boyer, and James C. Lester. 2019. "Development of a Lean Computational Thinking Abilities Assessment for Middle Grades Students." In *Proceedings of the 50th ACM Technical Symposium on Computer Science Education (SIGCSE '19)*. Minneapolis, 456–461. https://doi.org/10.1145/3287324.3287390.

Wilensky, Uri, and Kenneth Reisman. 2006. "Thinking Like a Wolf, a Sheep, or a Firefly: Learning Biology through Constructing and Testing Computational Theories—an Embodied Modeling Approach." *Cognition and Instruction* 24 (2): 171–209. https://doi.org/10.1207/s1532690xci2402_1.

Wolfram, Stephen. 2019. *Seeking the Productive Life: Some Details of My Personal Infrastructure* (blog). February 21, 2019. https://writings.stephenwolfram.com/2019/02/seeking-the-productive-life-some-details-of-my-personal-infrastructure/.

Zhao, Weinan, and Valerie J. Shute. 2019. "Can Playing a Video Game Foster Computational Thinking Skills?" *Computers & Education* 141: 1–13. https://doi.org/10.1016/j.compedu.2019.103633.

Zhou, Hao, Minlie Huang, Tianyang Zhang, Xiaoyan Zhu, and Bing Liu. 2018. "Emotional Chatting Machine: Emotional Conversation Generation with Internal and External Memory." *arXiv.org*. https://arxiv.org/abs/1704.01074v4.

5

LEARNING COMPUTATIONAL THINKING IN PHENOMENA-BASED CO-CREATION PROJECTS
PERSPECTIVES FROM FINLAND

Pasi Silander, Sini Riikonen, Pirita Seitamaa-Hakkarainen, and Kai Hakkarainen

INTRODUCTION

Societies and industries have changed significantly in recent decades. The emerging *innovation society* has resulted in the technological, sociological, and cognitive development of society. Our professional lives are highly digital, but K–12 education (both teaching and learning) is still taking its first steps in a digital transformation. To understand and become an active member of society, students have to learn to understand the technology behind digitalization. Understanding algorithms, such as procedural thinking, reasoning, and decision-making mechanisms, helps students understand technology and how it works. However, in addition to understanding algorithms and computational thinking (CT), students should be able to utilize them in their personal and collaborative thinking, problem-solving, and creative pursuits.

Modern society relies on advanced technologies, such as artificial intelligence (AI) and data analytics. To understand the automatic decision-making of online services and social media, students need CT skills. Moreover, the role of information that is processed and analyzed by AI is increasingly important in our everyday lives. For example, while banking or shopping, a customer receives information determined by the ads and customized services they see based on automatic decision-making by AI. When using a search engine or reading a newspaper online, the user is targeted by personalized content and ads based on the motives and content interests of service providers. Learners should be aware that the internet's search engines and social networking tools rate and censor search results and information based on various commercial and political motives.

The major challenge for the K–12 educational system globally is to help students develop critical thinking skills and creative capabilities, especially related to understanding computational processes and mechanisms. In the digital world in which we live, CT skills are a prerequisite for critical thinking. How can we ensure that K–12 educational systems are capable of helping students develop these skills? What methods do we need to use to learn and teach these skills? What wider changes in the organization of teaching and learning in educational institutions are needed?

COMPUTATIONAL THINKING AS A TWENTY-FIRST-CENTURY SKILL

Various definitions and frameworks for twenty-first-century skills (Trilling and Fadel 2009) have been used as a base for K–12 curricula to define transversal competencies and goals for education. Widely used frameworks in K–12 education usually include such competencies as collaboration, communication, citizenship, creativity, critical thinking, and character building. Most twenty-first-century skills frameworks are focused on so-called soft skills (Bereiter and Scardamalia 2012) and neglect, to a large extent, the importance of logic and mathematical or algorithmic reasoning. Wing (2006) introduced the idea of CT as a fundamental skill for everyone; nevertheless, none of the widely used frameworks have adopted it. Very often, CT is only linked to computer science or STEAM (science, technology, engineering, arts, and mathematics) education and is narrowly understood to only include coding or ready-made mathematical algorithms.

A common mistake is to talk about coding when we should talk about CT. Coding is often used as a generalized term for programming or, even more often, misused to describe some ill-defined activities with computers. To understand how to program, it is necessary to comprehend CT and system design. CT is not a new concept but has been studied and discussed mainly by computer scientists (Denning 2009; Tedre and Denning 2016; Wing 2006). However, it should be more extensively investigated by educational researchers and learning scientists when designing K–12 curricula and educational practices.

The importance of CT was introduced by Wing (2006) and more widely studied by Denning and Tedre (2019). Primitive forms of CT have existed in the form of mathematics and calculation throughout history, even in the time before computers. In modern terms, CT may be defined as cognitive skills and practices for designing computation and computing systems and for explaining and interpreting the world in terms of complex information processes (Denning and Tedre 2019). Wing (2008) has defined CT more compactly as analytical thinking utilizing abstractions, as she defines computing to be the automation of abstractions. However, CT is not only important for computing or for learning programming but it is also a highly generalized cognitive skill needed for critical thinking, media literacy, and knowledge production, as well as for comprehending ethical issues related to data-driven society and various aspects of AI and its ethically sustainable use.

LEARNING AND TEACHING COMPUTATIONAL THINKING IN MODERN K–12 EDUCATION

The utilization of CT in K–12 education is anchored in our conceptions of emerging digital technology, theories of learning, and technology-mediated practices of learning and teaching. It appears to us that CT requires a new level of epistemic fluency (Markauskaite and Goodyear 2017), interconnecting abstract and real-life phenomena by learners and teachers. When considering pedagogical applications of CT in K–12 education, it is not enough to address mere programming or coding. Programming in K–12 education is sometimes even simplified to routine procedures of giving directions to a computer or to a robot through individual commands. Coding does not equal CT (Wing 2006, 2008) or adequate computing skills; a wider approach than coding is needed for learning and understanding the computational aspects of problem-solving and analyzing, modeling, and automating abstractions (see figure 5.1). The focus should be on modelling and understanding real-world

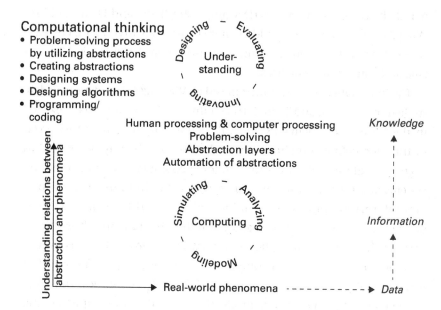

Computational thinking
- Problem-solving process by utilizing abstractions
- Creating abstractions
- Designing systems
- Designing algorithms
- Programming/coding

5.1 Framework for learning computational thinking in K–12 education, consisting of the computational system and human information processing.

phenomena by designing, creating, and utilizing abstractions and by creating algorithms and simulations. In addition, the focus of learning should be on systemic thinking, as in system theories or system design.

CT skills cannot be adequately learned in a decontextualized setting of programming or designing algorithms without a connection to real-world phenomena and their modeling. We argue that epistemic flexibility is essential to comprehending relations between the real-world phenomena (problems to be solved) and the abstractions (computational models or algorithms) that are used for problem-solving. The goal of learning should be a systemic understanding of the entire computational system, including real-world phenomena, computing, and human information processing.

The use of modern information technology and modern computing are fundamentally culturally mediated cognitive skills. CT (Wing 2006, 2008) can be associated with metacognitive skills and the sophisticated use of a repertoire of cognitive strategies. Using algorithms as a mental tool augments the power of human cognitive capacity and fosters the development of cognitive strategies. Simultaneously, computing and computers are used as tools for complex physically distributed cognition (Pea 1985; Salomon 1993). Computational power and computers are often used to solve problems that would be difficult or virtually impossible to solve with a human's information-processing capacity. A computational system consists of human cognitive processes, distributed cognition, and information processing on a computer (e.g., Pea, Kurland, and Hawkins 1985; Salomon, Perkins, and Globerson 1991), all embedded in the social practices of human communities (e.g., Ritella and Hakkarainen 2012). Human cognition and computer processing can be seen as intertwined agents of the cognitive system used for complex problem-solving. Moreover, the socially shared cognition mediated by computers boosts these intertwined agents of the cognitive systems that jointly may provide a crucial platform for creating novelty and innovations.

Ideally, when learners are provided with opportunities for cultivating CT skills in K–12 education, they should have generalizable capabilities for organizing, reorganizing, modeling, analyzing, utilizing, and computing information to problem-solve in any subject domain. This raises a pedagogical challenge for K–12 educational systems: How should CT be taught so that students gain adequate skills?

CT cannot be learned by reading books, by listening to teachers' lectures, or even by coding. Sociodigital processes combined with co-computational thinking are needed. The best way to ensure a holistic understanding of CT (see figure 5.1) is to connect it to a real-world phenomenon and to pursue complex projects that require the interrelation of concrete experiences with abstractions and associated formal languages. To learn novel skills needed for the future, such as CT and creativity skills, new epistemologies (see table 5.1) and metaphors for learning are needed. Beyond knowledge acquisition, these emerging metaphors of learning highlight the importance of learning through computational participation (Kafai 2016) and collaborative knowledge creation (Paavola and Hakkarainen 2005, 2014). Hence, co-creation and co-innovation are seen as crucial for learning CT and creativity.

Rather than merely digitalizing traditional acquisition-oriented and teacher-centered instructional practices (surface learning), it is critical to cultivate technology-enhanced practices of learning and instruction

Table 5.1 The epistemic approach for learning the traditional and new skills needed in a highly digitalized working life and in modern AI- and data-driven societies

	Surface learning	Deep learning	Phenomena-based learning
Goal	Recalling facts	Understanding	Creating new solutions
Outcome	Capability to apply information only in a narrow context, if at all	Capability to apply knowledge in various situations	Capability to create new solutions for various new situations
Methods	Information acquisition	Collaborative knowledge building	Co-creation and co-innovation
Focus	Facts	Knowledge	Thinking skills and strategies as well as innovation practices

that provide opportunities for social participation and collaborative creation of knowledge (Hakkarainen 2009; Paavola and Hakkarainen 2014). To appropriate sociodigital instruments as tools of everyday activity, it is necessary to transform everyday practices of learning and instruction as well as change the operational culture of schooling (Ritella and Hakkarainen 2012). Educational transformation is a systemic change and requires strong institutional support to succeed (Fullan 2016; Fullan and Quinn 2015). It is particularly important to develop novel epistemologies of learning and teaching, such as the phenomena-based approach, to integrate the entire community of the school and to promote the pedagogic transformations that the effective learning of CT will call for.

In addition to CT, we propose that computational creativity skills should be a goal of K–12 curricula. We cannot train our children to be merely computer players or even programmers in the future; we will have to train them to become computer composers with real computational creativity skills. To use a musical metaphor, it is not merely about pressing a piano's keys but about being able to interpret, compose, and create music. Computational creativity skills are not focused on the automation of existing processes or abstractions of the real world but rather on innovating and creating novel solutions, abstractions, and epistemic artifacts that may not yet exist. *Computational creativity skills* are used to create art and design artifacts, processes, and innovations by using computing, digital fabrication, and shared sociodigital processes.

PHENOMENA-BASED LEARNING AND CO-CREATION PROJECTS AS AN APPROACH TO LEARNING COMPUTATIONAL THINKING AND COMPUTATIONAL CREATIVITY SKILLS EDUCATION

Phenomena-based learning can be described as multidisciplinary inquiry learning in which teaching and learning, as well as curriculum, are based on holistic and authentic topics—not on traditional school subjects or decontextualized exercises. The key dimensions of phenomena-based learning are presented in table 5.2.

The basis of phenomena-based teaching and learning can be found in constructionism, which sees learners as active builders and creators of knowledge and artifacts. Knowledge is constructed as a result of problem-solving and creative production through the integration of little pieces into a comprehensive whole according to the situational needs and the information available at the time. When phenomena-based learning occurs in a

Table 5.2   Key dimensions of phenomena-based learning

Holism	The topics and concepts to be learned are chosen for their relevance in the real world, and a 360-degree perspective is offered through the integration of traditional school subjects.
Authenticity	The methods, tools, materials, and cognitive practices used in learning situations should correspond to ones in the real world: for example, in professional life.
Contextuality	Learners learn new things in their natural context and learn to move fluidly between contextualization and abstraction.
Problem-based inquiry learning	Learning and collaborative knowledge building are based on the questions and problems posed by learners, and solutions are created by them as well, allowing them to take an active role in designing the curriculum.
Learning as a nonlinear process	Learning is seen as a nonlinear process, which is activated, guided, and facilitated by open learning challenges and supporting structures.

collaborative setting (when the learners work in teams, for example), it supports the socioconstructivist and sociocultural learning theories, in which knowledge is not merely an internal element of an individual. Instead, knowledge is formed in a social context. Sociocultural learning theories focus on cultural artifacts (e.g., systems of symbols, such as language, mathematical calculation rules, and different kinds of thinking tools). Learning relies on the knowledge and tools that are transmitted by cultures, which are used generatively in novel contexts and for novel purposes.

Phenomena-based learning begins with the shared observation of holistic, genuine real-world phenomena in the learning community. The phenomena are studied as complete entities in their real context, and the knowledge and skills related to them are studied by crossing the boundaries between school subjects. Phenomena-based integrative study units frequently represent such holistic topics as climate change, the water cycle, and health and nutrition. This differs from traditional school culture, which is divided into subjects, where the things studied are often split into relatively small, separate, and decontextualized parts.

In phenomena-based teaching, understanding and studying the phenomenon start by asking a question or posing a problem (e.g., Why does an airplane fly and stay up in the air?). At its best, phenomena-based learning is cyclic inquiry learning, where the learners ask questions or pose problems about a phenomenon that interests them and then discover answers and find solutions together. The problems and questions are posed by the learners together—they are things the learners are genuinely interested in. Learners play a central role in creating and solving the learning challenges being pursued.

The observation is not limited to a single point of view; instead, the phenomena are studied from various points of view, crossing the boundaries between school subjects naturally and integrating subjects like mathematics, history, foreign languages, and psychology with a variety of themes. Phenomena-based structure in a curriculum actively creates better opportunities for integrating CT in various subjects and themes and for the systematic use of pedagogically meaningful methods, such as collaborative knowledge building (Scardamalia and Bereiter 2006), flipped classrooms (see, e.g., Bergmann and Sams 2012), and computational participation (Kafai 2016). The phenomena-based approach is also key to the versatile utilization of various digital learning environments (e.g., diversifying and enriching learning while using online learning environments).

In the learning process, new knowledge and skills are always applied to the phenomenon or the problem at hand, which means that the concepts, knowledge, and skills have immediate utility value that is evident in the learning situation. To absorb new knowledge and skills, it is very important that learners apply and use the knowledge and skills, such as CT, during the learning situation. Information learned only at the level of reading or theory (such as memorized physics formulas and calculation rules without real context or related problems) often remain superficial and separate details for the learners. They are unable to gain a comprehensive understanding and deeper knowledge of the real-world phenomenon and unable to internalize its meaning. Often it has been said that "you cannot learn to drive a car by using pen and paper" or that "cloze tests only teach how to answer cloze tests—there are no cloze tests in real life or professional life." Beyond encapsulated schoolwork, there are real communication situations where knowledge must be applied and messages must be transmitted clearly and comprehensively to another person.

The phenomena-based approach can significantly increase the authenticity of learning. This authenticity culminates in making the learner's cognitive processes and practices authentic. In a learning situation, the learner's cognitive processes, therefore, correspond to the cognitive practices required in the actual situation in which the knowledge and skills would be used. Toward that end, it is important to engage learners in creative activities that guide them to adopt the practices and epistemic games (Shaffer and Gee 2007) of computer scientists, designers, engineers, and scientists. In this authentic learning, the aim is to bring genuine practices and processes into learning situations in a pedagogically structured way when applicable, which allows the learner to participate in the expert culture of the field. Authenticity is a key requirement for the transfer and practical application of knowledge.

The new phenomena-based approaches for teaching and learning computational creativity skills are fostered by the novel affordances of sociodigital technologies that provide sophisticated professional-level tools for creative production. Associated practices involve, for instance, students learning by designing and building robots or utilizing 3-D HoloLens, 3-D printers, and sensors in their creative projects. The phenomena-based projects emphasize a way of thinking in which students solve authentic design challenges thorough various collaborative design activities, apply CT, and do actual coding, depending on the nature of the project.

Many Finnish schools are building educational makerspaces (see e.g., Peppler, Halverson, and Kafai 2016) by integrating arts and crafts, technology education, and science laboratories into other school subjects. Schools in Helsinki have organized codesign and co-invention projects that engage learners in designing complex artifacts that spark intellectual, engineering, and aesthetic challenges at lower and upper primary schools (Seitamaa-Hakkarainen and Hakkarainen 2017). Students work in small teams to solve an open-ended invention challenge using traditional craft and digital fabrication technologies. Their projects, in which they create various prototypes and products that assist in modeling the phenomenon, test and develop the learners' hypotheses and working theories. The challenge, which is co-configured with learners, might be, for example, to "design an intellectually challenging, aesthetically appealing, and personally meaningful complex artifact that makes daily tasks easier." It could be a new or an improved invention, and it should integrate both physical and digital (e.g., circuits or robotic) elements.

The role of teachers is not merely to facilitate learning but also to activate students' CT and learning processes. Toward that end, the learning-by-making activities are structured according to several stages, including skill building (e.g., working with microcontroller or other circuit boards), orientation (guided analysis of existing artifacts), and brainstorming with design challenges (in the classroom and at home with parents). They analyze design constraints (task requirements and resources), cluster design ideas, identify promising ones, and decide on their teams' design project. They share design ideas in the classroom, get feedback, seek knowledge (e.g., by visiting technical or design museums), experiment with design solutions, and construct prototypes of the design to arrive at their final solutions. It is also very important to organize exhibitions where teams can present their co-inventions to other students and parents. The analysis of Sinervo et al. (2020) of the designs of thirteen fifth-grade students (aged eleven to twelve years old) revealed that the details of their innovations varied considerably.

We categorized the teams' co-inventions according to their main function, such as improving cleanliness, providing reminders, or addressing hygiene, health, and nutrition issues. The inventions also reflected issues related to user values (health-related inequality, inclusion, or personalization), usage values (helping to resolve problematic situations), and environmental values (Sinervo et al. 2020).

Most of the teams' co-inventions were considered appropriate and promising, and only two co-inventions were not explicated clearly enough and could be considered quasi-creative and infeasible. Some very original ideas for known problems were found—for example, how to vacuum a carpet and the creation of a new gel comb for styling hair, even though these teams were not able to construct fully functional solutions. The gel comb team had a hard time figuring out how to get the gel out of the container. Some of the co-inventions were based on an already existing idea or product that was used in another context—for example, a pump bottle that was extended to help brush teeth with toothpaste more easily. In some cases, the co-invention was based on the adaptation of existing artifact designs by slightly modifying an existing product—for example, an automatic garbage container with an alarm that sounds when it is almost full. This long-term, open-ended invention project provided valuable learning opportunities for iterative problem-solving, shared meaning making, and collaboration that required a division of labor, organization, and personal responsibility. Phenomena-based learning empowers students to participate in the co-creation and co-innovation processes that are needed to learn CT skills and computational creativity skills. By using co-creation and co-innovation as learners' activities, the learning process is more insightful and inspiring. The role of the learner is not that of an object but that of an active subject of learning.

A more demanding example of a phenomena-based co-invention project was conducted with one class of seventh-grade students (aged thirteen to fourteen years). The project was initiated by the craft and visual arts teachers and involved the participation of mathematics, physics, chemistry, and information technology (IT) teachers, who provided their expertise to the inventors when needed. Eighth-grade digital technology students who had done a similar project the year before also helped the inventors during the project. The project started with two warm-up sessions for skill building. In the first session, the students built electric circuits using cards with copper tape, simple LEDs, and a coin cell battery. The aim of this warm-up session was to familiarize the students with basic electric circuits so that they would be able to use them in their inventions. The second warm-up session was organized by the eighth-grade students; they planned and held a workshop for the seventh graders about micro-controllers, basic programming with block-based coding, sensors, and DC motors. Many of the students had only done very simple Scratch programming tasks before this. After that, the actual collaborative invention project was initiated, and it ran for eight to ten weekly two-hour sessions. Also, in this project, the collaborative invention challenge was open ended: "Invent a smart product or a smart garment by relying on traditional and digital fabrication technologies, such as microcontrollers and 3D CAD." At the end of the project in May, the teams presented their inventions in an open invention exhibition held at the University of Helsinki.

This project proceeded much as the previous example had; it was initiated and led by the student teams. The teachers and tutors provided help when needed, but the project teams took most of the responsibility for the design and the construction. As the challenge required, student teams needed to use various digital technologies. It was also typical of the teams' processes that while ideating and experimenting, they confronted many phenomena related to physics, such as mechanics, electronics, and light and optics. Thus, they were exposed to numerous physics principles without being necessarily conscious of it. For example, one team (the banana light team) invented a banana-shaped LED light that attaches to a laptop lid and lights up the keyboard area. The features of their lamp included an RGB LED controlled by a microcontroller and a bendable structure that allowed the light to be directed to the keyboard.

During their design process, the team produced sixty-three design ideas in total, which can be divided into seven themes: (1) aesthetic features and name of the project; (2) materials; (3) light controls; (4) mounting to the laptop; (5) electrical connections; (6) directing light; and (7) other functions. The banana light team's invention process had many science-intensive steps. For example, when the team designed the structure of the lamp, some concepts of mechanics became relevant. With the joints, they experimented intensively with 3-D models and concrete prototypes. While the team searched for ways to attach the lamp to the lid of the laptop, the concept of friction came up. Furthermore, as the light was the main functionality of their invention, they spent a lot of time designing it and, thus, light and optics concepts were studied many times during the team's work. The microcontroller was used to operate the LED lights of the invention, and they tested several different options for controlling them, especially for turning them on and off. Understanding classical IF logic was particularly significant in these experiments in terms of learning programming and basic CT. Figure 5.2 shows a sketch and prototype of the banana light.

Furthermore, the team continued by testing different methods of turning the light on and off with predetermined event functions of the microcontroller, such as tapping the microcontroller twice or clapping their hands to create a loud sound. In the second prototype, they ended up using a simple button that they determined would be the most reliable when presenting the lamp to an audience in a noisy environment. Later, they decided to take their programming a bit further and added a functionality to control the brightness of the LED with the board's second button. The team was able to design a fully functional prototype meeting their specifications. These and other extensive maker-centered learning projects allow students to build epistemic flexibility in terms of interrelating concrete and abstract phenomena and, thereby, provide ample opportunities for system design and learning computational creativity and CT skills.

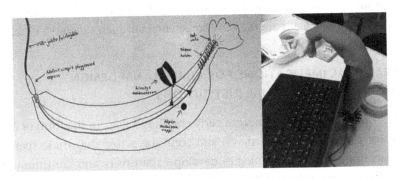

5.2 Illustrating, designing, and making a prototype of the banana light invention.

DISCUSSION

The activities of CT and programming are not equivalent to a human giving commands to a computer or a robot. Instead, they involve problem-solving and creativity, enhanced with computational tools and languages. It is not a matter of mastering certain commands or coding procedures but of engaging a designing system and creating digitally enhanced artifacts. How can we transform the educational system to help transform children from computer players to digital makers with real computational creativity skills?

To succeed in modern society, students should have advanced sociodigital and CT skills when they complete their K–12 education. These essential skills are needed across all fields of study, from the humanities to the sciences, including productive participation in knowledge-intensive work, and for becoming an active citizen in data- and AI-driven digital societies. CT cannot, however, be learned incidentally, for example, by playing computer games or by coding at home. Although informal interest-driven and creative participation is important for overcoming digital divides, formal education that deliberately cultivates innovative pedagogy and the associated teachers' expertise and guidance are urgently needed as well. The best way to provide CT skills and computational creativity skills for all students is to integrate them into K–12 education in curricula and in everyday teaching and learning practices in the form of phenomena-based co-creation projects. As we live in highly digital societies, we should also start discussing twenty-second-century skills, which will be focused on the innovation skills needed in an emerging innovation-driven society that is thoroughly based in AI and the smart use of big data. CT and computational creativity skills are the key competencies of such a society's citizens.

PRACTICAL IMPLICATIONS FOR CURRICULUM DESIGN AND FOR EDUCATIONAL INSTITUTIONS

Learning CT should begin from early childhood (e.g., in the form of cognitive games, songs, and plays) and continue across the whole span of education. Digital technologies develop expansively and continuously, so the process of learning CT and computational creativity skills should also be a sustaining, lifelong learning process. A significant challenge of teacher education is to help teachers develop digital and CT skills that they did not have the opportunity to learn during their own childhood education. Only by acquiring computational skills and practices can teachers work as builders of children's futures. To teach CT and creativity skills in K–12 education, both competent and educated teachers and the context and time for cultivating such competencies in teaching and learning are urgently needed. This creates a challenge for teachers' in-service training. How can teachers be trained in pedagogical skills and methods that will scaffold students' CT and computational creativity skills? Our experiences indicate that novel professional competencies become accessible when teachers are encouraged to collaborate with their colleagues and negotiate challenges through co-teaching. Teacher training should be thoroughly participatory and should engage teachers in co-creation and co-invention projects similar to those of young learners.

Traditional computer science and programming education do not offer ready-made solutions for learning CT or computational creativity skills in K–12 education. Instead, new practices and innovations require new pedagogical considerations in educational institutions on the level of the curriculum. An optimal impact on CT with phenomena-based learning and co-creation projects can be achieved by implementing the change comprehensively throughout the school's operating culture and by ensuring that CT and phenomena-based learning are integrated into the holistic reform of teaching and learning. The challenge is to implement the pedagogical change coherently and simultaneously at all levels (teaching, leadership, learning, technology, and curriculum). According to Fullan (2016), system improvement will result from a deep change in the culture of learning, local ownership of the learning agenda, and a system of continuous improvement and innovation that is simultaneously bottom-up, top-down, and sideways. Through systemic developmental efforts that integrate all levels, a permanent change in the operating culture can be achieved.

ACKNOWLEDGMENTS

This research was supported by the Academy of Finland (Grant 286837) and Strategic Research Grant 312527 of the Academy of Finland (Growing Mind Research Project).

REFERENCES

Bereiter, Carl, and Marlene Scardamalia. 2012. "What Will It Mean to Be an Educated Person in Mid-21st Century?" Gordon Commission on the Future of Education. https://www.ets.org/Media/Research/pdf/bereiter_scardamalia_what_will_mean _educated_person_century.pdf.

Bergmann, Jonathan, and Aaron Sams. 2012. *Flip Your Classroom: Reach Every Student in Every Class Every Day*. Washington, DC: International Society for Technology in Education.

Denning, Peter J. 2009. "The Profession of IT Beyond Computational Thinking." *Communications of the ACM* 52 (6): 28–30.

Denning, Peter J., and Matti Tedre. 2019. *Computational Thinking*. Cambridge, MA: MIT Press.

Fullan, Michael. 2016. "The Elusive Nature of Whole System Improvement in Education." *Journal of Educational Change* 17 (4): 539–544.

Fullan, Michael, and Joanne Quinn. 2015. *Coherence: The Right Drivers in Action for Schools, Districts, and Systems*. Thousand Oaks, CA: Corwin Press.

Hakkarainen, Kai. 2009. "Three Generations of Technology-Enhanced Learning." *British Journal of Educational Technology* 40 (5): 879–888.

Kafai, Yasmin B. 2016. "From Computational Thinking to Computational Participation in K–12 Education." *Communications of the ACM* 59 (8): 26–27.

Markauskaite, Lina, and Peter Goodyear. 2017. *Epistemic Fluency and Professional Education: Innovation, Knowledgeable Action and Actionable Knowledge*. London: Springer.

Paavola, Sami, and K. Hakkarainen. 2005. "The Knowledge Creation Metaphor: An Emergent Epistemological Approach to Learning." *Science and Education* 14: 535–557.

Paavola, Sami, and Kai Hakkarainen. 2014. "Trialogical Approach for Knowledge Creation." In *Knowledge Creation in Education*, edited by S. C. Tan, H. J. Jo, and J. Yoe, 53–73. Singapore: Springer.

Pea, Roy D. 1985. "Integrating Human and Computer Intelligence." In *New Directions for Child Development, No. 8, Children and Computers*, edited by Elisa L. Klein, 75–96. San Francisco: Jossey-Bass.

Pea, Roy D., D. Midian Kurland, and Jan Hawkins. 1985. "Logo and the Development of Thinking Skills." In *Children and Microcomputers: Formative Studies*, edited by Milton Chen and William Paisley, 193–212. Beverly Hills, CA: Sage.

Peppler, Kylie, Erica Halverson, and Yasmin B. Kafai. 2016. *Makeology: Makerspaces as Learning Environments*, vol. 1. London: Routledge.

Ritella, Giuseppe, and Kai Hakkarainen. 2012. "Instrument Genesis in Technology Mediated Learning: From Double Stimulation to Expansive Knowledge Practices." *International Journal of Computer-Supported Collaborative Learning* 7: 239–258.

Salomon, Gavriel. 1993. *Distributed Cognitions: Psychological and Educational Considerations*. Cambridge, MA: Cambridge University Press.

Salomon, Gavriel, David N. Perkins, and Tamar Globerson. 1991. "Partners in Cognition: Extending Human Intelligence with Intelligent Technologies." *Educational Researcher* 20 (3): 2–9.

Scardamalia, Marlene, and Carl Bereiter. 2006. "Knowledge Building: Theory, Pedagogy, and Technology." In *Cambridge Handbook of the Learning Sciences*, edited by Keith Sawyer, 97–118. New York: Cambridge University Press.

Seitamaa-Hakkarainen, Pirita, and Kai Hakkarainen. 2017. "Learning by Making." In *The SAGE Encyclopedia of Out-of-School Learning*, edited by Kylie Peppler. Thousand Oaks, CA: Sage.

Shaffer, David Williamson, and James Paul Gee. 2007. "Epistemic Games as Education for Innovation: Learning through Digital Technologies." *BJEP*, Monograph Series II, 5, 71–82.

Sinervo, Stiina, Kati Sormunen, Kaiju Kangas, Kai Hakkarainen, Jari Lavonen, Kalle Juuti, Tiina Korhonen, and Pirita Seitamaa-Hakkarainen. 2020. "Elementary School Pupils' Co-Inventions: Products and Pupils' Reflections on Processes." *International Journal of Technology Design and Education*. https://doi.org/10.1007/s10798-020-09577-y.

Tedre, Matti, and Peter J. Denning. 2016. "The Long Quest for Computational Thinking." In *Proceedings of the 16th Koli Calling International Conference on Computing Education Research*. New York, 120–129.

Trilling, Bernie, and Charles Fadel. 2009. *21st Century Skills: Learning for Life in Our Times*. New York: John Wiley.

Wing, Jeannette M. 2006. "Computational Thinking." *Communication of the ACM* 49 (3): 33–35.

Wing, Jeannette M. 2008. "Computational Thinking and Thinking about Computing." *Philosophical Transactions of the Royal Society A: Mathematical, Physical and Engineering Sciences*, no. 1881: 3717–3725.

6

COMPUTATIONAL EMPOWERMENT

Christian Dindler, Ole Sejer Iversen, Michael E. Caspersen, and Rachel Charlotte Smith

COMPUTATIONAL EMPOWERMENT: A CRITICAL COUNTERPART

In this chapter, we outline and position computational empowerment as an approach to digital technology in education. We trace the origin of computational empowerment through the participatory design tradition and discuss how it intersects with established ideas within computational thinking (CT). We use examples from teaching practice to illustrate how computational empowerment may be operationalized, and, on the level of curricula, we discuss the curriculum for the newly developed course, Technology Comprehension, for Danish primary and lower secondary education.

We define computational empowerment as a concern for the method used by students, as individuals and groups, to develop the capacity to understand digital technology and its effect on their lives and society at large and their ability to engage critically and curiously with the construction and deconstruction of technology (Dindler, Smith, and Iversen 2020). While this concern overlaps with the fundamental issues addressed within some parts of the CT literature, it also signals a critical approach that reaches beyond what is typically addressed in mainstream CT. Before unfolding the principles of computational empowerment in more detail, we trace the origin of the concept in the participatory design tradition.

A PARTICIPATORY DESIGN BACKGROUND

The participatory design tradition grew out of a series of projects in Scandinavia in the 1970s and 1980s, in which researchers and unions engaged in collaborative efforts to explore ways of democratizing the introduction of technology and ensuring quality of work and products for workers (Bjerknes et al. 1987). This fundamentally political commitment formed the backdrop of the practices of active user participation in technological development, using ethnographic methods to understand work practices and collaboratively constructing mock-ups of future technologies (Greenbaum and Kyng 1991) that have since proliferated beyond Scandinavia. The political commitment to empower people to understand and pose demands for technology also remains a topic in contemporary participatory design (Simonsen and Robertson 2013).

The notion of computational empowerment builds explicitly on the political, democratic ideas from participatory design and draws on the participatory practices that are used to realize these ideas. While the Scandinavian workplace of the 1960s and 1970s might seem an odd comparison to the challenge of educating young people in computing, we believe that there are parallels and that several principles from Scandinavian participatory design are more relevant than ever. In the early participatory design projects, unions and workers were fundamentally faced with a situation where they lacked the knowledge, organization, and power needed to understand and pose demands for technology. Similarly, the challenge facing many young people today is that they, generally speaking, have limited understanding of technology and computing, not only in terms of its construction but how it affects their lives. Hence young people have very limited capacity to pose demands for technology, make informed choices about technology in their lives, and take part in the development of technology and the cultures that surround it. Through the years, participatory design has developed several principles and practices for promoting democratic approaches to technology design, quality of products, and for empowering people to make informed decisions about technology. Here we draw out three principles from the participatory design tradition that have played a particularly prominent role in formulating the idea of computational empowerment.

The first is a concern for providing people with firsthand experience of technology in terms of how it is constructed and the consequences that it has. This concern has been evident throughout the history of participatory design, manifest in the archetypical participatory workshop, where users, designers, and stakeholders collaboratively explore technology and discuss its consequences and potential.

The second is a commitment to technology in use. This concern maintains that we need to understand technology not only as a technical issue but also through its consequences for people's everyday lives. In participatory design, this concern has been manifest in a long-standing tradition for using ethnographic methods to gain a detailed understanding of the practices for which technology was designed. Also, it is manifest in a critical stance toward how technologies shape work practices and the values inherent in these technologies.

The third is co-designing future technology. This concern reflects the view that people should not only be considered users and recipients of technology but also be invited to play an active role as co-designers. This concern may be traced in participatory design's catalog of methods (Hansen et al. 2019) and tools that invite future users to express their ideas and understanding in mock-ups and participation in prototyping activities.

The common goals of these (and other) participatory design principles have historically been to promote the agenda of democracy, quality of life, and empowerment of people to take an active role in technological development.

FROM PARTICIPATORY DESIGN TO COMPUTATIONAL EMPOWERMENT

The three principles outlined previously make up the background for computational empowerment. However, it is evident that the societal and technological landscape today is very different from the one in which participatory design emerged. So computational empowerment needs a contemporary articulation, which is the focus of this section.

Whereas the notion of "empowerment" in early participatory design was tied to empowering workers to have a say in the introduction of technology at the workplace, empowerment in the context of computing education is somewhat different. In education, the concepts itself carries with it a long history (Lawson 2011). Despite the fact that empowerment is explicitly mentioned as an objective in many contemporary papers based on computing education research, recent literature studies reveal that no clear definition of the term is provided in computing education research (Musaeus et al. 2021) nor in child computer interaction research (Van Mechelen et al. 2021). What comes closest to a definition is Shneiderman's manifesto entitled "Human Values and the Future of Technology: A Declaration of Empowerment," highlighting the need for empowerment at the intersection of human values and future technology. Here, Shneiderman (1990) argues that we, as researchers, designers, managers, implementers, and testers, must "recognize the powerful influence of our science and technology" and must commit ourselves to "studying ways to enable users to accomplish their personal and organizational goals while pursuing higher societal goals and serving human needs." This interpretation resonates well with that of computational empowerment. Here the term *empowerment* refers to a concern for providing students with the intellectual and practical capacity to understand and engage with technology. This may be fleshed out in three pillars of computational empowerment that are, effectively, contemporary articulations of the three participatory design principles mentioned in the previous section.

First, students should be provided with the means for engaging critically and curiously with the design of technology. This pillar reflects the idea that it is necessary for students to gain firsthand experience with technology, not only as something they use but also as a material that can be molded and used to build and construct things with. To some extent, this pillar resonates with the current focus on teaching students the basics of algorithms, programming, decomposition, and modeling. However, our concern is with the broader concept and approach of "designing" technology, which entails more than technical construction and modeling. Broadly speaking, design covers the entire iterative process including framing a problem, doing research, generating design ideas, constructing, and testing. Thus, this includes knowledge of how, for example, user research is done, and it requires knowledge of techniques for idea generation.

Figure 6.1 depicts a design process model developed through our work on computational empowerment (Iversen, Smith, and Dindler 2018)

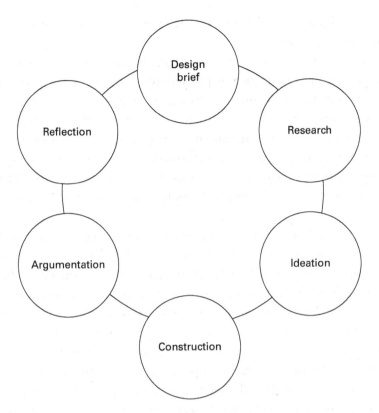

6.1 Process model for engaging students in research, ideation, construction, and reflection upon technology.

embodying the first pillar of computational empowerment. In some respects, the model is similar to other process models as it includes well-described activities such as research, ideation, and construction. However, it differs in at least two ways, and these reflect that the model is made in the interest of educating students in technology. First, besides well-known activities, it also includes "argumentation" and "reflection." These are deliberately included to make sure that design and construction in the interest of education are not only about making digital products but also about understanding how and why products are made to fit particular people and situations and encouraging students to reflect on what they learn by engaging themselves in design and construction. Second, the model is circular, suggesting that the goal is not a finished product (as is the case in most design models) but for students and teachers to iterate through the activities and develop their skills and knowledge.

This first pillar and the model inherently include knowledge and skills that are central to CT, such as programming and modeling. These are most clearly related to the "'construction" activity. These skills are an indispensable part of gaining firsthand experience with technology as a material that can be used to solve problems and shape our surroundings. As such, CT and computational empowerment are not competing ideas about engaging students in technology; they are complementary ideas. Next we provide a brief example of how the model can be used to scaffold teaching practice.

This example was centered on a project in which the task was to redesign an urban space in Aarhus, Denmark, to develop proposals for the city's upcoming year as EU Capital of Culture (2017). The design brief challenged the students to redesign a public park in accordance with the city council's aim of developing a more recreational space in the area for everyday leisure and social activities. The students had no prior experience with design processes or constructing with digital technology. The brief contained two important components to engage the students in the design process, namely authenticity and closeness, in terms of the local urban setting and neighborhood, to give the students an intrinsic motivation to engage in the design work. In the research phase, the pupils in groups explored the park and its visitors from different themes using observations, interviews, photo journeys, and mapping. Based on the design brief, their materials, and insights, the students worked to frame their unique challenges and collaborative ideation. Rather than developing specific technological artifacts, the design process emphasized an exploratory process, working with technology as a flexible and creative means. The role of the technology was downplayed in the initial activities and introduced during the ideation phase as students were able to work with and integrate relevant technologies into their projects in the construction activities. The availability of different technologies, such as Arduino, Makey Makey, and various software platforms, as flexible tools and materials to be integrated into the process with physical mock-up materials shifted the students' perceptions of technology from something involving fixed objects to digital means for creating their own alternative opportunities and solutions. This strategy was chosen to support the students in developing their own reflective stance toward designing with technology, which could form the basis of presentation and critical feedback in argumentation, as well as common discussions of the impact of technology and learnings from the process in reflection. The students designed a series of concepts for the park that they presented to visitors from the municipality, including automated bicycle stands to tidy up the park's many littered cycles, to new spaces for social activities and film screenings, and interactive waste bins that would nudge visitors to help create a more inviting public space. Students found the process challenging but exciting with its emphasis on problem-solving and technology design.

Second, students should be provided the means to analyze and reflect on how technology affects our lives as individuals, groups, and society. While the first pillar is concerned with how students can engage actively in the processes of researching, constructing, and reflecting on their designs, this second pillar is concerned with how students are equipped to engage with the technology that has been designed for them by others. This is a re-articulation of the central participatory design idea that technology shapes work practices and carries with it values embedded by those who designed the technology. It is a fundamentally analytical and reflective activity. Whereas the process described previously (figure 6.1) is concerned with design and construction, this second pillar is concerned with deconstruction. Figure 6.2 depicts the DORIT model developed for analysis and deconstruction. DORIT is short for "Do your Own Research In Technology." The model depicts six areas that each represent an individual analytical focus: technology prompts us to ask questions about the physical and digital materiality of the particular technology that we are analyzing. Say we are analyzing a smart watch, the technology area concerns the materials that have gone into the watch, the sensors and components used, and the programs running on the watch. If we move the focus to the purpose area, we ask questions concerning the purpose of the technology: What is the design meant to be used for; how is the interface arranged to support people in discovering the functionality? Moving to the area of use, we explore how the technology is actually used by people in a given situation. This will likely require observing people and perhaps interviewing them about their experience with the particular technology.

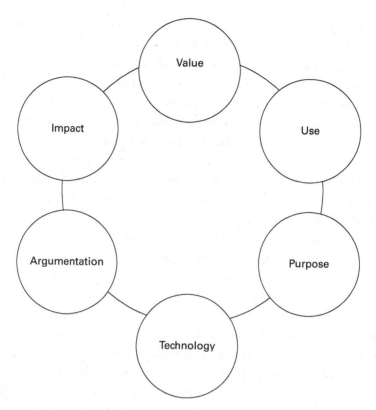

6.2 The DORIT model for engaging students in analyzing and reflecting on the technical construction, purpose, use, value, and impact of technology.

The next two areas, value and impact, are concerned with exploring the kinds of values that a particular technology reflects and the impact that the technology has. Finally, the area of argumentation asks us to look at the kinds of argument that the producer or the design itself provides for why we should use it. In sum, the six areas provide a structured way of analyzing, critiquing, and reflecting on the nature, use, and impact of technology.

Our example here is from a day in a Danish lower secondary school. Here, students worked with aspects of the idea of quantified self, using Garmin Connect watches during a whole school day. Based on the teacher's presentations of Garmin's website and the promotions of the product, the students were asked to analyze and reflect upon the artifact based on four dimensions of the model: argumentation, technology, value, and use. Small tasks included the categorization of statements concerning the aims, values, and intentions promoted by Garmin through their online communication and hence related to the area of "argumentation." Unboxing the watches, pupils explored data settings and submission of personal data (e.g., weight, height, age) to Garmin's system and did competitive running exercises around the school to carry out a simple analysis of use from a consumer perspective. Returning to the technology, students worked with the technical aspects of the watch by actively building a pedometer using simple Micro:bits (using MakeCode). This spurred a general discussion about the technical aspects of tracking movement and the technologies this could involve. Using screenshots of the Garmin watches' interfaces, the students were asked to analyze aspects of interactivity relating to the artifacts' composition and types of input/output data, before creating ideas for redesigns of new interfaces to suit their own everyday lives, values, and preferences. Such activities formed the foundations for discussions relating to impact, in which students were asked to critically reflect upon various aspects and layers of complexity in the digital artifact, from data privacy, intentionality, and system design to the personal and societal consequences of a device, such as a smartwatch, becoming part of our culture.

In this example, the teaching activities were arranged so as to move between the different areas in the model to include both technical exploration and design (building a pedometer) and more reflective task, including a discussion of the use, value, and impact of fitness tracker technologies.

The third and final pillar of computational empowerment is the idea of promoting democratic practices in the design and redesign of technology. In many respects, this pillar sums up the first two pillars. The prerequisite for taking part in technological development is an understanding of what technology is and how it is produced and a well-developed language for posing demands for technology. Democratization may, in this context, be understood at a number of levels. At the individual level, learning about design and construction as well as being able to critically analyze existing technologies provides students with the capacity to make informed decisions about their own use of technology. Moreover, it allows them to configure and perhaps redesign the technology of their everyday life. At the collective level, future generations that are well educated in terms of creating and assessing technology stand a better chance of making their voices heard when decisions are made about how technology is introduced and used and how it shapes our culture. This third pillar thus concerns the potential implications of the practices described in the first two pillars and hence it points to the larger aims of working with computational empowerment.

Taken together, the three pillars form the basis of computational empowerment. They also define two archetypal roles that students may assume in their engagement with technology. In the first role, students may engage in processes in which they design and construct technology for other people. These processes primarily concern the first pillar and include students researching, constructing, and reflecting on technology that they themselves create. In the second role, students may assume the role of analyzing and discussing the technology that others have designed for them. These processes relate primarily to the second pillar and the processes of analyzing the physical and digital construction, purpose, and actual use of a given technology. Figure 6.3 provides a simple depiction of these roles: the *arrows* at the top (moving left to right) illustrate processes of design and construction and the *arrows* at the bottom (moving right to left) illustrate processes of analyzing the technology made by others.

While computational empowerment is, in essence, different from classical articulations of CT, it shares concerns with a body of contributions

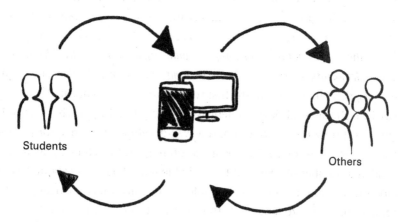

Students

Others

6.3 Students design and construct technology for others (*arrows left to right*), and students analyze and critique technology that others have designed for them (*arrows right to left*). (Adapted from Iversen, Dindler, and Smith 2019.)

within the field. In the next section we briefly review this literature to unveil the overlaps and points of resonance.

COMPUTATIONAL EMPOWERMENT AND COMPUTATIONAL THINKING

A concern for a broader framing of CT, including a more humanistic and critical approach to computing education, is present not only in the computational empowerment approach presented above but also in a series of recent contributions.

In their frameworks for studying and assessing the development of CT, Brennan and Resnick (2012) expanded the traditional conceptual understanding of CT to also include *computational practices* (the practices designers develop as they engage with the concepts, such as debugging projects or remixing others' work) and computational perspectives (the perspectives designers form about the world around them and about themselves). Brennan and Resnick (2012) combine CT, practices, and perspectives in their framework and thereby expand the scope of computing education to also include collaborative efforts in the design process as well as students' reflective understanding of digital technology.

This conceptual framework is also traceable in the realization of CT through making presented by Rode et al. (2015). Here, the authors envision competences related to aesthetics, creativity, and construction, visualizing multiple representations and understanding materials as integral parts of computing education. Rode et al. (2015) emphasize the importance of integrating arts in the science, technology, engineering and math focus, placing the "A" in STEAM.

Other prominent approaches include *computational participation* (Kafai and Burke 2013), focusing on creative engagement with computing and on moving beyond the individual to embrace wider social networks, and *computational fluency* (Resnick 2017), focusing on children expressing themselves through technology and becoming computational creators.

Wilensky, Brady, and Horn (2014) make the case for treating computation "as a core component in a broad-based cultural literacy" and express this concern through the notion of *computational literacy*.

The connection between computing and culture is also present in Tissen-baum, Sheldon, and Abelson's (2019) conception of *computational action*, in which they argue that learners have the capacity to have authentic impact in their lives through computing. They outline two key dimensions of computational action: *computational identity* and *digital empowerment*. Computational identity is a person's recognition that they can use comput-ing to have an impact in their lives and may have a place in the larger com-munity of computational problem solvers. Digital empowerment involves instilling in them the belief that they can put their computational identity into action in authentic and meaningful ways. They further argue that by focusing on computational action in addition to CT, computing educa-tion can become more inclusive, motivating, and empowering for young learners.

These approaches and characterizations are not conflicting; instead, they may be seen as focusing on different key aspects of CT. Nor does computational empowerment, as proposed in this chapter, take issues with the technical, creative, and cultural aspects of CT that are expressed in the work presented previously.

Computational empowerment accentuates two aspects in particular that contribute to the perspectives presented earlier. First, as noted in the second pillar earlier in this chapter and represented in model 3, we suggest that it is essential that children are provided with the means to analyze and reflect on the technology that surrounds them and makes up a central part of their everyday life. Engaging children in construction is not sufficient. Critical and curious deconstruction aided by model for analysis (such as the DORIT model) are necessary. In this sense, compu-tational empowerment accentuates the balance and potential interplay between construction and analysis. A similar concern is also expressed by Kafai, Proctor, and Lui (2019), who suggest that CT should also include "'pulling back the curtain' of the technological mechanisms underlying our existing computational systems in order to understand how these may cause inequities in and of itself" (104).

Second, computational empowerment accentuates the notion of design as the activity in which children, in addition to construction, do research, ideate, and reflect. Design is central to computational empowerment: it embodies the idea that technology is always imbued with values, it is always the product of choices, and these choices come with consequences for others and for ourselves. This concern has been inherited from participatory design and is fleshed out in the design model described earlier (figure 6.1).

COMPUTATIONAL EMPOWERMENT IN THE CURRICULUM

As noted earlier, we believe that CT and computational empowerment may complement each other to form the basis of an integrated approach to educating coming generations for a digitalized society. The two examples provided earlier demonstrate teaching activities that incorporate technical and reflective elements. To demonstrate how such an integration of CT and computational empowerment may be realized at the curricular level, we turn to the development of the new "Technology Comprehension" curriculum in Denmark.

An approach to embrace digital empowerment was present already in the Danish upper secondary Informatics curriculum developed in 2009 and 2010 and made permanent in 2016. One of six key competence areas was *use and impact of digital artifacts on human activity*. The purpose of this competence area was that students should understand that digital artifacts and their design have a profound impact on people, organizations, and social systems. Design of a system is not just design of the digital artifact and its interface, it is also design of the use and workflow that unfolds around the artifact. The purpose is that the students understand the interplay between the design of a digital artifact and the behavioral patterns that intentionally or unintentionally unfolds (Caspersen and Nowack 2013).

The curriculum for technology comprehension for primary and lower secondary education was developed by mandate of the Danish Ministry of Education in 2018 and is currently running on trial in forty-six schools for three years in Danish primary and lower secondary education. A committee of twenty-five appointed experts within education and research took part in the development of the curriculum. Based on previous research and impact of projects in both computational empowerment and CT (Caspersen et al. 2019; Smith and Iversen 2018), the authors of this chapter were invited to be centrally involved in the process: two of the authors acted as co-chairs for the working group, while a third author was involved in developing the content of the curriculum. In the choice of chairs, the Minister of Education signaled the importance of integrating humanistic and computer science approaches to computing education. Also, it was specified that the curriculum should embrace both technical as well as critical and design-oriented content.

The technology comprehension curriculum is based on four competence areas depicted in figure 6.4 (Danish Ministry of Education, n.d.).

Digital empowerment[1] refers to the critical and constructive exploration and analysis of how technology is imbued with values and intentions and how it shapes our lives as individuals, groups, and a society. It is concerned with the ethics of digital artifacts and promotes an analytical and critical approach to digital transformation.

Digital design and design processes refer to the ability to frame problems within a complex problem area and, through iterative processes, generate new ideas that can be transformed into form and content in interactive prototypes. It focuses on the processes through which digital artifacts are created and the choices that designers have to make in these processes, highlighting students' ability to work reflectively with complex problems.

Digital myndiggørelse

Digital empowerment
Critical, reflexive, and constructive examination and understanding of possibilities and consequences of digital artifacts.
Analysis of technology—intention and use | Evaluation | Redesign

Digital design og designprocesser

Digital design and design processes
Organization and implementation of iterative and incremental design processes considering the context of future use.
Problem framing | Ideation | Prototyping | Argumentation

Computationel tankegang

Computational thinking
Analysis, modeling, and structuring of data and data processes for automatic execution by a computer.
Data | Algorithms | Structuring | Modeling

Teknologisk handleevne

Technological knowledge and skills
"Mastery" of digital technologies (computer systems and networks), associated languages and programming.
Programming | Computer systems | Networks | Security

6.4 The four competence areas in the technology comprehension curriculum.

Computational thinking (CT) concerns the ability to translate a framed problem into a possible computational solution. It focuses on students' ability to analyze, model, and structure data and data processes in terms of abstract models (e.g., algorithms, data models, and interaction models).

Technological knowledge and skills concern knowledge of computer systems, digital tools and associated languages, and programming. They focus on the students' ability to express computational ideas and models in digital artifacts. This includes the ability to use computer systems and the associated language and to express ideas through programming. Working within this area aims at providing students with the experience and abilities needed to make informed choices about the use of digital tools and technologies.

Together, the four competence areas clearly integrate aspects of CT and computational empowerment as outlined earlier. The lineage from computational empowerment and participatory design is particularly evident in the areas of *digital empowerment* and *digital design and design processes*. It is, however, also evident when looking at the overall aim of the curriculum where the needs for skills to proactively engage in the digitization of society are accentuated: "In Technology Comprehension students gain skills to understand the capabilities of digital technologies and the implications of digital artifacts in order to strengthen students' capacity for understanding, creating and acting meaningfully in a digitized society where digital technologies and digital artifacts are catalysts for change" (Danish Ministry of Education, n.d., 1).

Moreover, technology comprehension is articulated as a support for intellectual freedom and a democratic citizenship among students in the Danish school system: "Freedom of spirit and democratic citizenship are widely cultivated in digital environments, which is why a well-founded understanding of technology is a prerequisite for being able to contribute constructively and actively in the development of relationships, communities and societies" (Danish Ministry of Education, n.d., 8).

These concerns for students' active engagement in technology development, democratic citizenship, and freedom of spirit run through the Technology Comprehension curriculum and can be traced throughout the four competence areas. *Design and design process* is participatory, emphasizing user studies as a prerequisite for new design; *digital empowerment* provides students with skills for analyzing and reflecting on the values, intentionality, and impact of digital technologies in our everyday lives. The areas of *computational thinking* and *technological knowledge and skills* represent core aspects of computing. Importantly, however, the four areas are not simply envisioned as separate entities that are positioned next to each other. In the very first sentence of the curriculum it is stated, "*There is in the description a balance between the four competence areas that in decisive ways enrichen each other and act as the premise for each other*" (Danish Ministry of Education, n.d., 1).

The integration of computational empowerment and CT form a balanced view and approach to computing education that is not found in other national curricula worldwide. Hence, it would appear that this curriculum is an ideal example of a balanced integration of computational empowerment and CT.

There are, however, a series of challenges and uncertainties relating to the development and implementation of the curricula in practice that are far from novel. The challenges include implementation in an existing national curriculum without educators' competences or resources, implementation of pipeline from preschool to higher education, and navigation of changing politics and priorities of education. These will, over time, determine whether the integration of computational empowerment and CT will endure in Danish primary and secondary education.

CONCLUSION

In this chapter, we make the case for computational empowerment—based on the legacy of participatory design—as a critical counterpart to mainstream CT. We envision computational empowerment as concern for how coming generations can develop the capacity and skills to make informed choices about technology and act critically and constructively as citizens in a digitized society. As such, the computational empowerment objectives resonate well with contemporary research efforts exploring computational practices and computational perspectives in computing education literature. However, as described in this chapter, computational empowerment accentuates the balance between construction and critical analysis of technology and the importance of engaging with the process of design.

We have illustrated how computational empowerment can be introduced into classroom teaching and how it has been adapted and introduced in the curriculum at a national scale. Our example from the Danish curriculum underpins how computational empowerment and CT can be tightly connected and mutually beneficial in the Technology Comprehension curriculum.

It could be argued that the Danish school system is relatively unique in terms of its statutory concern for critical perspectives on societal matters. However, we suggest that many school systems around the world could find inspiration in the Danish concern for computational empowerment to secure a conscientious digitization of our societies, in which future generations are provided with the educational means to engage actively and critically as citizens in an increasingly digital democratic society.

NOTE

1. In the Danish curriculum, "digital empowerment" is used independently of and with a different meaning than the term as used by Tissenbaum, Sheldon, and Abelson (2019).

REFERENCES

Bjerknes, Gro, Pelle Ehn, Morten Kyng, and Kristen Nygaard. 1987. *Computers and Democracy: A Scandinavian Challenge*. Aldershot, UK: Gower Pub Co.

Brennan, Karen, and Mitchel Resnick. 2012. "New Frameworks for Studying and Assessing the Development of Computational Thinking." In *Proceedings of the 2012 Annual Meeting of the American Educational Research Association*. Vancouver, Canada, 1: 25. scratched.gse.harvard.edu.

Caspersen, Michael E., Judith Gal-Ezer, Andrew McGettrick, and Enrico Nardelli. 2019. "Informatics as a Fundamental Discipline for the 21st Century." *Communications of the ACM* 62 (4): 58. https://doi.org/10.1145/3310330.

Caspersen, Michael E., and Palle Nowack. 2013. "Computational Thinking and Practice: A Generic Approach to Computing in Danish High Schools." In *Proceedings of the Fifteenth Australasian Computing Education Conference—Volume 136*. Darlinghurst, Australia, 137–143.

Danish Ministry of Education. n.d. "Danish Ministry of Education, Curriculum for Technology Comprehension." Danish Ministry of Education. https://www.uvm.dk/-/media/filer/uvm/aktuelt/pdf18/181221-laeseplan-teknologiforstaaelse.pdf?la=da.

Dindler, Christian, Rachel Charlotte Smith, and Ole Sejer Iversen. 2020. "Computational Empowerment: Participatory Design in Education." *CoDesign: International Journal of Cocreation in Design and the Arts* 16: 1, 66–80.

Greenbaum, Joan, and Morten Kyng. 1991. *Design at Work: Cooperative Design of Computer Systems*. New York: CRC Press.

Hansen, Nicolai Brodersen, Christian Dindler, Kim Halskov, Ole Sejer Iversen, Claus Bossen, Ditte Amund Basballe, and Ben Schouten. 2019. "How Participatory Design Works: Mechanisms and Effects." In *Proceedings of the 31st Australian Conference on Human-Computer Interaction*. Freemantle, Western Australia, 30–41.

Iversen, Ole Sejer, Christian Dindler, and Rachel Charlotte Smith. 2019. *En Designtilgang til Teknologiforståelse [A Design Approach to Understanding Technology]*. Frederikshavn, Denmark: Dafolo.

Iversen, Ole Sejer, Rachel Charlotte Smith, and Christian Dindler. 2018. "From Computational Thinking to Computational Empowerment: A 21st Century PD Agenda." In *Proceedings of the 15th Participatory Design Conference—Volume 1*, 1–11.

Kafai, Yasmin B., and Quinn Burke. 2013. "The Social Turn in K–12 Programming: Moving from Computational Thinking to Computational Participation." In *Proceedings of the 44th ACM Technical Symposium on Computer Science Education*. Denver, 603–608.

Kafai, Yasmin, Chris Proctor, and Debora Lui. 2019. "From Theory Bias to Theory Dialogue: Embracing Cognitive, Situated, and Critical Framings of Computational Thinking in K–12 CS Education." In *Proceedings of the 2019 ACM Conference on International Computing Education Research*. New York, 101–109.

Lawson, Tony. 2011. "Empowerment in Education: Liberation, Governance or a Distraction? A Review." *Power and Education* 3 (2): 89–103.

Musaeus, Line Have, Maarten Van Mechelen, Michael E. Caspersen, and Ole Sejer Iversen. 2021. "Empowerment through Computational Thinking: A Literature Survey." *Acta Didactica Norden*.

Resnick, Mitchel. 2017. *Lifelong Kindergarten: Cultivating Creativity through Projects, Passion, Peers, and Play*. Cambridge, MA: The MIT Press.

Rode, Jennifer A., Jennifer Booker, Andrea Marshall, Anne Weibert, Konstantin Aal, Thomas von Rekowski, Houda El mimouni, Akshay Sharma, Jordan Jobs, and Alexis Schleeter. 2015. "From Computational Thinking to Computational Making." In *Proceedings of the 2015 ACM International Joint Conference on Pervasive and Ubiquitous Computing and Proceedings of the 2015 ACM International Symposium on Wearable Computers—UbiComp '15*, 401–402. https://doi.org/10.1145/2800835.2800926.

Shneiderman, Ben. 1990. "Human Values and the Future of Technology: A Declaration of Empowermendermant." *Proceedings of the Conference on Computers and the Quality of Life—CQL '90*. https://doi.org/10.1145/97344.97360.

Simonsen, Jesper, and Toni Robertson. 2013. *Routledge International Handbook of Participatory Design*. New York: Routledge.

Smith, Rachel Charlotte, and Ole Sejer Iversen. 2018. "Participatory Design for Sustainable Social Change." *Design Studies* 59: 9–36. https://doi.org/10.1016/j.destud.2018.05.005.

Tissenbaum, Mike, Josh Sheldon, and Hal Abelson. 2019. "From Computational Thinking to Computational Action." *Communications of the ACM* 62 (3): 34–36.

Van Mechelen, Maarten, Line Have Musaeus, Arthur Hjorth, and Ole Sejer Iversen. 2021. "A Systematic Review of Empowerment in Child-Computer Interaction Research." In *Proceedings of the ACM Conference on Interaction Design and Children*. Athens, Greece, 119–130.

Wilensky, Uri, Corey E. Brady, and Michael S. Horn. 2014. "Fostering Computational Literacy in Science Classrooms." *Communications of the ACM* 57 (8): 24–28.

II

COMPUTATIONAL THINKING AND ARTIFICIAL INTELLIGENCE LITERACY IN K–12

7

THE COMPUTATIONAL THINKING AND ARTIFICIAL INTELLIGENCE DUALITY

Fredrik Heintz

Artificial intelligence (AI) is a new, general-purpose technology that will impact most, if not all, aspects of both our society and our personal every-day life. AI technology has enabled applications such as speech interfaces, vision-based object recognition, and machine translation. AI technology also makes recommendations about music, books, and movies for you, decides whether you will get a bank loan, and controls what posts you see on social media, all of which can have a major impact on your life. It is clear that AI technology will play a central role for most aspects of our professional and private lives, as well as society at large. Kevin Kelly predicts, "The business plans of the next 10,000 startups are easy to forecast: Take X and add AI" (2016). Andrew Ng says that AI is the new electricity—it is a fundamental part of almost all things (Lynch 2017).

Considering its expected impact, raising the awareness of what AI is and what it is not, as well as understanding some of the ramifications, are very important. Taking an educational perspective, it raises questions such as these: What does this mean for the need for competences, and what demands does it put on education? How can education retake its position as a positive force to provide individuals with the knowledge, skills, and attitudes they need to be constructive and critical actors in the major transformation that we are in? What competences are needed to effectively be able to use AI as the powerful tool it is?

The starting point is that people and AI complement each other. It is *humans **and** AI*, not humans **or** AI. It is clear that computers are significantly better than we are at well-defined tasks such as mathematical calculations, remembering huge numbers of facts, and repeating precise instruction over and over again exactly the same way. It is equally clear that people are significantly better than computers at understanding social interactions, making decisions from a holistic perspective, and dealing with vague or ambiguous situations. What is not clear is whether the progress of AI will eventually make computers better than humans at all these things. For the conceivable future, it is likely that humans will be better at some things and computers will be better at other things, and most things can be done better in collaboration than in isolation.

This means that we need to become better at solving problems together with computers powered by AI technology. Those who know how to do this effectively will have the best opportunities. The single most important competence to achieve this will most likely be computational thinking (CT): solving problems using concepts and techniques from computer science in such a way that computers can assist (Wing 2006).

AI and CT can actually be seen as duals with respect to problem-solving by computers and humans. AI is about providing computers with the ability to think like humans, while computational thinking is about improving the problem-solving capability of humans by leveraging the way a computer "thinks" when it solves problems.

Humans have developed increasingly powerful tools. Artificial intelligence is the latest—perhaps the ultimate—tool. AI is about understanding what intelligence would be sufficient to create intelligence in a computer or robot. A major challenge with this definition is that there is no commonly accepted definition of human intelligence (Legg and Hutter 2007). A computer can often do things that we assume requires intelligence without any effort, like solving difficult mathematical problems. At the same time, computers often are very poor when it comes to doing what appears to be really simple things, like learning a new concept from abstract descriptions, for example, the idea that a zebra is a horse with black-and-white-striped hair.

AI can also be described as systems taking input, analyzing the data, making decisions, and then acting based on these decisions. This approach is often called the Sense-Plan-Act approach (Russell and Norvig 2016). In many cases these systems learn to improve their performance over time from data collected (or given). These systems are often called agents, as they have a sense of agency that differentiates them from other computer programs. This also gives rise to a cognitive and social view on computation.

Machine learning is currently seen as the most interesting part of AI, both because many consider it an essential part of intelligence and because it allows computer programs to improve over time based on experience. This is important because it is hard for people to specify exactly what we want a system to do. Instead the machine can partly learn what to do and how to do it, as well as improve over time, by collecting data and modifying its behavior (Brynjolfsson and Mitchell 2017).

The scientific field of AI has many subfields, which study different aspects of intelligent behavior and cognition. Common topics at the main AI conferences include machine learning, knowledge representation and reasoning, heuristic search, planning and scheduling, natural language processing, computer vision, robotics, and multiagent systems. All of these topics have been studied since the 1950s. Most of them were in fact discussed already at the seminal Dartmouth conference in 1956.

Two of the most important subfields are machine learning and knowledge representation and reasoning. Knowledge representation and reasoning is the scientific study of how to represent knowledge in a computer and how to reason with this knowledge to draw valid conclusions. Machine learning is the scientific study of how a computer can learn things such as finding patterns, recognizing objects, and acting to achieve specific goals. Machine learning is mostly based on statistics and correlations (*black box* models), while knowledge representation and reasoning is mostly based on explicitly modeling cause and effect (*white box* models).

Currently, most of the attention is focused on machine learning, while knowledge representation and reasoning were the focus in the 1980s and 1990s, often in the form of expert systems. The next big step is likely the combination and integration of reasoning and learning, maybe in a similar manner as we humans do it with type, separate but somehow connected systems (Kahneman 2011). System I is the fast, automatic, and opaque system for perception and intuition with very limited introspection, which shares many similarities with data-driven machine learning approaches. System II is the slow, deliberate, and explicit system for analytical thinking and planning with a high degree of introspection, which corresponds roughly to formal, symbolic reasoning-based approaches.

Another significant trend is to study the implications of AI and to make sure that AI is developed in a way that benefits all. The EU is for example putting its weight behind the concept of *Trustworthy AI*, which requires AI systems to follow the applicable rules and regulations, live up to four ethical principles, and have a robust and safe implementation (High-Level Expert Group on AI 2019). A consequence of this is that the field of AI is broadening and today includes researchers from a wide variety of scientific disciplines, not only computer scientists.

Even if the goal is to make computers learn new things and act intelligently, it is important to remember that AI is still a tool. A tool is something people use to augment our capabilities (e.g., remember, move around, lift things, count) and to give us completely new capabilities (e.g., fly, travel in space, control processes in real-time, see in x-ray vision). Through digitalization, the effect and improvement rate of tools can grow exponentially, according to Moore's law. If these tools are connected in networks, their value can increase further because of the network effects.

We have seen a long history of automation in agriculture and manufacturing. Machines have taken over much of the work previously done through manual labor. Today, AI-based tools are enabling us to start automating tasks that require cognitive skills (Brynjolfsson and McAfee 2017). The development is still in a very early stage, but the trend is clear. More and more tasks are being automated. Automation often increases the efficiency, but it is rare that complete processes are automated. Rather, parts of the processes are automated, making people part of the resulting semi-automated processes.

An interesting question then becomes how this influences the role of humans. Humans and computers are fundamentally good at different things, which makes humans and computers complementary. Instead of complete automation, where we hand over the control completely to the computer, it is better if humans and computers solve problems together. Even if a computer is good at recognizing objects and classifying images, humans are still many times better at these tasks and definitely better at generalizing to other similar tasks. The role of humans then becomes to train and teach AI algorithms to do different tasks and monitor that they are actually doing the correct thing in an appropriate manner. The training most likely never will be completely finished, but rather incremental and continuous as new concrete examples of incorrect decisions and situations where the computer does not know what to do are collected. In these cases, we humans have to take over and provide the correct answer. A challenge for us humans then becomes what we think is correct, given our different perspectives and backgrounds.

Does this mean that the role of humans is determined by the ability of AI? Partly, but we are developing AI techniques to complement our selves and to do things that we find hard, like dealing with combinatorial problems and problems, which require detailed knowledge of vast amount of data. Similarly, humans are enabled to do what we are good at and what AI systems find hard, like understanding context and judge what is right or wrong from a societal or psychological perspective.

Does this mean that humans will eventually be marginalized? Probably not. First, by leveraging AI tools, humans will be able to do more and solve harder and more complex problems. Second, even if a computer could do the same things as a human, it is not necessary that it is cheaper, better, or even desired.

An interesting example is chess. We humans have no chance against the best chess computers and have not had a chance for over twenty years (Siegel 2016). At the same time, the quality of human chess playing is increasing, as we are practicing together with chess computers. Some claim that Magnus Carlsen is the best chess player in the world since he is the human who is the best at playing like a computer. This is natural to him as he has been practicing against the computer since he was a small child. What is even more interesting is that if you combine humans and chess computers in a team, called a centaur, they become better than both the best humans and the best computers. It is even the case that the team becomes even better if you include several people (Kasparov 2017). This is a concrete example of how the result improves when humans and computers collaborate to solve complex problems.

There is no dichotomy between humans and computers; it is not a question of either or, but rather humans *and* computers. Simplified, computers are good at doing, while humans are good at what should be done and why. We are good at asking questions, and computers are good at answering them. Examples are question-answering systems that are great at answering questions and planning systems that can generate elaborate detailed plans for how to achieve goals, but the questions and the goals have to be provided to the systems by human users.

An important observation is that it is a different skill to play chess with a computer compared to playing chess on your own. This means that even if you are an expert and are provided with the best possible tool, the result does not necessarily improve significantly from your performance without it. You might still perform worse than a person who is less of an expert in the subject but more of an expert on using the tool effectively.

To really leverage the computational power we need to both educate people in solving problems with AI tools and adapt the way we work to truly leverage the tools. Thus, relevant education, changed ways of working, and new organizational forms are required. A central capability is to transform business problems into computational problems. That is, to formulate problems in such a way that computers or computer tools can assist (Brynjolfsson and Mitchell 2017).

CT captures this general skill of solving problems in a way that computers can assist (Wing 2011). For computers to help us, we have to be better at understanding how a computer solves problems. Thus, CT is to a large extent about learning to understand how a computer "thinks" when it solves a problem.

When you solve problems with a computer, it is often about describing to the computer what should be done, rather than doing it yourself. Programs are descriptions of how to solve something that a computer understands. Traditionally, humans have to describe every step of the process in great detail. AI actually reduces this by enabling the computer to fill in some of the details.

CT is becoming a general basic skill (Wing 2006). We also need to teach about AI and how AI can be applied to different fields and problems. To do this well, you need to understand both the domain and the technology sufficiently well to make the right design choices or procure the right solutions. This leads to a challenge for all those school systems where subjects are taught independently. In the same way that AI breaks down the silos in organizations, AI requires different ways of teaching in school. Instead of treating each subject independently, there is a need to study both the subject matter and the AI tools and techniques used to help solve the subject matter problems.

AI and CT can actually be seen as two sides of the same coin. AI is about enabling the computer to solve problems we consider to require intelligence, or casually speaking, to enable computers to "think." CT turns this around and asks the question: How can people become better at solving problems by learning from how computers do?

We can now compare AI to the main CT activities.

AI tries to avoid step-by-step instructions through either (1) declarative programming, such as logic programming, in which an engine interprets declarative programs, stating what should be done and figuring out how to achieve this, or (2) through machine learning, which could also be called programming by example, in which a large set of examples together with an objective function are used to define what the program should do.

Breaking down problems into smaller problems, or to divide and conquer, is a classical problem-solving technique used, for example, in AI to provide dynamic programming solutions to optimization problems or as part of reinforcement learning (Sutton and Barto 2018). It can be questioned whether the computer really breaks down the problem itself, but in reinforcement learning the computer has the choice about what parts of the state space to explore, providing some freedom to select how to break down a problem.

Finding patterns is the main strength of deep learning neural network-based approaches (Goodfellow, Bengio, and Courville 2016; LeCun, Bengio, and Hinton 2015). Given sufficient (often large) amounts of relevant examples, these methods are able to find patterns in the data that are beyond what humans can do.

Abstraction is an area where AI-based approaches have had mixed success. On one hand, it could be argued that all approaches to representation learning are doing exactly this (Bengio, Courville, and Vincent 2013). On the other hand, the abstractions found are usually much more limited than the type of abstractions we humans create.

Designing algorithms to solve specific problems is an important part of CT. One way of characterizing AI, at least some parts, such as reinforcement learning and planning, is as a form of automated programming.

Some people even define AI as solving problems without being explicitly programmed (Brynjolfsson and Mitchell 2017).

The focus of traditional computer science, and CT, is to develop algorithms and programs that describe how to solve specific classes of problems with some guarantees. This usually involves understanding the problem in detail and then developing step-by-step instructions that allow a computer to solve problem instances repeatedly and with great precision.

The focus of modern AI is to develop algorithms and programs that can extract, or learn, general models or programs, from data where the problem is not really well defined. It is very hard to specify precisely what a cat or chair looks like, but it is relatively straightforward to create large collections of images with and without cats or chairs. The same is true for natural language.

By developing methods that do not require detailed specifications but rather can extract the underlying phenomenon from positive and negative examples, we increase the range of problems that can be addressed by computers. This is also significant for the skills required to leverage these techniques. Maybe there is a need for data thinking or machine learning thinking to capture the cognitive skills that highly skilled data science and machine learning engineers use to solve problems through data?

By studying AI and CT, we will learn more about both thinking and human intelligence, how to effectively solve problems with computers, and most importantly, how we humans can solve large scale complex problems together with AI. In consideration of the major challenges humanity is facing, such as providing everyone on the planet with food, energy, sustenance, and belonging in a long-term sustainable manner for both the climate and ourselves, this is absolutely essential.

REFERENCES

Bengio, Yoshua, Aaron Courville, and Pascal Vincent. 2013. "Representation Learning: A Review and New Perspectives." *IEEE Transactions on Pattern Analysis and Machine Intelligence* 35 (8): 1798–1828.

Brynjolfsson, Erik, and Andrew McAfee. 2017. "The Business of Artificial Intelligence." *Harvard Business Review*, 1–20.

Brynjolfsson, Erik, and Tom Mitchell. 2017. "What Can Machine Learning Do? Workforce Implications." *Science* 358 (6370): 1530–1534.

Goodfellow, Ian, Yoshua Bengio, and Aaron Courville. 2016. *Deep Learning*. Cambridge, MA: MIT Press.

High-Level Expert Group on AI. 2019. *Ethics Guidelines for Trustworthy AI*. European Commission, Brussels.

Kahneman, Daniel, 2011. *Thinking, Fast and Slow*. New York: Farrar, Straus and Giroux.

Kasparov, Garry. 2017. *Deep Thinking: Where Machine Intelligence Ends and Human Creativity Begins*. New York: Public Affairs.

Kelly, Kevin. 2016. *The Inevitable*. New York: Viking Press.

LeCun, Yann, Yoshua Bengio, and Geoffrey Hinton. 2015. "Deep Learning." *Nature* 521 (7553): 436–444.

Legg, Shane, and Marcus Hutter. 2007. "Universal Intelligence: A Definition of Machine Intelligence." *Minds and Machines* 17 (4): 391–444.

Lynch, Shana. 2017. "Andrew Ng: Why AI is the New Electricity." *Insights by Stanford Business*, 11.

Russell, Stuart J., and Peter Norvig. 2016. *Artificial Intelligence: A Modern Approach*. Upper Saddle River, NJ: Prentice Hall.

Siegel, Robert. 2016. "20 Years Later, Humans Still No Match for Computers on the Chessboard." *NPR.org*. https://www.npr.org/sections/alltechconsidered/2016/10/24/499162905/20-years-later-humans-still-no-match-for-computers-on-the-chessboard.

Sutton, Richard, and Andrew Barto. 2018. *Introduction to Reinforcement Learning*. Cambridge, MA: MIT Press.

Wing, Jeanette. 2006. "Computational Thinking." *Communications of the ACM* 49 (3): 33–35.

Wing, Jeanette. 2011. "Research Notebook: Computational Thinking: What and Why?" *The Link Magazine* 20–23. https://www.cs.cmu.edu/link/research-notebook-computational-thinking-what-and-why.

8

ARTIFICIAL INTELLIGENCE THINKING IN K–12

David S. Touretzky and Christina Gardner-McCune

HISTORY OF THE FIVE BIG IDEAS IN ARTIFICIAL INTELLIGENCE

The "Five Big Ideas in AI" were inspired by the 2017 CSTA (Computer Science Teachers Association) Computer Science Standards, which are organized around five big ideas in computing. Those five big ideas are: (1) algorithms and programming, (2) computing systems, (3) data and analysis, (4) impacts of computing, and (5) networks and the internet. Unfortunately, although artificial intelligence (AI) is an important branch of computer science, the standards contain only two sentences about AI, both in the eleventh- and twelfth-grade band, as shown in figure 8.1. Until recently, AI was considered too advanced for younger students.

The Five Big Ideas in AI are a way to introduce teachers, parents, and students to the essential concepts and major issues of a field often confused with science fiction (Touretzky et al. 2019). We argue here that studying AI can teach students about more than technology; it can help them better appreciate the complexity of humanity.

Each of the Five Big Ideas is described by a key phrase and a one-sentence statement; see figure 8.2. In a poster we published in 2019, each statement was unpacked in a paragraph of explanatory text. This poster has since been translated into fourteen languages, including Chinese, Korean, Hindi, Spanish, Portuguese, Hebrew, and Arabic, all available on

Describe how artificial intellgence drives many software and physical systems.	>	Algorithms & Programming	Algorithms	Communicating
Implement an artificial intelligence algorithm to play a game against a human opponent or solve a problem.	>	Algorithms & Programming	Algorithms	Creating

8.1   References to AI in the 2017 CSTA Computer Science Standards.

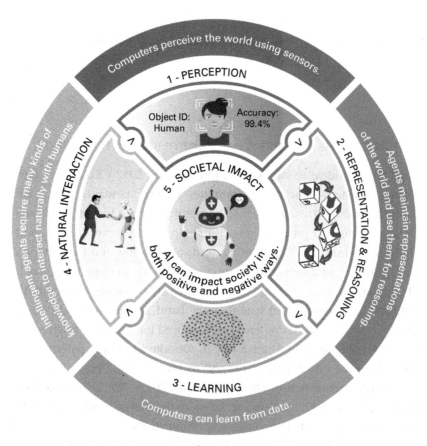

8.2   The Five Big Ideas in AI graphic from AI4K12.org.

the Artificial Intelligence for K–12 Students website (https://www.AI4K12 .org). In the guidelines, each Big Idea is broken down into a set of concepts and skills that form the rows of a table called a grade band progression chart. The columns are the four grade bands, and the cells define what students in that grade band should know about and be able to do with that concept or skill. At the time of this writing, the draft grade band progression chart for the first Big Idea, perception, has been released for public comment and is currently undergoing revision. An excerpt is shown in figure 8.3. The draft for the third Big Idea, learning, has also been released.

The ordering of the Five Big Ideas progresses from narrow areas of low-level processing (perception) to broad, high-level topics (societal impact). But they are not meant to be covered in sequence. Some curriculum developers have done this, such as ReadyAI's "AI + ME" overview (ReadyAI 2019). But there are many other ways to survey AI, such as by examining different application areas. A module on self-driving cars could touch on all five of the Big Ideas.

BIG IDEA #1: PERCEPTION

Big Idea #1, perception, says, "Computers perceive the world using sensors." The initial guidelines for Big Idea #1 start with a discussion of computer sensors, which connects with the computer science standards for computer hardware (under Computer Systems), and a discussion of human sensory capabilities, which naturally connects with human biology. But sensing isn't what this Big Idea is about.

The first major insight we want students to have is that perception is more than sensing. Specifically, perception is the extraction of meaning from sensory signals, using knowledge. An automatic door at a supermarket has a sensor, but it does not perceive anything. The signal from the pressure pad or ultrasonic transducer is too impoverished to carry much information, and the response of the door too simplistic to require any "meaning" beyond the raw signal. We want students to understand that not all devices exhibit intelligence. We would not be enjoying YouTube videos of wildlife wandering through supermarket aisles if their automatic doors could properly perceive who (or what) was entering.

AI4K12

Big Idea #1: Perception	Computers perceive the world using sensors.	Perception is the extraction of meaning from sensory information using knowledge	The transformation from signal to meaning takes place in stages, with increasingly abstract features and higher level knowledge applied at each stage.	LO = Learning Objective: what students should be able to do. EU = Enduring Understanding: what students should know.
Concept	**K-2**	**3-5**	**6-8**	**9-12**
Sensing (Living Things) **1-A-i**	LO: Identify human senses and sensory organs. EU: People experience the world through sight, hearing, touch, taste, and smell.	LO: Compare human and animal perception. EU: Some animals experience the world differently than people do. Unpacked: Rats and dolphins see sonar. Bees can see ultraviolet. Rats are have no color vision; dogs are red-green colorblind. Dogs and rats can hear higher frequencies than humans.	LO: Give examples of how humans combine information from multiple modalities. EU: People can exploit correlations between senses, such as sight and sound, to make sense of ambiguous signals. Unpacked: In a noisy environment, speech is more intelligible when the speaker's mouth is visible. People seem to know where a mouth with various actions (such as dropping an object) and can recognize when the sound doesn't match their expectation.	N/A - for AI purposes, this topic has already been adequately addressed in the lower grade bands. Other courses, such as biology or an elective on sensory psychology, could go into more detail about topics such as facial perception and vestibular organs. Possible enrichment material: look at optical illusions (Müller-Lyer illusion, Kanizsa triangle) and ask which ones are computer vision systems also subject to.
Sensing (Computer Sensors) **1-A-ii**	LO: Locate and identify sensors (camera, microphone) on computers, phones, robots, and other devices. EU: Computers "see" through video cameras and "hear" through microphones.	LO: Illustrate how computer sensing differs from human sensing. EU: Most computers have no sense of taste, smell, or touch, but they can sense some things that humans can't, such as infrared emissions, extremely low or high frequency sounds, or magnetism.	LO: Give examples of how intelligent agents combine information from multiple sensors. EU: Self driving cars combine computer vision with radar or lidar imaging, GPS measurement and accelerometer data to form a detailed representation of the environment and their motion through it.	LO: Describe the limitations and advantages of various types of computer sensors. EU: Sensors are devices that measure physical phenomena such as light, sound, temperature, or pressure. Unpacked: Cameras have limited resolution, dynamic range, and spectral sensitivity. Microphones have limited sensitivity and frequency response. Signals may be degraded by noise, such as a microphone in a noisy environment. Some sensors can detect things that people cannot, such as infrared or ultraviolet imagery or ultrasonic sounds.
Sensing (Digital Encoding) **1-A-iii**	N/A	LO: Explain how images are represented digitally in a computer. EU: Images are encoded as 2D arrays of pixels, where each pixel is a number giving the brightness of that piece of the image, or an RGB value indicating the brightness of the red, green, and blue components of that piece.	LO: Explain how sounds are represented digitally in a computer. EU: Sounds are digitally encoded by sampling the amplitude of the sound wave (typically several thousand samples per second), yielding a series of numbers.	LO: Explain how radar, lidar, GPS, and accelerometer data are represented. EU: Radar and lidar do depth imaging: each pixel is a depth value. GPS triangulates position using radio signals and gives a location as longitude and latitude. Accelerometers measure acceleration in 3 orthogonal dimensions. Unpacked: Radar and lidar measure distance as the time for a reflected signal to return to the device. GPS determines location by triangulating precisely timed signals from three or more satellites. Accelerometers use orthogonally oriented strain gauges to measure acceleration in three dimensions.

8.3 Part of the draft grade band progression chart for Big Idea #1, perception. The rows list concepts and skills; the columns are the four grade bands.

If the extraction of meaning from sensory signals requires knowledge, what does that knowledge look like? In the case of speech perception, this question leads to an examination of the many levels of language, starting with articulatory gestures (the motions made by the tongue, lips, and vocal tract), and progressing to phonology (sounds), morphology (word stems, prefixes, and suffixes), prosody (stress and intonation), syntax (grammar), and semantics (meaning). These are sophisticated concepts, but even young children can discuss the phonetic inventory of their native language and can understand why an intelligent agent like Siri or Alexa might have trouble understanding different accents or speech patterns.

The second major insight into perception we want students to come away with is what we call the *abstraction pipeline*: the transformation from signal to meaning takes place in stages, with increasingly abstract features and higher level knowledge applied at each stage. In the case of speech this progression is inherent in the structure of language, and early speech-recognition systems actually implemented the pipeline as a collection of distinct modules proceeding from the raw acoustic signal to phonemes, words, phrases, and meaning. In more recent systems based on deep neural networks there are many more stages of processing, and different types of knowledge co-exist across multiple levels. But even in these messier neural net implementations there is a general progression from more local, signal-based information to more global, meaning-based information as one moves through the layers.

Visual perception differs from speech perception in that language is something produced by *humans* for the purpose of transmitting meaning, while vision is concerned with *constructing,* meaning by sensing natural phenomena such as reflection and occlusion. The abstraction pipeline for vision starts with pixels and ends with 3-D scenes, but what lies between is a complex mix of edges, contours, boundaries, surfaces, parts, shadows, reflections, and objects. Marr (1982) called this the 2½-D sketch. The knowledge required to derive these representations is innate in humans and not easily articulated explicitly in a computer program.

The *abstraction* pipeline is a wondrous thing. Information flows backward as well as forward: for example, knowledge of the vocabulary of a language can influence the perception of ambiguous sounds, and knowledge about the shapes of objects can influence the interpretation of edges in a scene. Human perceptual processes are far from fully understood at present. Studying how AI attempts to mimic these processes offers a new route to appreciation of human perception.

How much of this can be conveyed in K–12 is still an open question, but at least the early stages of the pipeline can be exposed to students through interactive demos. Low-level vision can be *illustrated* by showing the real-time output of vertical and horizontal edge detectors (figure 8.4) applied to webcam images. Low-level auditory perception can be shown with real-time spectrograms (figure 8.5) and pitch trackers.

BIG IDEA #2: REPRESENTATION AND REASONING

Big Idea #2 states that "Agents maintain representations of the world and use them for reasoning." In computer science terms, representations are data structures, and reasoning is performed by algorithms. But how can the concept of representations be explained to children in the lower grades who are not yet familiar with data structures? Maps are a good place to

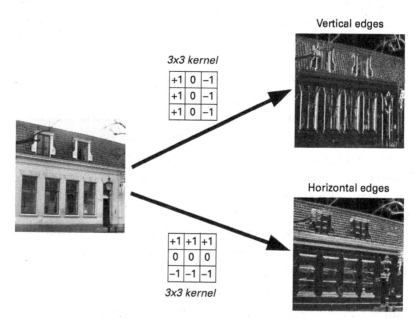

8.4 Edge detection is one of the first stages of computer vision. Vertical and horizontal edges are detected by convolving 3×3 kernels with the image.

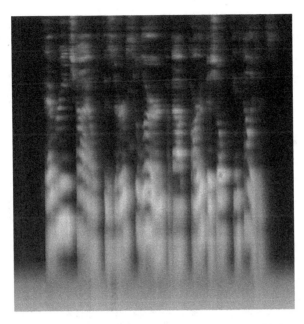

8.5 Real-time spectrogram of the first author saying, "Every child deserves to learn about artificial intelligence." The vertical axis is frequency; the horizontal axis is time; *shading* indicates the amount of energy in that frequency band. (Created with https://creatability.withgoogle.com/seeing-music.)

start. Even young children can grasp the concept of a map being a representation of a place. They understand that the map is not the territory, that maps abstract away many details, and that maps follow certain notational conventions, such as the way that roads or buildings are depicted. Having children construct a map of their house, their school, or their neighborhood brings these ideas home. Children can also appreciate that using a map to plan a route is a kind of reasoning and that a self-driving car must be doing a similar kind of reasoning. Thus, using maps, representation, and reasoning can be made accessible even in K–2.

A good next step in exploring representation and reasoning, appropriate for grades 3 through 5, is the *decision* tree. This can be introduced via the "guess-the-animal" game, where the goal is to guess the animal a person is thinking of by asking a series of yes-or-no questions, such as, "Does it swim?" or "Does it fly?" The questions form the nonterminal nodes of a binary tree, and the terminal nodes are the animals (figure 8.6). In playing

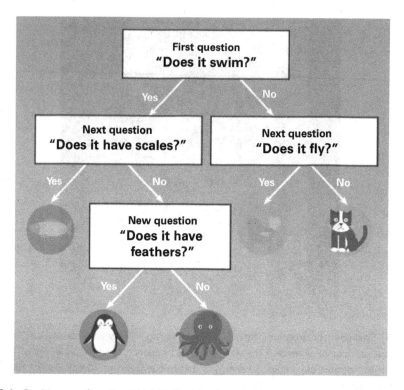

8.6 Decision tree learning. (*AI+ME: Big Idea 2—Representation & Reasoning: How AI Makes Choices.* AI+Me Series. Pittsburgh, PA: ReadyAI, 2020. Used with permission.)

this simple game children encounter fundamental concepts in representation and reasoning that they will be exploring further for years to come. First, the decision tree is drawn on the board so that everyone can follow the reasoning process. This introduces students to the notion of tree structures and serves as a simple formalism for encoding knowledge. Second, the procedure for playing the game is formalized. One always starts at the root node. Upon arriving at any nonterminal node, the student must ask that node's question and then follows either the "yes" or "no" branch to reach the next node. Upon arriving at a terminal node, one states the animal associated with that node and waits to see if the guess is correct. Asking students to explain this procedure in their own words prompts them to think about how the reasoning algorithm works.

Another valuable aspect of the guess-the-animal game is the procedure for growing the tree. If one reaches a terminal node and guesses "penguin," but the correct answer is "octopus," one has to obtain two pieces of information: (1) what question distinguishes between a penguin and an octopus, and (2) what is the correct answer for an octopus. The decision tree can then be updated by replacing the "penguin" terminal node with a nonterminal node containing the new question, "Does it have feathers?" Penguin and octopus become its two children. Following this *procedure*, especially when they choose the animals and questions themselves, gives children a feeling for how human knowledge can be encoded in a data structure, and how computers can learn.

A key insight we want students to have about this Big Idea is the interdependence of representation and reasoning. Reasoning algorithms need something to reason with, and representations are pointless if we have no way to put them to use. Consider the map example from earlier: the map representation needs a path-planning algorithm to find a route between two locations. It's also important to understand that representations are not just the input to an algorithm, they may also be constructed by the algorithm. The route constructed by the path planning algorithm is another representation. Likewise, game playing programs need another common AI representation, the search tree, to keep track of alternative moves as they search for the move that will lead to a winning game. The search tree is neither an input nor an output. It is constructed by the search algorithm as it searches. We express the representation/reasoning duality as follows: "Representation drives reasoning, and reasoning algorithms manipulate representations."

Older students can be introduced to a taxonomy of reasoning types to help them understand the variety of ways AI is used to make decisions. Classification and prediction (regression) problems are the most common applications of neural networks, although these problems can also be approached symbolically. Combinatorial search is one of the oldest parts of classical AI and still very important. Other reasoning approaches include logical deduction and theorem proving, constraint satisfaction, task planning, and numerical optimization. Some of these topics are too advanced for K–12, but it may be possible to provide a taste. For example, doing inference by resolution theorem proving using first-order predicate calculus is a topic for undergraduates, but we might give students in 9–12 a taste of logical inference by looking at how a computer can handle syllogisms, such as the classic "all men are mortal; Socrates is a man; therefore Socrates is mortal."

SYMBOLIC VS. FEATURE VECTOR REPRESENTATIONS

While much of the recent progress on the difficult problems of speech recognition, computer vision, and machine translation has resulted from advances in neural network technology, symbolic representations remain important, as evidenced by the resources Google and other large corporations have devoted to constructing knowledge graphs (Noy et al. 2019). The knowledge panel displayed on the right hand side of the screen in a Google search for "Thomas Jefferson" or "kiwi fruit" is generated from the Google knowledge graph. Hand-crafted symbolic representations used in classical AI are certainly easier to explain to children than the feature vector representations constructed by neural networks. But what should they understand about feature vector representations? In the remainder of this section we offer some speculation on how feature vector representations may influence students' views about word meanings.

Dictionaries and thesauruses are our traditional codifications of the meaning of words. With six hundred thousand words spanning one thousand years of usage, the *Oxford English Dictionary* (OED) is a landmark intellectual achievement, billing itself as "the definitive record of the English language" (Oxford University Press 2020). Dictionaries typically include usage examples—often famous quotations—that help put words into context. The OED contains 3 million quotations. All of this material was compiled over many years by committees of scholars. Similar efforts exist for other languages: for example, a special commission composed of members of the Académie Française produces the Dictionnaire de l'Académie Française, endorsed by the French government. Dictionaries are important cultural artifacts and are the original hand-crafted symbolic representations of words. But it is not easy for a computer to reason with this type of representation.

Computing technology has offered our culture a new type of word representation that now powers many natural language applications. This *feature vector encoding*, also known as a *word embedding*, represents each word as a point in a high-dimensional abstract space. To understand this encoding it is helpful to first consider a less abstract example. The following is inspired by the description of the word2vec family of models in Mikolov et al. (2013).

Suppose we want to represent the words "man," "woman," "boy," "girl," "king," "queen," "prince," and "princess." Imagine a 3-D space where the x coordinate encodes gender, the y coordinate encodes age, and the z coordinate encodes royalty (figure 8.7). Each of our eight vocabulary words can be mapped to a unique point in this space: for example, "man" might be $(0,1,0)$, and "princess" might be $(1,0,1)$. Euclidean distance in this space can serve as a heuristic for semantic similarity, allowing us to infer that "man" is semantically closer to "woman" than to "princess." We can go on to embed additional words in this space, even without adding more dimensions. "Son" would likely be close to "boy," although less definitive as to age, so perhaps its coordinates would be $(0, 0.3, 0)$. "Parent" is gender neutral but an adult, with no implication of royalty, so it might map to $(0, 0.5, 0)$, and so on.

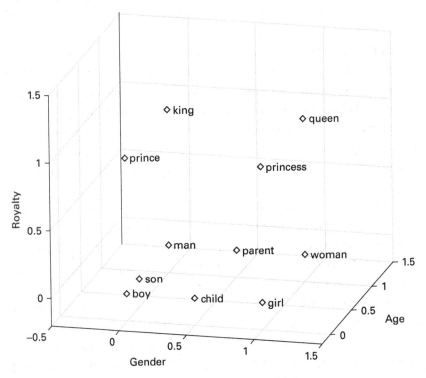

8.7 Representations of words as points in a 3-D semantic space.

Mikolov et al. (2013) showed that in addition to providing a similarity heuristic, feature vector encodings admit a simple type of analogical reasoning by vector arithmetic. Subtracting the vector for "queen" $(1,1,1)$ from the vector for "woman" $(1,1,0)$ yields a vector $(0,0,-1)$ that removes the royalty attribute from a word. Adding this vector to "prince" $(0,0,1)$ yields "boy" $(0,0,0)$. Adding it to "king" $(0,1,1)$ yields "man" $(0,1,0)$. Similarly, subtracting "man" from "boy" and adding the result to "parent" yields $(0.5,0,0)$, which is a plausible encoding for "child."

Representing a larger vocabulary requires a higher-dimensional feature space. Rather than designing those features by hand, they can be created using machine learning, specifically neural networks. We don't have a convenient way to train the network directly on word meanings, but since words with similar meanings tend to occur in similar contexts, it turns out that training the network to predict what words are likely to co-occur with a given word is an effective proxy for meaning. This approach captures more than pure syntactic and semantic features; it also captures information about usage: for example, which adjectives are typically applied to which nouns.

Unlike the carefully constructed dictionary definitions produced by human experts, feature vector representations are somewhat arbitrary. They depend on parameters such as the size of the context window (the number of words before and after the word whose features are being learned), the vocabulary set, the dimensionality of the feature space (number of units in the neural network's hidden layer), and the training corpus. Even if all these parameters are held constant, two separate runs of the learning algorithm will produce different representations because of the randomness of the network's initial weights. Heuristics used for speed training also influence the vector representation. And these vectors are not easily interpretable by humans, although one can sometimes find correlations between vector elements and semantic attributes by comparing the representations of several words, as in figure 8.8.

Despite their lack of definitiveness, statistical feature vector representations have significant practical uses. For example, they can be used to disambiguate homophones during real-time speech recognition. Tell a chatbot you want "<u>two</u> coffees, not <u>too</u> hot, <u>to</u> go" and it will get every word right. Neural machine translation systems use feature vectors as their

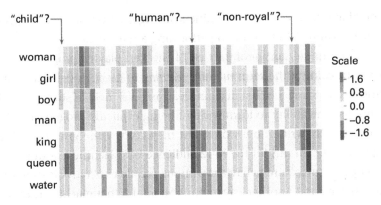

8.8 Feature vector representations of words in word2vec. (Figure modified from Alammar 2019.)

input and output encodings, as do some question answering systems such as Siri, and machine translation applications such as Google Translate.

There are already simple online demos that allow people to explore word-2vec vocabularies and experiment with the analogy via vector arithmetic. Demos that are friendlier to K–12 users will surely follow. eCraft2Learn, a children's AI programming framework built on top of Snap!, recently added blocks for working with feature vectors (Kahn and Winters 2020). Allowing students to experiment on their own with feature vector representations is the twenty-first-century version of teaching them to explore a dictionary: it will enrich their appreciation of language. It will also give them insight into the workings of the AI systems they interact with in their daily lives.

BIG IDEA #3: LEARNING

Big Idea #3 says "Computers can learn from data." It's important to distinguish human learning from what the computer is doing, so the guidelines begin with a comparison. Machine learning mostly follows one of two approaches: finding patterns in data, or optimizing behavior based on trial and error. Humans do those things too, but they also learn in other ways, such as by being told, by observing others, by asking questions, by experimenting, and by making connections to past experience. Human learning, because it is part of a larger cognitive architecture, is general and flexible, while machine learning is accomplished by specialized algorithms and focuses on performing a specific task.

Arthur Samuel, author of the first AI checkers playing program, is credited with coining the term *machine learning* in 1959. A definition often attributed to Samuel is that machine learning is a "field of study that gives computers the ability to learn without being explicitly programmed." He didn't actually write those words, but they convey the gist of his thinking.[1] Our take on this for the K–12 audience is: "Machine learning allows a computer to acquire behaviors without people explicitly programming those behaviors." Another way to think about it is that machine learning is a way to *construct* a reasoner. So humans program the learning algorithm, the learning algorithm constructs a reasoner with the desired behavior, and the reasoner is then employed in some task such as recognizing cats in images or deciding whether an email is spam.

One of the things we want students to be able to do is construct a reasoner themselves. Several tools allow children to train an image classifier on small numbers of examples using deep neural networks and transfer learning. Probably the best known tool is Google's Teachable Machine, which conveniently runs in the browser. The demo can use images captured from a laptop's camera and doesn't require any programming. Similar capabilities now exist in children's programming frameworks, such as App Inventor, Cognimates (based on Scratch), and eCraft2Learn (based on Snap!). Using a tool like Teachable Machine, students can train a classifier to recognize a thumbs-up gesture, a peace sign, and a "no gesture" condition. They can then measure its accuracy on new images and experiment with adding more varied training examples to help it perform better. This makes a compelling educational experience for adults as well as children. It's a great way to approach machine learning, but it has some limitations, which must be addressed through other activities.

To enhance their understanding of machine learning, we would like students to experience what it *feels* like to acquire a concept by finding patterns in data. The problem with training Teachable Machine to recognize cats or thumbs-up gestures is that we start out already knowing those concepts, even if the machine does not. Training a classifier on familiar concepts cannot help one experience what it's like to be the trainee.

To address this, the guidelines have students play the role of machine learner for concepts they don't already know.

This exercise can be done as early as in grades K–2 by showing labeled examples of cartoon creatures and asking students to figure out a rule that predicts the labels. For example, the images could be of cartoon fish of various colors, with different shaped heads, bodies, fins, and tails. The labels could be "eats seaweed" and "doesn't eat seaweed." Labeled instances would be presented one at a time, and after seeing a sufficient number the students could begin positing what the pattern is that predicts a fish eating seaweed. A simple case would be that it's the purple fish that eat seaweed. More challenging cases may involve a conjunction of features (only purple fish with pointy heads eat seaweed), or for older students, a negated value (purple fish except those with small tails), a disjunction of conjunctions (purple fish with pointy heads or orange fish with small tails), or something even more complex.

In later grade bands, students are asked to simulate learning algorithms in more detail. For example, in grades 3–5, instead of verbally stating a classification rule, they may be asked to construct a decision tree, where each node tests a single feature such as color or head shape. In 9–12 they may be asked to train a classifier or predictor to fit a set of noisy training points by turning knobs to adjust parameters, eyeballing the quality of the fit. Such a model may predict a person's height given their age, or the price of a used car given its mileage. For a linear model $y = mx + b$, they would adjust the slope (m) and intercept (b), but they could also train nonlinear models such as logistic functions or cubic polynomials the same way.

CHANGES IN INTERNAL REPRESENTATIONS
Another insight we want students to have is, "Learning of new behaviors is brought about by changes in internal representations." In other words, what the learning algorithm is doing is not magic; it is simply adjusting a data structure. This is the second drawback to Teachable Machine and similar transfer learning tools: they are black box demos whose internal representations are unobservable. Given the complexity of deep neural network representations, even if there were a practical way to display

them, it's not clear how their hidden layer activations could be made interpretable by non-experts. There is, however, interesting work on giving qualitative insights into what these networks are doing, such as displaying which areas of a scene a network is attending to, or finding the optimal stimulus for triggering a learned feature detector. As our methods for analyzing deep neural networks improve, the way we teach them will evolve.

For now, we advocate approaching "changes to internal representations," using hand simulations of symbolic learning applications. We can help students recognize that the decision trees they built in grades 3–5 or the parameter values they adjusted in grades 9–12 are the internal representations that learning algorithms manipulate. We can also draw on some "glass box" machine learning tools that disclose their representations. For example, MachineLearningForKids allows students to construct a classifier using decision tree learning, and a recent enhancement added the ability to draw the decision tree. While the tree can be very complex for multivariate datasets, such as the Titanic survivor data used as one of the illustrative examples, for simpler data the tree is easily interpretable.

For exploring changes in neural net representations, Google's Tensor-Flow Playground is an ideal tool. It allows students to train small feed-forward neural networks that are graphically displayed in the browser. Every connection is explicitly represented and gets thicker or thinner as the magnitude of the weight increases or decreases; the sign of the weight determines its color. By hovering over a connection, students can read the exact weight value. What we want students to appreciate is that the weights constitute an internal representation of a set of feature detectors that the learning algorithm (backpropagation) is incrementally adjusting. Exactly how those adjustments are calculated can be left to more advanced classes. In deep neural networks, these feature detectors are complex and hard to interpret, but for the shallow networks and simple 2-D input patterns supported by TensorFlow Playground, it is possible to exactly visualize what each feature detector is doing.

TYPES OF LEARNING

"Finding patterns in data" is a broad concept that encompasses both supervised learning, where the data are labeled, and unsupervised learning, where they are not. It can be used to produce both classifiers and predictors. Classification is a special case of prediction in which the output is drawn from a discrete set (the class labels) rather than a continuous range. The other type of machine learning covered in Big Idea #3, "learning from experience," involves something radically different.

In supervised learning the algorithm is provided with the correct answer (the label) for every training example. All it has to do is adjust the internal representations to make the model more likely to produce this answer. In learning from experience, known as reinforcement learning, the algorithm is only provided with a scalar value, the reinforcement signal, which indicates how well things are going. It is not told what it should do differently to make things go better; it has to figure that out for itself.

The other reason reinforcement learning is radically different is that reinforcement learning is used for sequential decision problems. While classification and prediction are one-shot problems where a single input is mapped to a single output, sequential decision problems involve a series of action choices, where each action affects the choices available in the next step. An example would be playing a game like chess, where each move constrains the choices available for the next move. We want students to appreciate two things about reinforcement learning. First, the computer is not being trained by a teacher; it is generating its own data by making a choice at each step and seeing where that choice leads, that is, how much reinforcement it ultimately receives. Computers that have become expert game players through reinforcement learning generated their training data by playing against themselves. Second, because we are not required to provide the algorithm with the correct answer at each step, it is possible for the algorithm to discover solutions to problems in which we don't know ourselves what would be the best choice to make.

Reinforcement learning is worth teaching in K–12 because it has led to some significant achievements for AI, such as AlphaGo's 2016 defeat of world champion Go player Lee Sedol. But like deep neural networks, the details of reinforcement learning algorithms are too complex for all but the most advanced high school students. Hand-simulating the algorithm would be tedious because of the large number of trials required even for simple tasks. But tiny grid world simulations with only a handful of states and actions can provide a glimpse into how reinforcement learning works.

Some other topics covered in Big Idea #3 are the design of feature sets, development and use of large datasets, and sources and effects of bias in training data.

BIG IDEA #4: NATURAL INTERACTION

Big Idea #4 covers a range of topics relating to how computers interact with people. The one-sentence description reads: "Intelligent agents require many kinds of knowledge to interact comfortably with humans." The major topics that make up this Big Idea are natural language understanding, common sense reasoning, affective computing, and consciousness/theory of mind.

Natural language understanding includes making sense of human requests to intelligent agents, extracting information from text, and translating from one language to another. Language is often syntactically ambiguous, so finding the most likely meaning of a text requires some semantic analysis. For example, "John saw the man from the restaurant" could mean either that John was gazing out from the restaurant when he saw the man, or that John saw the man who had some previous connection to the restaurant. Further context is necessary to decide which meaning the speaker intended.

Speaking with an intelligent agent incapable of *common sense reasoning* would be tedious because everything would have to be spelled out in detail. Common sense reasoning includes naive physics: understanding the properties of solids and liquids and how they behave in response to forces such as gravity. Winograd schema sentences such as, "The trophy would not fit in the suitcase because it was too [large/small]," illustrate how an understanding of naive physics, in this case volume and physical containment, determines whether "it" refers to the trophy or the suitcase.

Another requirement for common sense reasoning is knowledge about the world: for example, knowing that cats are living things, or what chairs are used for. This also includes sociocultural knowledge, such as when to pay at a restaurant, or what makes a good gift for a child.

Today's AI systems show little common sense reasoning ability. Google can translate text into over one hundred languages but can't answer questions about a short story that a five-year-old would find trivial. AI systems try to make up for this deficiency by focusing on retrieval from huge knowledge bases. But retrieval is not the same as inference. For example, ask Google how much an alligator weighs, and it will answer five hundred pounds. Ask how much an ostrich weighs, and it will say 250 pounds. But ask it, "Does an alligator weigh more than an ostrich?" and, as of April 2021, it doesn't even understand the question. Retrieval alone doesn't cut it—usually. Sometimes it does. Ask Google, "Is Microsoft bigger than IBM?" and it finds articles where people have discussed that question. But ask it, "Is Intel bigger than Pfizer?" and it falls apart, despite the fact that it can retrieve the number of employees and market capitalization of these companies, either of which could be used to compare their size.

To achieve human-like common sense reasoning would require something called Artificial General Intelligence, or AGI. One of the essential understandings we want children to come away with is the difference between the narrow AI reasoners we have today and the broad AGI reasoners depicted in science fiction. One way to drive this idea home is to try to have a conversation with an intelligent agent such as Alexa or Siri. At present they do not maintain context from one utterance to another, so one can't have a meaningful discussion with them. AI developers are currently working on this. Chatbots, which are more specialized than "agents" such as Alexa, address the problem by relying on templates for common interactions such as inquiring about the availability of a product, or placing an order. But if the conversation veers outside the anticipated scenarios, the chatbot is lost. We want children to be aware of these limitations so that they do not attribute more intelligence to an AI agent than it deserves.

A third topic in Big Idea #4 is *affective computing*, or recognizing and dealing with human emotional states. This includes sensitivity to tone of voice, facial expressions, and body language, and the ability to adjust interaction style to effectively respond to indications of frustration, boredom, or excitement. If robot companions were as responsive as dogs to our emotional states, they might truly capture our hearts.

The final topic in Big Idea #4 is *consciousness and theory of mind*. These terms are normally addressed in university-level philosophy courses. But because today's children are growing up with intelligent agents, and in a culture filled with fictional robots with human-like personas, they are primed to appreciate questions about whether computers really do have minds, or could in principle have them. Concepts such as the Turing Test, or Searle's hypothetical Chinese room, can be introduced in high school, and should be.

MORE PLAYING WITH LANGUAGE

We both enjoyed learning about sentence diagramming in school. In this section we draw a connection between sentence diagramming and AI, specifically the question of how a natural language understander begins to make sense of a sentence. We speculate that playing with AI language tools may instill in future generations of students an appreciation for the formal structure of language that we got from experimenting with diagramming.

Sentence diagramming was invented in the 1840s by Stephen W. Clark, a rural New York schoolmaster, as a means of helping students learn to "parse" (grammatically analyze) sentences (Florey 2012). The notation was refined by Alonzo Reed and Brainerd Kellogg in 1877 into a form that became widely used in nineteenth- and twentieth-century middle and high schools. Diagramming is less frequently taught today and is not included in the Common Core (Thomas 2014). English teachers argue and research has shown that isolated direct grammar instruction does not help students become more effective writers. Nonetheless, readers of a certain age may have fond memories of learning to diagram sentences (Florey 2006), perhaps because they were a first exposure to formal representations. Diagrams are also something like data structures, a fundamental concept in computer science.

Sentence diagrams are a simplified version of the syntax trees used in modern linguistics to represent the syntactic structure of sentences. Diagrams use only a few graphical devices, mainly horizontal, vertical, and diagonal lines, as in figure 8.9. Some of these devices serve multiple roles, whereas syntax trees label every node with an unambiguous grammatical class.

Some linguistic theories are phrased in terms of transformations on tree structures: for example, a sentence in the active voice can be transformed into the passive voice by switching the subject and direct object subtrees and modifying the verb phrase, so "John saw Mary" becomes

As Gregor Samsa awoke one morning from uneasy dreams
he found himself transformed in his bed into a monstrous vermin.

Kafka, *Metamorphosis*

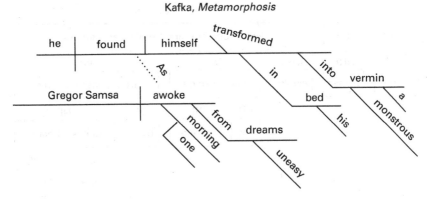

8.9 Diagramming a sentence. (Courtesy of Pop Chart Labs.)

"Mary was seen by John." Ambiguous sentences such as "John saw the man with a telescope" are compatible with multiple tree structures, for example, one in which "with a telescope" is attached to "saw," and one in which it is attached to "man."

AI systems must parse sentences in order to understand them. While syntactic analysis is only one part of language understanding, it is an essential component. The widespread availability of natural language parsers presents an opportunity to introduce students to grammar in a new way: by having them experiment with automated parsers. Figure 8.10 shows a parse tree provided by the online demo page for the Berkeley Neural Parser.[2]

Figure 8.11 shows the same parse in traditional syntax tree notation.

Students could learn to draw syntax trees by comparing their efforts to computer-constructed syntax trees like the ones shown here. They could explore the topic of syntactic ambiguity by constructing sentences and seeing if the parser generates more than one parse tree. And they could learn to write simple rules in a phrase structure grammar and see those rules used to generate parse trees (whose terminal nodes form sentences) by iterative expansion of nonterminal nodes. With a well-designed graphical interface to manage the rules, and automatic generation of many examples from

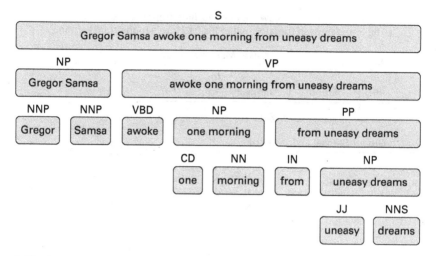

8.10 Parse tree produced by the Berkeley Neural Parser (https://parser.kitaev.io). NP indicates a noun phrase, VP a verb phrase, and PP a prepositional phrase.

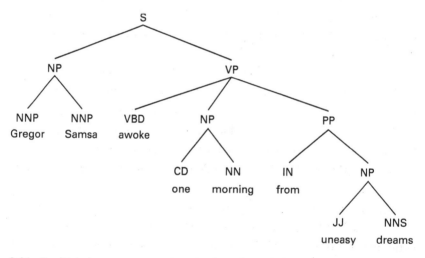

8.11 Traditional syntax tree notation, also from the Berkeley Neural Parser.

the current rule set, students would have a grammar "sandbox" in which to explore syntax and the relationship between parsing and generation.

The linguist Mark Liberman has remarked that because of diagramming instruction, "grammar-school children of the 19th century learned more about linguistic analysis than most graduate students in English departments do today" (Liberman 2012). Interactive language tools designed specifically for K–12 could remedy that.

What about semantics? Modern AI has leveraged statistical learning over large datasets to construct practically useful natural language tools for tasks such as machine translation or text summarization. These tools use heuristics to resolve ambiguity from local context. The approach is a powerful one but does not achieve true "understanding" in the human sense, as evidenced by the limitations these systems still exhibit. For example, given "John saw the man with binoculars," the Berkeley Neural Parser attaches "with binoculars" to "man," while most humans would prefer "saw." But given "John easily saw the man with binoculars," the Berkeley Neural Parser attaches "with binoculars" to "saw." It's not just the presence of "easily" that changes the attachment, because given "John easily saw the man with groceries," the prepositional phrase attaches to "man," as it should. The interaction of the noun with the adverb to influence attachment is not the result of some explicitly formulated rule, nor is it the result of commonsense reasoning. Rather it reflects the statistics of the corpus the model was trained on, captured in a deep neural network. Another example is the parser makes different but plausible attachment choices for "John saw the man with one eye" (attached to "saw") versus "John saw the man with one leg" (attached to "man"). But it does not do so well on "John saw the man with one ear." Statistics can only get you so far.

One way students can explore machine understanding of language is by comparing how AI parsers resolve ambiguous sentences with their own preferred interpretations of those sentences, as we've done above. It's even more fun than sentence diagramming.

BIG IDEA #5: SOCIETAL IMPACT

Big Idea #5 is that "AI can impact society in both positive and negative ways." We want students to be aware of these potential impacts, especially since there is so much apprehension today about AI putting people out of work, enabling unprecedented levels of government surveillance, or unleashing killer robots on the world. All of those things are likely to happen to some extent. But there are also many benefits to be realized from AI, such as improved medical diagnoses and treatment, faster drug discovery, robotic assistance for disabled or elderly persons, increased productivity in industry, and personalized instruction for learners of all ages. Students need to be shown a balanced picture.

We've listed four subtopics for this Big Idea: (1) ethics of AI making decisions about people, (2) economic impacts of AI technology, (3) AI and culture, and (4) AI for social good.

A great deal of attention has been paid to bias in AI-powered systems. One source of bias results from training a system on an unrepresentative dataset: for example, a face-recognition engine expected to work for everyone but that was trained primarily on Caucasian faces. A trickier problem is automated decision-making systems found to treat different groups of people unequally based on criteria we do not consider appropriate. People don't set out to build systems that discriminate based on race or gender. They may even withhold that information from the AI system in an attempt to ensure neutrality. But race and gender correlate with other variables and so can be implicitly present. The problem is that machine learning systems trained on data that are unbalanced for historical reasons can acquire biases that perpetuate these imbalances because they want to correctly predict the training data. A famous example is Amazon using information from past technical hiring decisions to train a system for screening resumes only to find that it had learned to assign negative values to keywords that correlate with being female (Dastin 2018).

An important message for students to hear is that it is possible to take steps to mitigate the negative impacts of technology. Face recognition engines can be required to undergo testing to ensure that they perform equally well for all populations. Automated decision-making systems, whether AI-powered or not, can be required by regulation to be transparent in their reasoning and can be explicitly tested for disparate treatment of protected groups based on inappropriate criteria.

ARTIFICIAL INTELLIGENCE AND CULTURE

Until recently, AI's contributions to popular culture have been entirely through science fiction. Speculation about possible futures remains an engaging pastime: will we be happily coexisting with R2D2 and Lieutenant Data, or fleeing the Terminator? Instilling a basic understanding of AI helps students recognize that neither scenario is imminent. But now, actual AI applications are appearing in popular culture. Intelligent assistants modeled after Siri and Alexa are showing up in commercials and TV show episodes. Radio station promos advise listeners to "tell Alexa to play your favorite AM station." Meanwhile, children's interactions with Alexa have sparked a debate about whether they should be taught to treat intelligent agents with politeness (Elgan 2018). As Elgan observes, "Preparing kids for the future means more than mere manners. It means teaching them to appreciate the difference between real human people and mere machines designed to create the illusion of humanity."

We will soon have many more humble robots in our lives. Shelf-scanning robots are appearing in department stores and supermarkets, small-item delivery robots are trundling the halls of hospitals and high-end hotels, and food and package delivery robots are beginning to share the sidewalk with pedestrians. There is already a new genre of YouTube videos showing mishaps with self-driving cars. Today's children will grow up in a culture where we routinely share our living space with machines that, although not very bright, can navigate effectively through the world. iRobot founder Colin Angle reported that 90% of Roomba owners named their vacuums (Barker 2018). How will they respond to robots that can see and hear?

CONCLUSION

In recent years there have been concerted efforts to introduce children to "computational thinking" (Wing 2006), including its four cornerstone concepts of problem decomposition, pattern recognition, abstraction, and algorithms. ISTE (the International Society for Technology in Education) and CSTA offer a joint operational definition of computational thinking (CT, ISTE 2011) that includes five dispositions or attitudes: (1) confidence in dealing with complexity, (2) persistence in working with difficult problems, (3) tolerance for ambiguity, (4) ability to deal with open ended problems, and (5) ability to communicate and work with others to achieve a common goal or solution.

AI thinking implicitly draws upon the core concepts and dispositions of CT. The Big Ideas of perception, reasoning, and learning are all realized as algorithms, while representations are examples of abstraction. And introducing students to AI topics such as the richness of language or the subtleties of visual understanding asks them to grapple with problems that are complex, difficult, ambiguous, and open ended. But AI thinking also goes beyond classical CT in this sense: it asks students to consider that computation can actually *be* thinking. Not in the fully human, "strong AI" sense that Turing envisioned in his seminal paper on machine intelligence (Turing 1950), but at least in the specialized, narrow form known today as "weak AI." CT is exactly what humans need when they try to understand how machines can think.

These are the early days of K–12 AI education. It's a dynamic area that is developing rapidly. Here is what we see at the frontier:

- New tools and demos are coming online, making it easier to give students hands-on experiences with AI technologies. Since many of these tools run in the browser, they are accessible even to low-resource schools.
- As more states adopt standards mandating computing instruction for all K–12 students, programming is making its way into the lower grades, which means students will be more computationally sophisticated when they learn about AI.
- AI professional development opportunities for teachers will begin to have an impact. Computer science in general is poorly represented in the schools: many computing teachers have no formal computer science training. Even so, they at least understand how a digital computer works and have elementary programming skills. But few of these teachers claim to know anything about AI, or can even define it. Over the next few years we hope to see AI become more integrated into computing curricula and teachers become more confident about introducing AI topics in their classes.
- AI technologies continue to progress. Intelligent agents are becoming better conversationalists. Robot companions that are not vacuum cleaners will find a niche where they can be successful, while robots in

the workplace become common. Fully autonomous, go-anywhere self-driving cars are probably still two decades away, but less demanding applications such as freight hauling or fixed-route shuttle services are already being deployed. As AI becomes a larger part of our lives and culture, the need to demystify AI in K–12 will be widely recognized.

NOTES

1. See https://datascience.stackexchange.com/questions/37078/source-of-arthur-samuels-definition-of-machine-learning.

2. Try the Berkeley Neural Parser at https://parser.kitaev.io/.

REFERENCES

Alammar, Jay. 2019. "The Illustrated Word2vec." http://jalammar.github.io/illustrated-word2vec/.

Barker, Colin. 2018. "Automation: How iRobot's Roomba Vacuum Cleaner Became Part of the Family." *ZDNet.com*, June 15, 2018. https://www.zdnet.com/article/automation-how-irobots-roomba-vacuum-cleaner-became-part-of-the-family/.

Computer Science Teachers Association (CSTA). 2017. "CSTA K12 Computer Science Standards, Revised 2017." https://www.csteachers.org/standards.

Dastin, Jeffrey. 2018. "Amazon Scraps Secret AI Recruiting Tool that Showed Bias against Women." *Reuters*, October 9, 2018.

Elgan, Mike. 2018. "The Case against Teaching Kids to Be Polite to Alexa." *Fast Company*, June 24, 2018. https://www.fastcompany.com/40588020/the-case-against-teaching-kids-to-be-polite-to-alexa.

Florey, Kitty Burns. 2006. *Sister Bernadette's Barking Dog: The Quirky History and Lost Art of Diagramming Sentences*. New York: Melville House.

Florey, Kitty Burns. 2012. "A Picture of Language." *New York Times*, March 26, 2012.

International Society for Technology in Education (ISTE) and the Computer Science Teachers Association (CSTA). 2011. "Operational Definition of Computational Thinking for K–12 Education." https://cdn.iste.org/www-root/ct-documents/computational-thinking-operational-definition-flyer.pdf.

Kahn, Ken, and Niall Winters. 2020. "A Guide to AI Extensions to Snap!" https://ecraft2learn.github.io/ai/, chapter 5, "Working with Words and Language."

Liberman, Mark. 2012. "Diagrammatic Excitement." *Language Log*, March 27, 2012. https://languagelog.ldc.upenn.edu/nll/?p=3868.

Marr, David. 1982. *Vision*. Cambridge, MA: MIT Press.

Mikolov, Tomas, Ilya Sutskever, Kai Chen, Greg Corrado, and Jeffrey Dean. 2013. "Distributed Representations of Words and Phrases and Their Compositionality." *Advances in Neural Information Processing Systems* 26: 3111–3119. https://dl.acm.org /doi/10.5555/2999792.2999959.

Noy, Natasha, Yuqing Gao, Anshu Jain, Anant Narayanan, Alan Patterson, and Jamie Taylor. 2019. "Industry-Scale Knowledge Graphs: Lessons and Challenges." *Communications of the ACM* 62 (8), 36–43. https://doi.org/10.1145/3331166.

Oxford University Press. 2020. *The Oxford English Dictionary.* https://www.oed.com.

ReadyAI. 2019. "AI+ME." https://edu.readyai.org/courses/aime/.

ReadyAI. 2020. *AI+ME: Big Idea 2—Representation & Reasoning: How AI Makes Choices.* AI+Me Series. Pittsburgh, PA: ReadyAI.

Thomas, Paul L. 2014. "Diagramming Sentences and the Art of Misguided Nostalgia." https://radicalscholarship.wordpress.com/2014/08/24/diagramming-sentences -and-the-art-of-misguided-nostalgia/.

Touretzky, David, Christina Gardner-McCune, Fred Martin, and Deborah Seehorn. 2019. "Envisioning AI for K–12: What Should Every Child Know about AI?" In *Proceedings of the Thirty-Third AAAI Conference on Artificial Intelligence (AAAI-19).* Palo Alto, CA, 9795–9799. https://doi.org/10.1609/aaai.v33i01.33019795.

Turing, A. M. 1950. "Computing Machinery and Intelligence." *Mind,* LIX (236): 433–460. https://doi.org/10.1093%2Fmind%2FLIX.236.433.

Wing, Jeannette M. 2006. "Computational Thinking." *Communications of the ACM* 49 (3), 33–35. https://doi.org/10.1145/1118178.1118215.

9

PREPARING CHILDREN TO BE CONSCIENTIOUS CONSUMERS AND DESIGNERS OF AI TECHNOLOGIES

Daniella DiPaola, Blakeley H. Payne, and Cynthia Breazeal

"How many of you watch YouTube every day?"

A sea of eleven-year-old hands shot up. Every student in our summer artificial intelligence (AI) workshop had not only heard of YouTube but used it daily.

Although a bit jarring, this makes sense. In the 2019 Common Sense Media Report, 56 percent of tweens (ages eight to twelve years) reported watching online videos daily, and 76 percent reported regular usage of YouTube specifically. These statistics have almost doubled from 2015, suggesting that children's online video consumption is on the rise. At the same time, we see TV consumption declining, with children watching about a half-hour less television than four years ago (Rideout and Robb 2019).

We asked the same group of students, "Who uses AI every day?"

The answer looked a bit different, with about half of hands hesitantly going up. It became clear that students were not aware that some of their favorite technologies, like YouTube or Snapchat, are powered by artificially intelligent systems. Without knowing how these AI systems work, students are unable to make choices about how they would like to interact with them. AI is very much part of children's technology landscape, and it has implications for how they navigate their digital world. If children are able to use AI, they must be able to identify it, know how it works, and understand that they have the agency to change it. We need to give students these skills so that they are empowered to decide how they would like AI to fit into their lives.

To meet this need, we developed a curriculum with three primary goals:

1. Students should be conscientious consumers of AI.
2. Students should be ethical designers of AI.
3. Students should be able to participate in democratic discussions around AI.

CONSCIENTIOUS CONSUMERS OF ARTIFICIAL INTELLIGENCE

If children are touching AI-powered systems every day, they really should be aware of it. For example, our middle schoolers shared that they often rely on YouTube's recommendation algorithm to determine what videos to watch. According to YouTube, the recommendation algorithm uses the consumer's viewing history as one of the main factors for determining which videos to recommend (Covington, Adams, and Sargin 2016). By recommending videos based on what the user has previously watched, YouTube hopes that the user will stay on the site for longer. The longer viewers watch content, the more ads will sell. For the most part, YouTube is successful in this endeavor. In 2018 Neal Mohan, YouTube's chief product officer, reported that the recommendation algorithm accounted for 70 percent of watch time on the platform (Solsman 2018).

In February of the same year, the *Wall Street Journal* published an article entitled, "How YouTube Drives People to the Internet's Darkest Corners," which recounted an investigation the publication had done into YouTube's recommender system (Nicas 2018). The recommender system seemed to suggest increasingly conspiratorial or extreme content to its users, regardless of whether the user was searching for it. The article shows screenshots of "suggested videos" that were recommended to a brand-new user with no previous viewing history. When the new user searched for "the pope," suggestions included videos containing conspiracy theories around the Pope ("How Dangerous Is the Pope?"). When the user searched for "lunar eclipse," videos implying that the Earth is flat ("Lunar Eclipse Doesn't Work on Your Globe!") were suggested (Nicas 2018). Viral conspiracy videos become even more of an issue when popular teen YouTubers spread these theories, like a popular YouTuber, Logan Paul, uploading a video trailer promoting the Flat Earth theory in early 2019 (Schoenberg 2019).

YouTube is one example of the many systems that children use. Snapchat, Instagram, Amazon Alexa, and Google Search are other common examples of AI that children touch every day. These systems make decisions, like recommending content, and children are often not aware of the mechanics by which the systems make such decisions. AI education is essential in raising conscientious consumers of these systems.

FUTURE ETHICAL DESIGNERS OF ARTIFICIAI INTELLIGENCE

Given the pervasive impact AI is having on the global economy and society, for good or for bad, it is imperative to educate an AI literate citizenry. If we're to educate and train the next generation of AI makers, we need to empower them with the tools and conceptual frameworks to design these systems ethically. Present-day technologists and designers are beginning to realize the long-term societal consequences of the AI-powered systems that they create. Major AI tech companies have been criticized when their products did not work as intended or behave equitably for everyone. Amazon's facial recognition technology has been shown to have high error rates for darker-skinned minorities (Vincent 2019). Uber's self-driving car neglected to account for pedestrians who jaywalked (Marshall and Davies 2019). Google has been called out for search algorithms that perpetuate harmful stereotypes (Manjoo 2018). AI can do tremendous good, but these stories are a call to action for the technology community. Software developers need to adopt ethical practices in the design and development of AI systems. Classrooms that are introducing AI for the first time are a great place to start.

It's not enough for students to be conscientious consumers of AI; they must become ethical designers of it as well. Universities teach computer science and are preparing students to enter a workforce that develops AI systems. AI has already had an incredible impact on fields like medicine and renewable energy, and we want future generations to continue to make positive contributions to society through AI. If computational thinking (CT) is starting to enter K–12 education, what about learning about AI? In 2018 the David E. Williams Middle School in Coraopolis, Pennsylvania, became the first school to integrate AI into its curriculum. Students in grades 5 through 8 are learning about and designing their own AI systems through courses such as Introduction to Pattern-Finding through Gaming and Recognizing Computer Patterns Virtually and Through Algorithms. AI education has been integrated into their elective courses, and there is interest in integrating AI literacy into their core curriculum, too (Aglio 2018).

K–12 AI literacy is in its infancy but gaining momentum. Schools like David E. Williams are early adopters of AI curriculum. Traditional STEM programs such as iD Tech summer camps are beginning to offer AI courses, and new programs such as ReadyAI and Technovation are creating new spaces for this content to emerge (Artificial Intelligence Summer Camp: Machine Learning for Teens 2020; Empowering All Students to Improve Our World with AI 2019). The AI4K12 initiative, jointly sponsored by Association for the Advancement of Artificial Intelligence (AAAI) and the Computer Science Teachers Association (CSTA), is working toward national guidelines for AI K–12 education akin to national K–12 computer science standards. As these groups set the precedence for AI education, we must make sure that they include ethical design tools and practices.

TOMORROW'S DEMOCRATIC, AI-LITERATE CITIZENS

Even students who will not grow up to be future technologists should be responsible users and conscientious consumers of AI. AI isn't only affecting our personal technologies and online circles. It's entering our communities as well, and citizens should be able to make informed decisions about its use. Consider the case where facial recognition technology is being used by law enforcement to detect criminal suspects. Many have expressed concerns that this technology, which is known to consistently misidentify darker-skinned faces, could further exacerbate racial inequality or could increase the amount of surveillance within communities. In June of 2019 the residents of Somerville, Massachusetts, a town located near Harvard University and MIT, passed legislation placing a moratorium on facial recognition technologies in the city. The city councilor of Somerville, Ben Ewen-Campen, credits the bill to the technocentric community. The residents of Somerville know enough about the technology to believe that it is not yet ready to be given authority in the legal system. Cities around Silicon Valley are beginning to ban the technology as well (Wu 2019).

As AI continues to enter and alter our cities, it is important that young people grow up being well equipped to handle these democratic processes. Like the constituents of Somerville, we want our students to have the knowledge and skills to be able to make informed decisions in their own communities.

CURRICULUM DESIGN

For these reasons, we have developed, piloted, and evaluated a hands-on AI and ethics curriculum for middle school that can be integrated into formal or informal learning contexts. The second author, Blakeley H. Payne, developed the curriculum and teacher training guide as part of her master's thesis. The curriculum has three major goals. The first is to teach young people how to be conscientious consumers when using their own devices powered by AI. The second is to give students knowledge and perspective so that they can participate in democratic discussions around these technologies. Finally, we want to empower them to be ethical designers as they begin to build these systems themselves. Three principles inform the design of this curriculum: the idea that ethics education should be integrated alongside technical education; the value of "unplugged" activities as a complement to those that use technology; and the value of peer collaboration and discussion with opportunities for creative learning.

First and foremost, this curriculum sought an integrated approach to ethics and AI topics. Although integrated approaches are beginning to gain traction at the collegiate level (Grosz et al. 2019; Saltz et al. 2019; Skirpan et al. 2019), research shows that most university machine learning courses do not teach ethics issues at all or relegate ethics as its own class (Saltz et al. 2019). Within the K–12 setting, almost all activities that mention ethics do so as the last module of a larger unit (Lissitsa 2019). Such approaches are problematic because research suggests that isolating ethics from technical content often leads students to perceive ethics as unrelated to their technical studies (Davis and Walker 2011; Spradling, Soh, and Ansorge 2008). To offer a more holistic educational experience, we introduce ethics concepts as frequently as technical ones, anchored in familiar scenarios that are meaningful to students. For example, when we teach students how machines learn to classify objects, we make sure to have a discussion about how classifiers can encode biases, and the potential consequences for society when such systems are used to make important decisions, such as the use of facial recognition technology in policing.

We intentionally designed our AI and ethics curriculum to be low cost and accessible to students and schools from all economic backgrounds. To truly democratize AI, it is important to remove as many barriers as possible that may hinder or prevent low-income and minority students—students who are most likely to be negatively affected by these technologies—from understanding how AI works, the current impact AI has on society, and the impact AI could have on society in the future. For these reasons, our curriculum is largely unplugged (requiring only pencil and paper; two lessons require access to the Chrome web browser) and is open source for noncommercial use (CC-BY-NC; https://creativecommons.org/licenses/by -nc/4.0). Furthermore, our unplugged activities are designed to engage students in highly kinesthetic or creative activities with a sense of playfulness (Bell et al. 2009). Many of the activities throughout the curriculum follow a constructivist approach in which the teacher acts as a facilitator. Instead of lecturing students, we leverage topics that middle schoolers are comfortable with, like YouTube, and allow them to shape classroom discussion. We found that students were often expert users when it came to these technologies and were able to apply their learning to their everyday life. We learned a lot from their experiences and observations.

We piloted the complete curriculum, comprising two plugged and six unplugged activities, in a week-long workshop with twenty-eight middle school students (eight female students) in the summer of 2019 (see figure 9.1). We recruited participants under an approved IRB protocol through a local science, technology, engineering, and mathematics (STEM) enrichment program, Empow Studios. Students were divided into two groups, fifth through seventh graders (led by the Blakeley H. Payne) and seventh through ninth graders (led by Daniella DiPaola). Each group

9.1 A group of fifth through seventh grade AI designers in front of their "Hopes + Concerns about AI" mural.

also had a mentor from Empow Studios who assisted in classroom facilitation and was trained in the workshop material. These students had a wide range of previous computer science experience, ranging from no prior experience to more than seven years. Very few had ever formally learned about AI. Given this varied background, we first had to answer the challenge of how to bring middle schoolers from being uninitiated to ethical designers of AI. In the remainder of this chapter, we highlight three different modules to show the range of activities and how middle school students engaged with them.

WHAT IS ARTIFICIAL INTELLIGENCE?

The first activity in the curriculum is designed to help students identify AI systems in their everyday lives. For simplicity, we ask students to look for three components in an AI system: a dataset, learning algorithm, and a prediction. When students propose a technology that may be powered by AI, we walk them through the following questions:

1. Is your system trying to predict something? If so, what?
2. What data does the system use to predict this?

At first, students were focused on the embodied examples of AI, such as Amazon Alexa or a self-driving car. We nudged them to think about more software or web systems, such as a spam filter on their email.

Once students were able to identify the parts of an AI system, we went into a more detailed explanation of algorithms themselves, and how specific objectives can be designed into them. Students learn that, like a recipe, an algorithm is made up of a specified input transformed by many specific steps to achieve a desired outcome. In introductory computer science courses, students are commonly asked to write the steps to make a peanut butter and jelly sandwich as a way to learn the specificity required to construct a useful algorithm. We had our students do the same exercise, but instead of writing instructions for a regular PB&J, we asked them to find a partner and write instructions for the *best* PB&J.

After the activity, we had students reflect on their recipes. We asked, "If you could replace the word *best* with another word, what would you choose?" A pair of students said the word *best* meant the most sugar, and they added hazelnut spread, sprinkles, and marshmallows to a classic PB&J. Another pair decided that *best* meant "most allergy-friendly" and decided to omit the peanut butter from their recipe. Not surprisingly, none of the students said the word "healthy" or "cost-effective," but we did brainstorm what that might look like, including a "healthy" PB&J with bananas instead of bread.

Students could clearly see that, based on their definition of *best*, their algorithms had very different outcomes from their peers. Once an algorithm tries to optimize, it is essentially encoding an opinion about what is important to prioritize. To quote the well-known AI ethicist, Cathy O'Neil, "Algorithms are opinions embedded in code" (O'Neil 2017). In the same way, AI and machine learning algorithms used in commercial products are optimized for different objectives based on who creates them—in fact, they are not as objective as we would like to think. Words like *best* are words that we commonly see used with software solutions, but it may mean very different things from algorithm to algorithm. For example, Google search strives to give the "most relevant" results, although *relevant* is not clearly defined. Is "most relevant" the link that I will most likely click on? Is it what will make Google the most money? Is it what will give me the answer I was hoping for? Whatever it is, it is referred to as what the search engine *optimizes* for. Just as Google gets to decide what their search engine optimizes for, our middle schoolers got to decide what their PB&J sandwiches optimize for. Words such as *relevant* and *best* are not neutral, and their definitions change based on who is creating them. Algorithms hold the opinions of their creators.

Then we pose the following challenge to students: How do we decide what our peanut butter and jelly algorithms should optimize for? To aid in decision-making, we introduced students to a tool called the *ethical matrix*. Originally a tool used in bioethics, Cathy O'Neil has written about how it can be used in the context of AI (O'Neil and Gunn forthcoming). An ethical matrix is a 2-D table where stakeholders are listed on the *y* axis and the values those stakeholders hold in the system are listed on the *x* axis. Designers can then go row by column and identify where stakeholders' values align and where they conflict. Designers can also identify which conflicts in values may produce the most harm for any of the stakeholders involved. In filling out the matrix, designers are forced to empathize with multiple perspectives of a diverse set of stakeholders.

Our students brainstormed various stakeholders and values for PB&J sandwiches and practiced creating ethical matrices of various sizes. Students identified stakeholders such as *kids, parents, doctors*, and *supermarkets* with values such as *taste, health, cost*, and *efficiency*. They compared all stakeholder-value pairs to determine which stakeholders care about various values (see example, figure 9.2). After they had laid out the matrix, we asked them to decide on *which* value they should optimize for, after reflecting on how stakeholders and values relate within the system. They saw that depending on the particular stakeholders and values that they accounted for, there were varied results. For example, a matrix with stakeholders like *parents, doctors*, and *dentists* may value *health* more than one with *kids, teenagers*, and *supermarkets*.

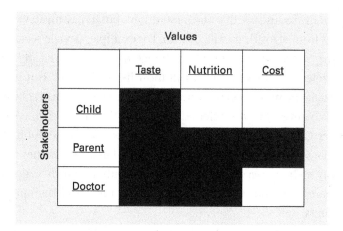

9.2 An example of a completed ethical matrix for PB&J with *child, parent,* and *doctor* as the stakeholders.

SUPERVISED MACHINE LEARNING AND ALGORITHMIC BIAS

In the PB&J activity, students learn that algorithms can be optimized toward subjective goals. Building on their learning, this activity shows another way in which algorithms can produce nonneutral outcomes. In an example of a "plugged" activity, we focused on a specific class of AI algorithms called *supervised machine learning.* Supervised machine learning finds patterns by being shown labeled examples of data points. For instance, a supervised ML algorithm may be given examples of emails labeled as "spam" or "not spam" with the goal of classifying unseen emails as "spam" or "not spam" in the future. Recent studies have shown that many of these supervised machine learning systems—from facial recognition to hiring algorithms, to advertising algorithms—tend to predict worse outcomes for members of minority groups. This phenomenon is called *algorithmic bias.* A common reason for these biases comes from the data that trains the algorithms. If a dataset underrepresents or incorrectly characterizes a certain group, the algorithm will also mischaracterize that group (Barocas and Selbst 2016). For example, it is known that many commercial facial recognition algorithms meant to classify faces as male or female will misidentify darker-skinned female faces as male faces because of the fact that these algorithms were trained primarily on lighter-skinned male faces (Buolamwini and Gebru 2018). In this way, classification systems that are trained on historical data that encode societal biases will perpetuate those same biases.

Often these supervised machine learning classifiers are referred to as "neural networks." To demonstrate how a neural network is trained, how it works, and how it can lead to algorithmic bias, we utilized Google's Teachable Machines platform. Teachable Machines has an easy user interface that allows students to train a deep neural net classifier by taking or uploading photos or audio. Without any code or even any typing, students can train an algorithm in a matter of minutes. This opens up the possibility for many more students to play with the pieces of a machine learning algorithm, manipulate them, and see how they impact the performance of the code.

During the workshop, we had students create their own classifier system using a training set of provided cat and dog images. The goal of the classifier was to distinguish between pictures of cats and pictures of dogs. However, unknown to the students, the provided training dataset was biased. It contained more images of cats than dogs, and the images of cats contained a greater variety of breeds than did the images of dogs. After the training period, we gave students a new collection of cat and dog images to test out their classifier. After testing out each image of a cat or dog, the students recorded whether the algorithm correctly classified the image, and at what confidence level their classifier performed (figure 9.3). From this data, students quickly realized that their systems worked much better on cats than dogs. They were then tasked with re-curating their training datasets to produce fairer outcomes between cats and dogs. Students decided to include an equal number of more diverse cats and dogs and found that their algorithms worked much better.

Next, we showed the students a video about Joy Buolamwini's "Gender Shades" work on algorithmic bias in facial recognition systems (MIT Media Lab 2018). Buolamwini explains that many facial recognition systems work better on pale skin and male faces and work especially poorly on darker-skinned female faces. We asked the students what they would do if they were in charge of improving the system. Many students responded that they would create a dataset that was much more representative of all skin tones and gender. They were able to make the connection between the simple cat and dog classifier and the advanced face recognition systems used in commercial settings. If the system works better for one group than

9.3 A group of students test their classifiers and record the confidence level for each item of test data.

another group, changing the training data to be more representative is one method designers can use to improve the system to make it behave more equitably.

The importance of this topic became deeper for the students as they watched live as Buolamwini testified before Congress, which serendipitously aired on C-SPAN during the workshop. Buolamwini answered questions on how facial recognition systems worked and why they were biased toward specific groups of people. Students were not surprised by her answers, but they were surprised that members of Congress were not aware of the impact of these technologies. Our students were able to see that what they were learning in our workshop had real implications for what was happening in the world around them. At the end of the day, one child reflected on what they had learned: *"I still think that facial recognition is not fair, because they still—these companies have not changed the fact that . . . it only works properly for adults that are males and are pale white. And it's not fair to people with colored skin or like younger people or people who are girls."*

REDESIGNING YOUTUBE

In the last days of the workshop, the final activity is a collaborative paper-prototyping project where students are tasked with redesigning the You-Tube recommendation algorithm. Working in pairs, students were asked to first identify stakeholders invested in YouTube's recommendation algorithm and the values those stakeholders hold. Next, they created an ethical matrix for their own system design, similar to those for PB&J at the beginning of the week. After creating a matrix, students were asked to discuss it and use their conversation with other student pairs to identify the goal of their new system and provide a rationale for that goal. Some examples of these matrices can be found in figure 9.4.

This work guided students in paper-prototyping their new YouTube design. In the same pairs, students were provided craft supplies and worked together to draw out a new version of YouTube with features that served their identified goal. They used these initial drawings to get feedback from other classmates. Peer feedback guided changes made for the final paper prototypes (figure 9.5).

Stakeholder-value pairs from the ethical matrices were recorded and summed across all students. The stakeholder-value pairs that guided the students' redesigns were YouTube-money (9), kids-entertainment (7), YouTubers-money (6), YouTube-entertainment (6), and Youtubers-entertainment (6). These responses are visualized in figure 9.6. These pairs were used to determine the goals for the recommendation algorithm. The most common goals for the system were entertainment (6) and profit (2). Most students chose goals that aligned with the most stakeholder-value pairs: "because the most stakeholders have the value of entertainment." Others took a more nuanced path, such as one group that justified their decision to optimize for profit: "YouTube and YouTubers can use the profit to increase the quality of the site and videos." Many students identified more than one goal for their system, such as being entertaining while also being kid-friendly: "[our design will have] all kid-friendly videos that will make you laugh and any inappropriate content will be deleted."

Next we spotlight three examples of student projects.

Step 3: Fill out the following ethical matrix from your answers above:

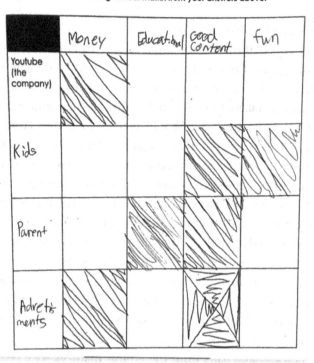

	Money	Educational	Good Content	fun
Youtube (the company)	▨			
Kids			▨	▨
Parent		▨	▨	
Advretisments	▨		▧	

Step 3: Fill out the following ethical matrix from your answers above:

	Profit	Quality	Reccomndt	Appropriated
Youtube (the company)	✓		✓	✓
Viewers		✓	✓	✓
Yotuba	✓	✓		✓
Adrtisng	✓		✓	

9.4 Examples of ethical matrices for the YouTube Redesign Project. The image on the top decided to optimize for "good content," and the image on the bottom chose to optimize for "profit."

9.5 Student drawing out a paper prototype for the YouTube Redesign Project.

| | **Value** | | | | | |
Stakeholder	Money	Entertainment	Safety	Ads	Popularity	Other
YouTube						
Kids						
YouTubers						
Advertisers						
Viewers						
Parents						
Adults						
Sponsors						
Media						
Doctors						

9.6 A heatmap of stakeholder-value pairs for the YouTube Redesign project. Darker and larger shapes denote pairs that were used most often.

PROJECT 1: OPTIMIZING FOR PROFIT

This rising seventh grader and eighth grader decided that YouTube should maximize profit. They identified YouTube, YouTubers, viewers, and advertisers as their stakeholders with the values of profit, quality of videos, recommendations, and appropriateness. Like previously mentioned, students chose this goal because "YouTube and YouTubers can use the profit to increase the quality of the site and videos." Their paper prototype, seen in figure 9.7, shows features including additional ads in the sidebar or the inability to skip through ads in videos.

PROJECT 2: OPTIMIZING FOR ENTERTAINMENT

This pair of rising fifth graders decided to optimize their new version of YouTube around entertainment. Students identified YouTube, kids, parents, and advertisers as their stakeholders along with the values of money, educational, good content, and fun, where most stakeholders were interested in "good content." The students wrote, "We decided on this goal because having fun is very fundamental but being appropriate

9.7 Student shows her "profit-maximizing" YouTube prototype.

is also needed." When asked how they would achieve this goal, the students wrote, "We would also teach it to give us clean content or videos that don't have swears. It will have a child safety mode to make sure there are no swears or inappropriate content." Their paper prototype is pictured in figure 9.8 and includes features like a slider, where users can choose levels of "rudeness" that appear in their videos and a child safety setting.

PROJECT 3: OPTIMIZING FOR TIME WELL SPENT

This pair of rising eighth graders decided to optimize for a version of YouTube that was less addictive or as the students wrote, "[Users] are also aware of how long they spend on the platform." This group identified a number of non-AI features that could help achieve this goal, such as "screen pops up after an hour of usage" or "can set a time limit." Their paper prototype appears in figure 9.9.

9.8 An example of "Entertainment" YouTube. Students put filters on the left side of the webpage to help the user tweak what they would like to see.

9.9 An example of "Time Well Spent" YouTube. The first image shows a pop-up window that lets the user know how long they have been on YouTube. The second picture shows the home page. The bottom right sticky note reads, "This shows a history of recently watched videos and time spent on YouTube session."

SOCRATIC SEMINAR

During the week of our workshop, the *Wall Street Journal* published an article about the children's content on YouTube. With so many known consumers being minors, the FTC was pushing for YouTube to create a separate app to house all kids' content to be compliant with federal laws such as the Children's Online Privacy Protection Rule, commonly known as "COPPA." This new, hypothetical app would collect less data, remove ads, and remove the AutoPlay feature.

We abridged the article and read it out loud with our students. Since the results from this case could very well change the way that they use YouTube, we were curious about their reactions and how they might apply their ethical design skills to this real-world situation. We opened up the conversation by asking about the various stakeholders involved with the article. Kids were able to identify many stakeholders, including Google executives, Google as a company, kids, parents, consumers of YouTube, and advertisers. When we asked them whom the *most* important stakeholder was, many said the kids impacted by the FTC's ruling: *"Because it's a lot about the safety of kids and what they watch because kids get easily influenced. So when they see something's happening around them, they obviously think, 'Oh, they're more experienced; we should copy whatever they're doing.' So, it could be really bad; that's why they take a long time to make sure everything's cautious and there's no bad content that could get released into the world of children."*

One student mentioned that Google is a big stakeholder as well. "I think Google would be like one of the major ones because, for one thing, it's making lots of money on YouTube."

We asked the students if they thought that YouTube should move forward and move all of the content. The majority of students thought yes, they should. One student thought that kids' safety was a reason to move it, "because then even if YouTube doesn't make as much money as they used to, it's still important that kids don't watch grown-up stuff." Another thought that YouTube would actually lose viewers and money if they didn't move their content over: "It's good to have a separate app, because less people might start watching it, if they don't."

One student thought YouTube should keep things the way that they are because they might lose money if they moved everything to another platform. This student thought that there was a problem with content, but recommended an alternative fix: *"I think this would be a bad thing. Because, YouTube would be losing a lot of money. And the way that they could fix it is add a different setting. Maybe find a better way to do the restrictive mode, or something like that. Or add another setting that would help restrict, like a child mode setting that will only have, that would send them to a different part which is all kids' videos."*

Regardless of their view on the situation, we asked students how they would feel if their parents forced them to use the YouTube Kids app instead of the regular app. Many expressed frustrations and felt like they could maturely handle the content on the app as it was: *"I would feel like, 'Shucks.' Because, I've been using YouTube a very long time. And I didn't even know what YouTube Kids was until a couple weeks ago . . . And so it's like I don't know. People just totally . . . now you have to go to this new app called YouTube Kids now. I'd be very confused. I also, if I didn't know that at first, I'd just be looking around YouTube for my favorite channels and videos that I watch, and be like, 'Where'd they all go?'"*

Perhaps one of the most important parts of the discussion happened when children were able to identify the different outcomes of new policies and features: *"I would remove AutoPlay because it was, when it first came out . . . People's definition of what's mature and what's not mature is different. It would feel like a more . . . Well, I'm kind of split on the issue. It would be a much more simple and easier decision to just remove the AutoPlay. That way, a kid and parents could choose at will what they want to watch. But then, again, moving it all to a safer site will generally be more secure. You feel more secure."*

This discussion allowed students to apply what they had learned to a concrete, timely, and relatable societal issue. Students had studied how the AutoPlay feature worked, how to identify the stakeholders and their values related to YouTube, and how to modify a design to change those stakeholders' interactions with the system.

A few months after the workshop Google and YouTube settled the lawsuit for 170 million dollars and an agreement that they would no longer collect data for videos labeled for children ("Google and YouTube Will Pay Record $170 Million for Alleged Violations of Children's Privacy

Law," Henderson 2019). Some of the students' concerns were addressed in the lawsuit, such as feeling safer that they will not get content that is too mature for them, yet still accessing videos through the familiar YouTube site. Other student concerns, such as the impact of these changes on content creators, remain hotly debated (Ray 2019). We are interested in following up with students to understand their perspectives on this recent change.

CONCLUSION

The first day of our workshop, some students came in with high-level questions such as, "What is AI? How does it work?" and "What are examples of AI that we use in everyday life?" The students who had more specific definitions of AI often included science fiction references, such as the characters Hal from *2001: A Space Odyssey* and Jarvis from the Iron Man franchise. Their understanding of AI was limited to far-off dystopian narratives, yet they were using these technologies daily. Through the workshop, we were able to help them identify AI, understand how it works, and give them the tools to design it to be more equitable.

AI can be complex, but we chose activities and technologies that the students were already familiar with, like YouTube. It was evident that when students arrived, even though they knew little about AI, they held expertise on the topic of YouTube. Students could name their favorite content creators and name ways in which YouTube's recommendation algorithm either assisted their favorite content creators or disadvantaged them. However, many students did not realize that the recommendation algorithm was a form of AI.

Once we redirected them to talk about AI technologies in terms of a system that they were familiar with, their conversations about ethics of AI were much more focused and realistic, and at times quite nuanced. As they were exposed to the curriculum, we saw their conversations transition into discussions around fairness and equity in their daily technical tools and that they were capable of empathizing with a broader set of stakeholders.

We observed increasingly more questions about agency as the students became confident in their ability to identify the positives and negatives of various AI systems. They expressed interest in systems that would benefit many stakeholders: "I hope AI benefits everybody, not just one or two groups of people." They began to question others' knowledge of these systems as well. One student reflected on watching Congressional hearings and asked, "Why does Congress not know about today's modern tech?"

As students reflected on their week at the workshop, we saw their new understanding of AI and its impact on society change their feelings of agency over the AI-enabled technologies they use. Many students expressed interest in presenting their ideas to various stakeholders, especially when it came to their YouTube redesign project. Our activities throughout the week became a means for them to question, vocalize, and create the sociotechnical systems that they would like to see. One student commented, "I wonder if my parents will like my YouTube redesign," while another questioned, "Will YouTube pay attention to our ideas?"

Our students came in with a wide range of exposure to technical concepts as well as practical experience with coding. For some students, the prospect of enrolling in an AI course with no prior knowledge was intimidating. The parents of one student, Sarah, approached the instructors at the beginning of the week to say, "I want you to know my child is a little nervous about having no coding experience. She thinks she'll be behind, but she is excited about the societal impact of things." However, the curriculum was designed in a way that any child, regardless of background, could understand and contribute to the activities. The activities were also designed to work with a variety of learning styles and interests, including some that used computers and others that relied on creative writing or drawing. We feel that the students not only could grasp the material we were teaching, both ethical and technical, but were able to apply it to the technologies they use every day. This was evident during the last day of the workshop, where students presented their YouTube Redesign projects to their parents and members of the MIT community, often highlighting the processes they took to get to their final product. The YouTube Redesign Activity was successful because students were able to create a prototype based on what they had learned. We recommend including more hands-on, project-based activities in future iterations of this curriculum. While the unplugged nature helped students to initially grasp concepts, many students were excited by the idea that they could continue to learn about AI through a more technical course. At the end of the course, Sarah's parents returned to say, "She loved it and wants to sign up for a more technical course next time, especially something that might involve web programming."

As students build on their knowledge of AI through technical courses, we encourage educators and education policymakers to ensure that ethics is embedded in the course requirements. We saw the impact of a focus on ethics in our final YouTube projects, where students' outcomes took multiple perspectives into consideration. The implications of doing this kind of work is not only to make children more AI literate but also to change the norms and culture associated with the technology industry. Education practices that promote perspective taking and thinking about consequences will lead to expectations by the public that industry designers and engineers will draw on these same skills.

The shift in students' thinking from being consumers to conscientious users of AI-enabled apps and services brought with it a new level of optimism around the future of AI. Through our activities, we were able to have deeper conversations about philosophical topics such as fairness, bias, and perspective taking. AI became a tool for us to ask the question, "What kind of world do we want to make?" Students were able to reflect on the world as it is and were given the tools to design it to be what they wanted it to be. They were not only capable of understanding the larger implications of AI, but they had excellent ideas on how to improve it to make a more inclusive and just world.

For your own use, the materials used in this workshop can be found at bit.ly/mit-ai-ethics.

ACKNOWLEDGMENTS

The authors would like to thank Maeve Ronan, Danny Plouffe, Carolyn Song, and Ilana Pelzman-Kern for teaching and mentoring our students and for their feedback on the curriculum. Thank you to Empow Studios for recruiting. Lastly, thank you to the MIT Media Lab Consortia for funding this work.

REFERENCES

Aglio, Justin. 2018. "Coming This Fall to Montour School District: America's First Public School AI Program." *Getting Smart*, July 19, 2018. https://www.gettingsmart.com/2018/07/coming-this-fall-to-montour-school-district-americas-first-public-school-ai-program/.

Barocas, Solon, and Andrew D. Selbst. 2016. "Big Data's Disparate Impact." *California Law Review* 104: 671–732.

Bell, Tim, Jason Alexander, Isaac Freeman, and Mick Grimley. 2009. "Computer Science Unplugged: School Students Doing Real Computing Without Computers." *New Zealand Journal of Applied Computing and Information Technology* 13 (1): 20–29.

Buolamwini, Joy, and Timnit Gebru. 2018. "Gender Shades: Intersectional Accuracy Disparities in Commercial Gender Classification." In *Proceedings of Machine Learning Research 2018 Conference on Fairness, Accountability, and Transparency*. New York, 1–15.

Covington, Paul, Jay Adams, and Emre Sargin. 2016. "Deep Neural Networks for YouTube Recommendations." In *Proceedings of the 10th ACM Conference on Recommender Systems*. New York, 191–198.

Davis, Janet, and Henry M. Walker. 2011. "Incorporating Social Issues of Computing in a Small, Liberal Arts College: A Case Study" In *Proceedings of the 42nd ACM Technical Symposium on Computer Science Education*. New York, 69–74.

Grosz, Barbara J., David Gray Grant, Kate Vredenburgh, Jeff Behrends, Lily Hu, Allison Simmons, and Jim Waldo. 2019. "Embedded EthiCS: Integrating Ethics Broadly across Computer Science Education." *Communications of the ACM* 62 (8): 54–61.

Henderson, Juliana G. 2019. "Google and YouTube Will Pay Record $170 Million for Alleged Violations of Children's Privacy Law." Federal Trade Commission, November 20, 2019. https://www.ftc.gov/news-events/press-releases/2019/09/google-youtube-will-pay-record-170-million-alleged-violations.

iD Tech. n.d. "Artificial Intelligence (AI) Summer Camp: Machine Learning for Teens: 2020." Accessed May 20, 2020. https://www.idtech.com/courses/artificial-intelligence-and-machine-learning.

Lissitsa, Katherine. 2019. "Why Teach Kids About AI?" *Kids Code Jeunesse*, May 6, 2019. https://kidscodejeunesse.org/blog?b=2019-05-06-Why-Teach-Kids-About-AI.

Manjoo, Farhad. 2018. "Here's the Conversation We Really Need to Have About Bias at Google." *New York Times*, August 30, 2018. https://www.nytimes.com/2018/08/30/technology/bias-google-trump.html.

Marshall, Aarian, and Davies, Alex. 2019. "Uber's Self-Driving Car Didn't Know Pedestrians Could Jaywalk." *Wired*, November 5, 2019. https://www.wired.com/story/ubers-self-driving-car-didnt-know-pedestrians-could-jaywalk/.

MIT Media Lab. 2018. "Gender Shades." https://www.gendershades.org.

Nicas, Jack. 2018. "How YouTube Drives People to the Internet's Darkest Corners." *The Wall Street Journal*, February 7, 2018. https://www.wsj.com/articles/how-youtube-drives-viewers-to-the-internets-darkest-corners-1518020478.

O'Neil, Cathy. 2017. "The Era of Blind Faith in Big Data Must End." Filmed April 2017 in Vancouver, Canada. TED video, 13:19. https://www.ted.com/talks/cathy_o_neil_the_era_of_blind_faith_in_big_data_must_end/transcript?language=en.

O'Neil, Cathy, and Gunn, Hanna. "Near term AI." *Ethics of Artificial Intelligence* (forthcoming).

Ray, Cory. 2019. "YouTube Family Vlogger Petitions FTC Ahead of 2020 COPPA Enforcement." *Rogue Rocket*, November 7, 2019. https://roguerocket.com/2019/11/07/youtube-coppa/.

ReadyAI. n.d. *Empowering All Students to Improve Our World with AI*. Accessed May 20, 2020. https://www.readyai.org/.

Rideout, Victoria, and Michael B. Robb. 2019. The Common Sense Census: Media Use by Tweens and Teens. *Common Sense Media*. https://www.commonsensemedia.org/sites/default/files/uploads/research/2019-census-8-to-18-full-report-updated.pdf.

Saltz, Jeffrey, Michael Skirpan, Casey Fiesler, Micha Gorelick, Tom Yeh, Robert Heckman, Neil Dewar, and Nathan Beard. 2019. "Integrating Ethics within Machine Learning Courses." *ACM Transactions on Computing Education (TOCE)* 19 (4): 1–26.

Schoenberg, Nara. 2019. "Controversial YouTube Star Brings Flat-Earth Conspiracy Theory to New Audience: Kids." *Chicago Tribune*, March 13, 2019. https://www.chicagotribune.com/lifestyles/ct-life-flat-earther-kids-03132019-story.html.

Skirpan, Michael, Nathan Beard, Srinjita Bhaduri, Casey Fiesler, and Tom Yeh. 2018. "Ethics Education in Context: A Case Study of Novel Ethics Activities for the CS Classroom." In *Proceedings of the 49th ACM Technical Symposium on Computer Science Education*. New York, 940–945.

Solsman, Joan E. 2018. "Ever Get Caught in an Unexpected Hourlong YouTube Binge? Thank YouTube AI for That." *CNET*, January 10, 2018. https://www.cnet.com/news/youtube-ces-2018-neal-mohan/.

Spradling, Carol, Leen-Kiat Soh, and Charles Ansorge. 2008. "Ethics Training and Decision-Making: Do Computer Science Programs Need Help?" In *Proceedings of the 39th SIGCSE Technical Symposium on Computer Science Education*. Portland, OR, 153–157.

Vincent, James. 2019. "AI Researchers Tell Amazon to Stop Selling 'Flawed' Facial Recognition to the Police." *The Verge*, April 3, 2019. https://www.theverge.com/2019/4/3/18291995/amazon-facial-recognition-technology-rekognition-police-ai-researchers-ban-flawed.

Wu, Sarah. 2019. "Somerville City Council Passes Facial Recognition Ban." *The Boston Globe*, June 27, 2019. https://www.bostonglobe.com/metro/2019/06/27/somerville-city-council-passes-facial-recognition-ban/SfaqQ7mG3DGulXonBHSCYK/story.html.

COMPUTATIONAL THINKING AND PHYSICAL COMPUTING EDUCATION IN K–12

10

EXAMINING THE MULTIDIMENSIONAL LEARNING AFFORDANCES OF ROBOTICS FOR COMPUTATIONAL THINKING AND SCIENCE INQUIRY

Florence R. Sullivan

ROBOTICS PROBLEM SPACES

Computational thinking (CT) is an integral aspect of learning and work in the science, engineering, technology, and mathematics (STEM) fields (Lee et al. 2020). Indeed, the Next Generation Science Standards (NGSS) (2013) have defined mathematics and CT as one of the eight core disciplinary practices of science activity. Robotics is a robust learning environment that supports the development of CT and science literacy (Sullivan 2008; Sullivan and Heffernan 2016). Foundational to robotics learning is integrated interaction in the three problem spaces typical of all robotics learning environments, including the device itself, the screen-based programming environment, and the actual physical environment in which students are testing their robotic device. This chapter begins with a description of each of the problem spaces, individually, and proceeds with examples of student learning drawn from fifteen years of research on the topic. Specifically, I discuss student engagement in both science literacy practices (e.g., systems thinking, inferential reasoning) and CT practices (e.g., abstraction, creative problem solving, and algorithmic thinking) as both are supported by engagement in robotics learning. The chapter concludes with thoughts for future research directions. These observations derive from both cognitive and sociocultural viewpoints, with early work grounded in task analysis and mental representations (Roth 2001), and later work grounded in a socio-cultural framework (Vygotsky 1978).

THE FIRST PROBLEM SPACE: THE ROBOTIC DEVICE

We have focused primarily on using the LEGO Mindstorms robotics kit with students. Therefore, in this chapter, I describe this device as the first problem space. However, any robotic device that includes the same elements as the LEGO kits will support student learning in the same way. A micro-computer, called a brick, is at the heart of the LEGO Mindstorms kit; the brick was developed at the MIT Media Lab in the mid-1990s (Resnick et al. 1996). This brick, which is in its third iteration, is currently called the EV3. The EV3 is a device that can fit into the palm of an adult's hand (see figure 10.1). The brick has four ports in which output devices, such as servo motors, can be plugged in with connecting wires, and another four ports in which input devices, such as digital sensors, can be connected. There are three motors that come with the kit, two large motors and one small motor. The larger motors are typically used when children are building a vehicular robot. Once the vehicular robot is constructed, the motors are attached to wheels, and as the motor spins, so do the wheels. The third, smaller motor can be used to operate a robotic arm that may be affixed to the vehicular robot. While building a robotic vehicle is a popular approach, many other types of machines can be built with the materials.

In addition to the brick and the motors, each robotic kit comes with several digital sensors, including a color sensor, a touch sensor, and an ultrasonic sensor. These sensors can be used in one of two ways (both of which are important for science inquiry and are discussed in greater detail later). The first mode is a data collection and display mode; the second is a wait-for mode that can trigger a specific event, once a threshold has been met or crossed. The kit also includes a number of LEGO pieces, called Technics, which fit together around the brick and the motors to create any number of structures or vehicles.

The design of the robotic device is dictated by the challenge that students are attempting to solve. As noted previously, often a robotic vehicle

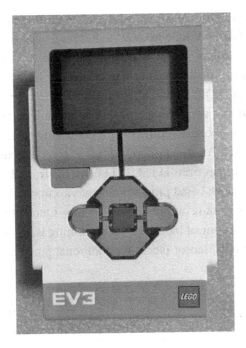

10.1   The LEGO Mindstorms EV3.

is constructed and sensors are then added to the vehicle to aid in navigation. For example, the ultrasonic sensor measures the distance between the sensor and objects in its path; using this sensor, a program can be written that will allow the robot to circumnavigate obstacles in the room. The design of the robot as a problem space revolves around accurate design, physical construction, and correct wiring of the motors and the sensors. While students may initially develop a robotic device that they think is adequate, through the process of working out a solution to the given challenge, students will often need to revise their design. So, while we may think of the design of the device as the first problem space, it is a problem space that is returned to throughout the duration of problem-solving activity.

THE SECOND PROBLEM SPACE: THE SCREEN-BASED PROGRAMMING ENVIRONMENT

At this point, several types of software can be used to program the LEGO EV3 robot: the actual software created by LEGO called LabVIEW for LEGO MINDSTORMS (LVLM); an extension that can be used in the 2-D animation and game programming environment, Scratch (Scratch, n.d.); EV3python; RobotC; and other programming environments (LEGO Engineering, n.d.). For the purposes of this chapter, I focus our discussion by drawing examples from LVLM. LVLM (see figure 10.2) is designed as a drag-and-drop, block-based programming environment. It provides action blocks for programming output devices (motors, sound, display, and/or the brick light), flow control blocks for programming wait for loops and sensor triggered events, sensor blocks for additional programming of sensors

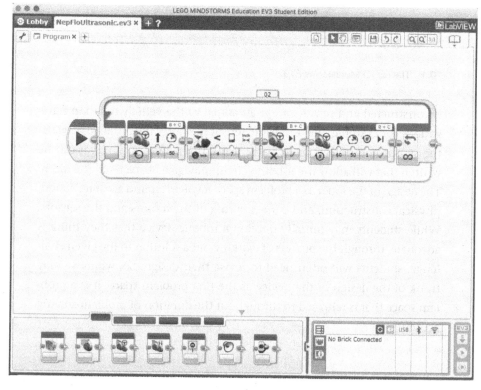

10.2   The LabVIEW for LEGO Mindstorms (LVLM) programming environment.

including data collection, data operations blocks for working with data that have been collected, advanced blocks (including message blocks, and Bluetooth-enabled operations), and finally a "My Blocks" section, where users can create their own blocks.

In addition to the programming blocks, the software includes a utility in the bottom right-hand corner of the interface that, when the EV3 is connected to the laptop, allows the user to quickly verify which ports the motors are connected through, which port a sensor is connected to, and whether that sensor is actually reading environmental data. This, along with a context-sensitive help utility, which can be selected from a drop-down menu, allows students to learn about the programming environment and also verify that all parts of the robot are functional.

THE THIRD PROBLEM SPACE: THE PHYSICAL ENVIRONMENT

For the purposes of this chapter I describe a specific environment, developed by the FIRST LEGO League, which is an international, nonprofit organization that publishes a thematic robotics challenge and holds regional robotics events each year in which children participate. While this is a specific physical environment, the reader should bear in mind that robotics environments can be created in any room, and/or one could do robotics outdoors. Indeed, any physical space could be a potential robotics environment. The FIRST LEGO League challenge map is four feet wide by eight feet wide, which can be laid on the floor or set on a table with similar dimensions. The challenge map comes with specific pieces that are placed in specific spots on the map. For the purposes of this chapter, I provide an image of one such challenge map created by the FIRST LEGO league (2011). This challenge map was used in 2011 and is known as the Food Factor Challenge (see figure 10.3). In this challenge, children were tasked with completing specific large-scale food production robotic tasks on the challenge board, while considering the environmental effects of such production (e.g., the long-term effects of over-fishing). The board consists of fifteen different challenges. All of the challenges include a description of a real-world problem that the challenge attempts to solve.

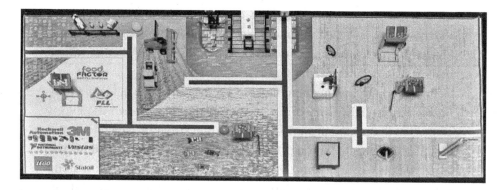

10.3 The Food Factor Challenge Board by FIRST LEGO League.

LEARNING IN THE MULTIDIMENSIONAL PROBLEM SPACE

From a Vygotskyan (1978) perspective, students learn in the robotics environment through interaction with the tools and dialogue with each other and the teacher. It is important to note that the learning outcomes described in the following pages are made possible through a pedagogical approach that affords open-ended, collaborative learning. It is children's free movement within the space that also contributes to their learning (Dewey 1938/1997). In other words, while children should be given a specific challenge to solve, within the activity itself, children should have freedom to explore various solutions and various approaches. It is through collaborative exploration that children are able to engage in practices that support their learning. In our research, we have found support for student learning and growth in the following areas: systems learning, science literacy, inferential reasoning, abstraction, creative problem-solving (including the role of play), problem-solving strategy development, and computational concepts (Sullivan 2008, 2011; Sullivan and Keith 2018; Sullivan and Lin 2012; Sullivan, Söken, and Yildiz 2019). This learning and growth are supported by the design affordances of the multidimensional robotics environment. I address each aspect of learning with robotics in turn.

SYSTEMS LEARNING

A system is defined as a collection of parts or processes (Penner 2000). Hmelo-Silver, Holton, and Kolodner (2000) define a complex system as one in which part of a system interacts with other systems; to understand a complex system, students must engage with the "causal interactions and functional relations" (p. 248) among systems. The three problem spaces that make up the robotics learning environment function as a complex system (Sullivan 2008). This is so because each problem space can be seen as a system in its own right. And, while the problem spaces are tightly coupled to create the learning environment, one must often master and troubleshoot errors in each system, as well as across the complex system, to solve challenges. For example, students often build a vehicular robot with the LEGO pieces and wheels when they are working with robotics. If the vehicle is constructed poorly, it will affect the performance of the entire system. Therefore, students would need to work on fixing the building error to continue with any challenge solution.

Meanwhile, the program may contain an error that prohibits it from executing when transferred to the robot. In this instance, the feedback students receive is simply no feedback: the robot will not execute the program, it will not move. Students then must return to the programming space to puzzle through the error. Importantly, students are learning about the robotic system through these debugging activities. In this way, it is easy to see how learning to think computationally (debugging a robotics problem) is connected to science inquiry (learning about systems). In our prior research, we found that students' understanding of systems improved after a long summer course in robotics. A total of twenty-six fifth-grade students, ages ten to twelve years, worked in a three-week, 105-hour robotics course. Results on a systems thinking test created by Cooper (2004) indicated that students' ability to think about systems improved significantly from before to after (Sullivan 2008).

SCIENCE LITERACY

Science literacy has been variously defined as the ability to engage in the activity of inquiry, including "making observations, posing questions, planning investigations, reviewing what is already known in light of experimental evidence, using tools to gather, analyze, and interpret data, proposing answers, explanations, and predictions; and communicating the results" (National Research Council [NRC] 1996, 23). Science literacy as defined by the Next Generation Science Standards (NGSS 2013) includes knowledge of disciplinary core ideas (specific to each area of science), science and engineering practices (including the practices identified previously by the NRC), and cross-cutting concepts (including concepts that apply to all domains of science). In robotics learning environments, students have the opportunity to engage in many of the practices defined by the NRC and the NGSS. In our prior research (Sullivan 2008), we identified some of the cross-cutting concepts students engage with, including cause and effect, systems and system models, and structure and function. For example, we found that the feedback loop created by the activity of writing and executing programs on the robotic device (problem spaces one and two) support student engagement with cause and effect, whereas building a robotic device to carry out specific tasks in a specific environment (problem spaces one and three) supports engagement with the concepts of structure and function. Finally, as noted earlier, students engage with and improve their understanding of the concept of systems as they work in the robotics learning environment (Sullivan 2007, 2008).

The NGSS (2013) refers to science and engineering practices as including observing, questioning, and planning, as well as designing, testing designs, analyzing results, and modifying the design accordingly. Importantly, these practices fall well within the CT construct as defined by other researchers (Barr and Stephenson 2011; International Society of Technology in Education and the Computer Science Teaching Association 2011). For example, planning is an aspect of problem-solving; designing is an aspect of programming activity; and testing designs, analyzing results, and revising designs constitute debugging activity.

In prior research, I identified a very regular set of activities that students engage in while working with robotics, which I have termed the troubleshooting cycle (TSC) (Sullivan 2011). The TSC consists of designing and building the robotic device, writing a program for the device, testing the program, diagnosing errors, debugging the program, and/or revising the design of the device, and retesting the program. This iterative practice encompasses action and interaction across the three problem spaces. The duration of a TSC is variable, it can last a few minutes, several minutes, or longer. However, the actual troubleshooting activity is very stable, it always consists of these six activities, and so it is an excellent unit of analysis for educational research; it can also serve to organize and support student learning and activity. For example, in one curricular implementation we studied, the teacher developed a note-taking worksheet that prompted students to record their trials, including what the students did, the problems they encountered, and their solutions to the problem. This worksheet is akin to a researcher's journal (Sullivan 2007). The troubleshooting cycle is a computational activity that is clearly an aspect of science and engineering practice as identified by the NGSS.

INFERENTIAL REASONING

As noted in the NGSS, "cause and effect" is a cross-cutting concept in science. In our research, we have found that interaction across the three problem spaces of robotics supports both hypothesis development, through debugging activity (Sullivan 2008), and inferential reasoning with data collected by sensors attached to the robotic device (Sullivan, Söken, and Yildiz 2019). Indeed, we have found that the sensors play an instrumental role in supporting student engagement in science and engineering practices in the robotics setting. The sensors are designed to monitor and/or collect data in the physical environment (the third problem space). The robotic device can be programmed to respond to a specific result when sensors are used to monitor the environment. The device can also be used as a means of collecting, storing, and then transmitting data to another device. In this way, the device, equipped with a programmed sensor can function as a scientific instrument for data collection.

We conducted a study in a sixth-grade science classroom, in which we followed a focal group of students as they worked to solve challenges that centered on heat and light energy topics (Sullivan, Söken, and Yildiz 2019). The students in the study were twelve years old; they were working with the second LEGO iteration of the brick (called the NXT) and a programming environment created at Tufts University called Robolab. Robolab is equipped with science investigation utilities, including a data graphing capability that allowed students to interpret the data numerically or through creating various graph-based visualizations of the data (see figure 10.4). The challenge the students were solving in this class was called Cave Explorer. This challenge asked students to explore three simulated cave environments to find out which one may be the most

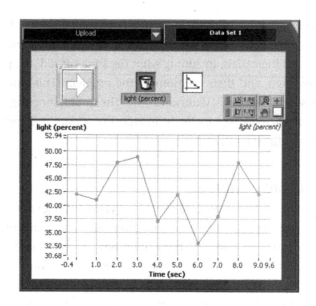

10.4 Screenshot of the Robolab Datalogger.

comfortable to sleep in; the three simulated caves were actually three cardboard boxes, prepared with varying levels of light and heat inside. Students designed their robots with light, heat, and touch sensors and programmed them to navigate into the caves, collect data, and navigate back out. Table 10.1 presents a conversation among the students as one of them makes an inference from the data collected by the light sensor for one of the caves.

As can be seen in table 10.1, S makes an observation related to the differences in the numerical readings and then she makes an inference about where the data was collected. In line one, S has decided that the last three collected readings were collected outside of the cave, because of the numerical difference in the first three numbers as compared to the rest of the numbers in the data readout. Each of the "caves" was darker than the actual classroom itself. So, she infers that the light readings that were significantly higher in number were collected outside of the cave. Meanwhile, J interprets the last two readings as being outside the cave. In line seven, S notes that it is not just the last three but also the first light reading that was taken outside of the cave. In line 12, S begins to explain her reasoning to I (the third student in the group). While S is consistently interrupted by J, we

Table 10.1 School A student discussion—Making inferences from numerical data

Line	Speaker	Utterance	Researcher interpretation
1	S:	The, the last three [readings] are from outside.	Sara reads a numerical presentation of the collected light data and makes an inference based on it.
2	J:	What?	Javier asks Sara to repeat herself.
3	S:	The last three make, I think they're from outside because you know how when they came out there was two separate readings?	Sara repeats the comment and expands with some reasoning.
4	J:	No, the last two.	Javier interprets the data slightly differently.
5	S:	The last three.	Sara repeats claim.
6	J:	The last two.	Javier repeats claim.
7	S:	Three and then the first.	Sara continues to read the displayed data and interpret.
8	J:	Mister we got five hundred and two readings, why?	Javier asks the teacher a question about the printout.
9	S:	Yeah.	Sara affirms question.
10	T:	Oh, you got (?)	Teacher remark is partly unintelligible.
11	J:	You do it go and do it.	Javier instructs Sara to continue.
12	S:	Yeah, you know you're inside you're inside look, look he came out Ilana this . . .	Sara interprets the readings for Ilana.
13	J:	No don't (show it her) cause she's gonna say that's not gonna work.	Javier interferes with Sara's interpretation to Ilana.
14	S:	Look at this look at the light.	Sara continues interpreting.
15	J:	It's not gonna work.	Javier continues to interfere.
16	S:	These two are from outside.	Sara continues interpreting.
17	J:	It's not gonna work.	Javier continues to interfere.

(continued)

Table 10.1 (continued)

Line	Speaker	Utterance	Researcher interpretation
18	S:	And then . . .	Sara continues interpreting.
19	J:	It's not gonna work.	Javier continues to interfere.
20	I:	So, we got to do it all over again?	Ilana expresses confusion between Sara and Javier's comments.
21	J:	No.	Javier continues to interfere.
22	S:	And then these last these last three are from outside, and so feels right.	Sara continues interpreting and suggests the last cave "feels right."

can see that in lines 12, 14, 16, and 22, S points out to I how the amounts of reflected light are different and how that indicates where the readings were taken. In this example, it is possible to see that S is making inferences from the data. She is engaged in deductive reasoning from the data, and she is engaging in the cross-cutting concept of cause and effect—since the device is outside of the box, the light readings are higher. This is a powerful learning moment for these students that included both CT and science literacy elements. It is made possible by virtue of working in the multidimensional problem space of robotics; each of the problem spaces mattered in this interpretation, the designed device, the data read-out (part of problem space two), and the physical "cave" in which the robot collected data.

ABSTRACTION

In addition to supporting systems thinking and science literacy practices, the multidimensional problem space and iterative nature of robotics support the process of abstraction. Abstraction is an important computational concept. Abstraction refers to the stripping away of detail to reduce the complexity involved in a problem. The goal in abstraction is to identify the generalizable elements of a problem, which may be seen as foundational. It is when the foundational elements are clear that new representations of the problem can be developed, and these new representations can help lead to solutions. The three problem spaces of the robotics learning environment support abstraction in an *after the fact* mode. This is so because the physical robot and physical environment constitute 3-D representations of the problem, and the 2-D programming space offers an abstract representation of the 3-D movement of the robot. While working in the troubleshooting cycle, students move back and forth between the 3-D challenge environment and the 2-D programming environment. As they do so, they reason about the program they have written and the movement of the robotic device. In this way, the shift in attention, back and forth between the 2-D representation to the 3-D representation, supports students' model development and abstract thinking ability. Since the 2-D environment is provided to students, they do not have to create the abstraction (hence the after-the-fact mode). However, they do need to learn how to interpret the abstraction, and this work is supported by the 3-D aspects of the activity.

We have observed this behavior over and over again in our work. To demonstrate the phenomenon, we provide a vignette from a recent study (Sullivan and Keith 2018). Seventeen girls (ages eight to fourteen) participated in this case study. The case study focused on girls learning robotics in a one-day introduction to the FIRST LEGO league. Students worked collaboratively in groups of two or three to solve the challenges provided. Table 10.2 presents a short vignette featuring a conversation that one focal group of students had as they worked to solve a challenge. The conversation begins at the challenge board (lines 1 to 8), as the group observes the functioning of the robot, and continues as they move back to their worktable, where they were programming their robot.

As can be seen in table 10.2, the vignette begins with the students testing their robot. It does not work completely (lines 2–8), so they diagnose the problem, and then they move back to the 2-D representation and, as can be seen in line 17, L gesture and talk through what each icon programs the robot to do. While they are talking through the program, they are thinking back to what they just saw happen on the 3-D challenge board. In line 18, F pinpoints the block she believes should be programmed differently. It is this same activity that supports the students' ability to think more abstractly about the problem—each time the students execute the program, they must re-examine the icons used to program the robot to gain a better understanding of how to revise the program. This constant interplay between the 2-D and 3-D aspects of the activity provides students

Table 10.2 Abstraction dialogue

Line	Student	Utterance	Location	Researcher interpretation
1	L:	Okay, try that, I think that might have been what we have.	Challenge Board	Three students stand around the game board to test their executable program.
2	F:	Yeah, I think we just need to make *that* distance longer. What? Okay.	Challenge Board	Possible solution is forwarded by F. F is surprised by the robot's movement.
3	L:	Well . . .	Challenge Board	L makes an utterance while watching the robot.
4	F:	No.	Challenge Board	F articulates the failure of the program.
5	S:	It's crashing.	Challenge Board	S narrates the movement of the robot.
6	F:	Alright let's fix that.	Walking toward work table	F suggests group activity.
7	L:	Okay, what do we need to switch?	Challenge Board	L asks aloud what needs to be done.
8	S:	Okay, we need to make things that when it goes that way it's longer.	Challenge Board	S offers a potential solution.
9	F:	Yeah, we need one of the distances to be longer.	Walking toward worktable	F agrees with S's analysis.
10	S:	Haba	Worktable	S tries to sit in F's chair.
11	F:	S!	Worktable	F asks S to move (with tone implies S should quit fooling around).
12	L:	S!	Worktable	L agrees with F.
13	S:	Sorry.	Worktable	S apologizes for lack of focus.

Table 10.2 (continued)

Line	Student	Utterance	Location	Researcher interpretation
14	F:	Come on.	Worktable	F asks S to refocus.
15	S:	Okay, so what are we doing?	Worktable	S refocuses.
16	F:	Uh . . .	Worktable	F begins a verbalization.
17	L:	So it goes forward, turns, forward, turns when, when does it go wrong?	Worktable	L (looking at the computer screen) thinks aloud and moves her hands as if they were the robot moving across the table.
18	F:	I think it was that one.	Worktable	F (pointing at the screen) points at the block that needs to be programmed differently.

with strong supports for developing the ability to program and to think abstractly about the movement of the robot. Essentially, the 3-D activity of testing the executable program on the challenge board transforms student understanding of the 2-D programming icons. In this way, the three problem spaces work together to support learning about abstraction.

CREATIVE PROBLEM-SOLVING

In addition to supporting engagement in CT and science literacy practices, other modes of learning are strongly supported by robotics. These modes include play and creativity. Both of these modes of interaction support student engagement in problem-solving and learning with robotics. I argue that robotic devices are inherently playful; typically, the robotic device spurs student curiosity, and observing the movement of the device immediately raises a number of questions in students' minds about what the robot is and how it is doing what it does. Anecdotally, I have witnessed many students become intrigued with the device and express a desire to play with it; this desire to play with the robot serves as a means for learning more about it.

Playfulness can lead to resourcefulness when students are attempting to solve a robotics challenge. In a study conducted with students in a sixth-grade science classroom (Sullivan 2011), I used a Bakhtinian (Bakhtin 1986, 1981) lens to identify the reified and spoken voices that influenced students' collaborative development of a creative idea to solve a particular challenge. Integral to this analysis is the notion that the designed device itself embeds the intentions of the designers and affords certain types of interactions. Resnick (2003, 2006, 2014) has often discussed the role of play at the heart of the technologies he develops, such as the LEGO brick. This is in line with Papert's (1993) strong support for the idea of tinkering with technologies to learn more about them, but also to make them one's own. Moreover, the manipulative nature of the robotic device (i.e., one can hold it in one's hands), coupled with the fact that the device can be designed to roam around a room as a wheeled vehicle, affords a high degree of student interaction and provides an opportunity for students to think creatively about how to use the physical environment (the third problem space) to help them solve challenges.

In this particular study (Sullivan 2011), the students repurposed an item from the LEGO materials not used in the creation of the robotics device to help them solve the challenge. The repurposing of the item was an instance of bricolage (Lévi-Strauss 1966). Bricolage is the idea that one should use what is "ready-to-hand" to address current problems, regardless of the intended use of an object. This type of practice leads students to develop environmentally influenced problem-solving strategies and algorithms to solve robotics challenges.

In addition to creating environmentally influenced problem-solving strategies, we have also found that students developed strategies that entail the use of the device itself. For example, in a case study conducted with twelve students attending the three-week, 105-hour robotics camp referenced earlier in the chapter, we identified a problem-solving strategy we termed "simulating the movement of the robot" (Sullivan and Lin 2012). This strategy includes holding the robot (the first problem space) and moving it about the physical environment that constitutes the challenge space (the third problem space). We observed that, as students engaged in this activity, they often verbalized the program that needed to be written to solve the challenge. Here, one can recognize this activity from Vygotsky's

(1978) perspective as the role of externalized verbalizations and the use of tools in mediating student learning in the robotics environment.

Finally, in addition to engagement in problem solving, our research has indicated that students engage in a number of activities that emphasize computational concepts while working across the three problem spaces that make up the activity of learning with robotics. In our early work (Sullivan and Lin 2012), we examined the computational concepts that fifth-grade children engaged with while solving robotics challenge. For example, we have found that children had the opportunity to engage with conditional reasoning, program control and flow elements, and the basic idea of input/process/output. In our later work (Sullivan and Keith 2018; Sullivan, Söken, and Yildiz 2019), we developed a computational concepts coding scheme to assist in the analysis of student problem-solving conversations and activities across two different studies. In each of these studies we collected video data of focal student groups solving robotics challenges. We transcribed these data and analyzed student talk at the level of the utterance.

Our computational concepts coding scheme was both data driven and theoretically influenced from the literature (Barr and Stephenson 2011; Grover and Pea 2013; Wing 2006). The scheme includes five CT codes as follows: analysis, algorithmic thinking operations, algorithmic thinking variable, designing, and debugging. We split the algorithmic thinking code in two because of the relative sophistication of setting the variable parameter of a coding block (algorithmic thinking variable) versus simply selecting a coding block to use in the program (algorithmic thinking operation). In two different case studies, we observed students intensely involved in computational discussions regarding designing (problem space one), algorithmic thinking (problem space two), and analysis and debugging (problem spaces one, two, and three). Characteristic of student involvement was a relationship between the difficulty of the challenge attempted and the sophistication of the solution. In this way, we observed a phenomenon originally discussed by Dorst and Cross (2001) regarding the co-evolution of the problem definition and the designed solution; as students became more familiar with the problem spaces in which they were working, the more sophisticated the designed solutions became, both at the building level (problem space one) and the programming level (problem space two).

CONCLUSION

In summation, robotics is an integrated learning system comprising three interwoven, multidimensional problem spaces. Interaction within and among these problem spaces supports students' development of CT and their science inquiry abilities. A future research direction derived from our research is further investigation of the intersection of CT and disciplinary practices. As Lee et al. (2020) have pointed out, there are a number of newer areas of inquiry in STEM that blend computation and science: for example, computational biology. Future CT research should seek to further explicate the interdisciplinary relationships endemic to these new areas, such that powerful curriculum and pedagogical practices can be developed to support students' learning.

REFERENCES

Bakhtin, Mikhail Mikhailovich. 1981. *The Dialogic Imagination,* edited by Michael Holquist; translated by Caryl Emerson and Michael Holquist. Austin, TX: University of Texas Press.

Bakhtin, Mikhail Mikhailovich. 1986. "The Problem of Speech Genres." In *Speech Genres and Other Late Essays,* translated by Vern W. McGee, edited by Caryl Emerson and Michael Holquist, 60–102. Austin: University of Texas Press.

Barr, Valerie, and Chris Stephenson. 2011. "Bringing Computational Thinking to K–12: What Is Involved and What Is the Role of the Computer Science Education Community?" *ACM Inroads* 2 (1): 48–54.

Cooper, Tim. 2004. "A Systems-Based Robotics Curriculum." Unpublished master's thesis, New York: Teachers College, Columbia University.

Dewey, John. 1938/1997. *Experience and Education.* New York: Simon and Shuster.

Dorst, Kees, and Nigel Cross. 2001. "Creativity in the Design Process: Co-evolution of Problem–Solution." *Design Studies* 22 (5): 425–437.

FIRST LEGO League, 2011. *Food Factor.* http://www.firstlegoleague.org/sites/default /files/food-factor/food-factor-challenge.pdf.

Grover, Shuchi, and Roy Pea. 2013. "Computational Thinking in K–12: A Review of the State of the Field." *Educational Researcher* 42 (38): 38–43. https://doi.org/10.3102 /0013189X12463051.

Hmelo, Cindy E., Douglas L. Holton, and Janet L. Kolodner. 2000. "Designing to Learn about Complex Systems." *The Journal of the Learning Sciences* 9 (3): 247–298.

International Society for Technology in Education and the Computer Science Teachers Association. 2011. *Operational Definition of Computational Thinking for K–12 Education*. http://www.iste.org/docs/ct-documents/computational-thinking-operational-definition-flyer.pdf?sfvrsn=2.

Lee, Irene, Shuchi Grover, Fred Martin, Sarita Pillai, and Joyce Malyn-Smith. 2020. "Computational Thinking from a Disciplinary Perspective: Integrating Computational Thinking in K–12 Science, Technology, Engineering, and Mathematics Education." *Journal of Science Education and Technology* 29, 1–8. https://doi.org/10.1007/s10956-019-09803-w.

LEGO Engineering. n.d. *LEGO Engineering*. http://www.legoengineering.com/alternativeprogramming-languages/.

Lévi-Strauss, Claude. 1966. *The Savage Mind*. Chicago: University of Chicago Press.

National Research Council. 1996. *The National Science Standards*. http://www.nap.edu/readingroom/books/nses.

Next Generation Science Standards. 2013. *Next Generation Science Standards*. https://www.nextgenscience.org/search-standards.

Papert, Seymour. 1993. *The Children's Machine: Rethinking School in the Age of the Computer*. New York: Basic Books.

Penner, David, E. 2000. "Cognition, Computers, and Synthetic Science: Building Knowledge and Meaning Through Modeling." *Review of Research in Education* 25: 1–35.

Resnick, Mitchell. 2003. "Playful Learning and Creative Societies." *Education Update* VIII (6).

Resnick, Mitchell. 2006. "Computer as Paintbrush: Technology, Play, and the Creative Society." In *Play = Learning: How Play Motivates and Enhances Children's Cognitive and Social-Emotional Growth*, edited by Dorothy Singer, Roberta Mitchnik Golikoff, and Kathy Hirsh-Pasek, 192–208. Oxford: Oxford University Press.

Resnick, Mitchell. 2014. "Give P's a Chance: Projects, Peers, Passion, Play." *Constructionism and Creativity Conference*, opening keynote speech, Vienna, Austria, August 19, 2014.

Resnick, Mitchell, Fred Martin, Richard Sargent, and Brian Silverman. 1996. "Programmable Bricks: Toys to Think With." *IBM Systems Journal* 35 (3&4): 443–452.

Roth, Wolf Michael. 2001. "Learning Science Through Technological Design." *Journal of Research in Science Teaching* 38: 768–790. https://doi.org/10.1002/tea.1031.

Scratch. n.d. *Scratch*. https://scratch.mit.edu/.

Sullivan, Florence, R. 2007. "Learning Through Building and Programming: Thinking and Reasoning with Robotics." Invited presentation, the STEM Education Institute, University of Massachusetts, Amherst, October 23, 2007.

Sullivan, Florence, R. 2008. "Robotics and Science Literacy: Thinking Skills, Science Process Skills, and Systems Understanding." *Journal of Research in Science Teaching* 45 (3): 373–394.

Sullivan, Florence, R. 2011. "Serious and Playful Inquiry: Epistemological Aspects of Collaborative Creativity." *Journal of Educational Technology and Society* 14 (1): 55–65.

Sullivan, Florence, R., and P. Kevin Keith. 2018. "Computational Thinking and Doing with Robotics in an All-Girl Workshop Setting." Paper presentation at the annual meeting of the American Educational Research Association. New York, April 13–17, 2018.

Sullivan, Florence, R., and John Heffernan. 2016. "Robotic Construction Kits as Computational Manipulatives for Learning in the STEM Disciplines." *Journal of Research on Technology in Education* 48 (2): 1–24.

Sullivan, Florence, R., and Xiaodong Lin. 2012. "The Ideal Science Student Survey: Exploring the Relationship of Students' Perceptions to their Problem Solving Activity in a Robotics Context." *Journal of Interactive Learning Research* 23 (3): 273–308.

Sullivan, Florence, R., Ali Söken, and Ozkan Yildiz. 2019. "Robotics and Science Inquiry: The Affordances of Sensors for Learning About Data." Paper presentation at the annual Conference of the American Educational Research Association. April 5–9, 2019, Toronto, Ontario, Canada.

Vygotsky, Lev Semyonovitch. 1978. *Mind in Society: The Development of Higher Psychological Processes,* edited by Michael Cole, Vera John-Steiner, Sylvia Scribner, and Ellen Souberman. Cambridge: Harvard University Press.

Wing, Jean. 2006. "Computational Thinking." *Communications of the ACM* 49 (3): 33–35.

11

TOWARD A RESEARCH AGENDA FOR DEVELOPING COMPUTATIONAL THINKING SKILLS BY SENSE-REASON-ACT PROGRAMMING WITH ROBOTS

Nardie Fanchamps, Marcus Specht, Lou Slangen, and Paul Hennissen

INTRODUCTION

Programming is important for pupils to develop computational thinking (CT) skills (Kennisnet 2016; Serafini 2011). CT comprises the thought processes that play a role in formulating and solving problems so that the solutions are presented in a form that can be effectively conducted making use of computer science concepts (Wing 2006). CT encompasses a range of analytic and problem-solving skills, dispositions, habits, and approaches used, such as the ability to break down complex tasks into simpler components, pattern recognition, pattern generalization, parallelization, and abstraction (Silk, Schunn, and Shoop 2009; SLO 2017; Toh et al. 2016). Using CT in search for solutions also means gaining insight into the design of algorithms (Fanchamps et al. 2019).

Programmable robots provide excellent opportunities to develop CT skills as they combine the production of code with immediate tangible results and feedback (Catlin and Woollard 2014; Slangen 2016). More specifically, such a robotic programming environment can ensure that programming actions and their results are immediately perceptible by pupil and teacher (Sapounidis, Demetriadis, and Stamelos 2015). When pupils can immediately test the response of their programming action against the effect in reality, they will be better able to judge the effect of their programming action(s) (Wang, Wang, and Liu 2014). In this way, robotic environments function as direct manipulation environments (DMEs), which make it possible to obtain direct feedback on the effect of the programming operation (Jonassen 2006; Rekimoto 2000).

A robot that needs to anticipate changes in its environment requires a different program than one carrying out an unchanging, predictable task. By making use of sense-reason-act (SRA) programming, a robot can react to changes in its surroundings (Slangen 2016). To enable the construction of such SRA programs, a variety of encoding components are available. SRA programming is the skill of using encoding components in such a way that, by its program, a robot can anticipate and react autonomously to changes in the environment. Selecting and using the proper encoding components in a robotic problem environment require understanding variable solution strategies and the deployment of powerful cognitive skills, which we here define as SRA thinking. SRA thinking is characterized by the deployment of cognitive skills such as analyzing, synthesizing, elaborating, imagining, parallel thinking, cause-effect reasoning, and problem decomposition (Slangen and Sloep 2005). Moreover, the application of these cognitive skills is closely related to principles of CT (Yadav et al. 2017). Therefore it seems logical to operationalize these SRA characteristics in the learning of CT skills. In addition, the perception of the type of execution of the robot's programming task appears to make a difference. A different level of abstraction occurs when a physically present and concretely observable robot executes programming commands than when the execution of the programming task only occurs on a screen (Weintrop and Wilensky 2015).

The timing and kind of teacher interventions also contribute to pupils' decision-making skills when learning how to solve robot programming problems (Valcke 1985). Teacher support can help or hinder (Slangen 2016). For teachers it seems to be difficult to be sufficiently reticent at crucial moments (Sentance and Csizmadia 2017). Instead of exercising a certain restraint, teachers often intervene to inform pupils when difficult problems must be solved or when misconceptions are likely to arise (Petrou and Dimitrakopoulou 2003). In addition to providing support and guidance, teacher interventions can also disrupt pupils' ongoing thinking and can interfere with learning processes (Dekker and Elshout-Mohr

2004). Therefore the reticence of the teacher is an important condition to enable pupils to develop programming problem-solving skills through the route of inquiry-based learning and problem-solving action (Yadav et al. 2017).

McWhorter (2008) has found positive effects of programming robots on pupil motivation, their use of learning strategies, and their agency in selecting learning objectives, mediated by self-regulation skills, autonomy, and competence of the pupils. Pupils' autonomy appears to increase motivation and performance and is one of the basic psychological needs, together with the need for building relationship and competence (Baard, Deci, and Ryan 2004). The attention for these basic needs is an underlying cause of a number of quality differences between intrinsic and extrinsic motivation. Moreover, learning to program from meaningful contexts where one has a sense of control can influence the autonomy and competence development of the learner (Rovai, Wighting, and Lucking 2004).

Previous research conducted by Fanchamps et al. (2019) has shown that primary school pupils are capable of arriving at a certain level of SRA programming but that pupils often do not apply SRA independently, even when they have previously experienced the benefits of the SRA approach. This research also anticipated that the instruction method used by the teacher (a scaffolding-based approach versus direct instruction) would show a characteristic difference on the development of self-efficacy, but this could not be demonstrated.

Elaborating on the findings set out previously, our overarching research proposal sets out to examine if the type of programming problem and task design have an impact on evoking SRA thinking and to what extent the influence of teacher interventions are of importance. We also want to examine whether these variables affect the effectiveness of the interventions.

THEORETICAL FRAMEWORK

From our literature review and previous research, we are generally interested in the question of whether the type of programming environment and task design can evoke SRA thinking and therefore strengthen the development of CT. We also specifically want to know if the instruction variant used influences SRA thinking and indicates the level of the effectiveness of the intervention.

From prior research we know that primary school pupils, when programming robots, primarily use linear programming structures, even when they have previously experienced the benefits of parallel programming and sensor use (Slangen 2016). In the pupils' linear approach, all commands are invariably sequenced in long strings, without several handling routines being operational at the same time (Wyeth, Venz, and Wyeth 2003). We also showed that pupils have considerable difficulties in understanding and applying SRA programming and find it challenging to use sensors or sensor programming (Slangen, van Keulen, and Gravemeijer 2011). In an SRA program, there is always a conditional encoding component, based on sensing (i.e., detection of change), that necessarily influences the handling of the program. This is different from straight-line programming, in which each encoding component is a stand-alone command that is arranged in the correct sequence (Wyeth, Venz, and Wyeth 2003). SRA programming has its origins in the robotics world and connects physical reality with the virtual world based on observation, decision-making, and action. Understanding SRA programming means that pupils can explicitly relate processes in which a robot: (1) records observations based on sensor use (sense), (2) compares these observations with internal values of the external situation and decides which path to follow (reason), and (3) reacts according to a subsequent process in which the program "tells" the robot what action to take (act). SRA programming involves complex elements, such as the "if-then-else," the "nested loop," "when," "while," "wait-until," "event handling," and "simultaneous running parallel routines" that pupils find difficult to understand (Gregg et al. 2012). Understanding the functionality of the use of sensors also appears to be an abstract task.

A functional application of SRA when programming robots, whether combined with the applicability of sensory input, requires pupils to apply logical reasoning in programming environments (Pea and Kurland 2007), which we define here as SRA thinking. These insights enable pupils to program a robot that can anticipate changes in its environment through its program. In other words, it requires system thinking—the understanding of the interactions and interdependencies between programming and the sensors and actuators used (Slangen, van Keulen, and Gravemeijer 2011).

CT is the process-based (re)formulation of a problem in such a way that it becomes possible to solve the problem with computer technology (Barr, Harrison, and Conery 2011; Wing 2006). CT instrumentalizes an iterative process based on three phases: (1) problem definition, (2) solution expression, (3) implementation and evaluation (Wong 2014; Yadav, Hong, and Stephenson 2016). CT also refers to skills such as problem decomposition, pattern recognition, data formation, generalization, abstraction, and algorithmization (Voogt and Roblin 2010).

SRA programming with functional sensor use can be applied in different programming contexts and can be regarded as a smart way of programming (Gregg et al. 2012). However, our previous research shows that if pupils are still able to use linear programming structures, they do not recognize the added value of SRA programming (Fanchamps et al. 2019; Wyeth, Venz, and Wyeth 2003). This seems to be caused by the fact that when a programming task is based on the use of an unchanging, static environment, in which pupils are not confronted with changing events that must be anticipated, they maintain a predictable approach to the programming task (Slangen, van Keulen, and Gravemeijer 2011). However, if the programming environment in which a robot has to perform its tasks is dynamic in nature, and therefore unpredictable because the environment is constantly changing, then the solution requires the use of SRA programming in which sensors, conditionals, and routines must be used to successfully solve the programming problem (Demetriou 2011; Dragone et al. 2005).

SRA programming requires a degree of abstract thinking. It means being able to analyze the robotic task environment—being able to recognize the conditional and iterative conditions and translate them into the correct application of programming instructions (Caci and D'Amico 2002; Pea and Kurland 2007). If pupils understand that the reasoning process of a robot is based on principles of logic, conditional, causal, and iterative reasoning and thinking in parameters and variables, this would be recognizable in their created programs (Slangen and Rohaan 2018). Code that is produced according to SRA principles contains such complex principles of programming, conditionals, and loop structures. Analyzing pupils' code reveals information about pupils' SRA thinking skills such as efficiency, creativity, higher-order reasoning, analyzing, synthesizing, and judgment.

DMEs are innovative learning tools that combine ICT (information and communications technology) control technology and programmable logic controllers with the construction of a concrete, material model (movable structures linked to motors, actuators, and sensors) (Jonassen 2006; Rekimoto 2000). Characteristic for DMEs is the "direct" feedback from the technology that provides pupils with feedback on their thinking and actions (Slangen, van Keulen, and Gravemeijer 2011). Examples of such tools are TechnoLogica, VEX IQ, Arduino Makeblock, and LEGO Mindstorms EV3, with which pupils can build a working robot or machine that must then be programmed to carry out predefined assignments (Jonassen 2000; Slangen, Fanchamps, and Kommers 2008; Slangen, van Keulen, and Gravemeijer 2011; Slangen, van Keulen, and Jochems 2009). The use of DMEs imposes requirements on the environment and the task and the type of guidance and is very suitable for inquiry-based learning and a problem-solving approach.

Self-efficacy is an important requirement for pupils to be able to work on a robotic programming task in a creative, targeted manner independently of the teacher (Dignath and Büttner 2008; Spin 2015). It is the teacher's task to create and support opportunities and possibilities in which pupils can conduct their assignment in a self-effective way (Dignath-van Ewijk and Van der Werf 2012). This asks for learning contexts in which learners can make their own choices and decisions and in which there are possibilities for direct feedback. As mentioned previously, DME robotics programming environments seem to be suitable for solving programming tasks in a self-effective way.

According to Stevens (2004) and Broeck et al. (2010), pupils' self-effectiveness is built on competence, autonomy, and relationship. Competence refers to the feeling and belief in one's own ability. To let pupils experience what they are capable of requires challenge and motivational strengthening elements. A combination of high (but realistic) expectations and the availability of help and support are necessary for developing a strong sense of competence. Autonomy is having the confidence to be independent in such a way that pupils can make their own decisions and choices. It is pupils feeling that they are capable of doing a task on their own. Autonomy is only possible if tasks and instrumentation are carefully aligned to the potential and needs of pupils. Relationship is the feeling of belonging and being part of a community. Pupils need relationships, both with their teacher and with other pupils, based on providing safety, space, guidance, and support. Pupils and the teacher should collectively feel responsible for a good atmosphere in the classroom, and pupils should feel they can count on the support and guidance of the teacher (Rovai, Wighting, and Lucking 2004).

Apart from the coaching and instruction of the supervising teacher, the pedagogical needs of the learner play an important role (Vosniadou et al. 2001). Our previous research showed that, when working with programmable robotics contexts in which pupils have to solve programming problems with LEGO robots, the type of instruction offered (scaffolding-based versus direct instruction) does not make a significant difference in relation to the yield, solution, and efficiency of the constructed program (Fanchamps et al. 2019). However, the teacher should adapt the pedagogical offer to the pupils' characteristics and associated pedagogical needs in such a way as to achieve maximum learning efficiency (Alfieri, Brooks, and Aldrich 2011).

Interventions by teachers can influence pupils' final learning efficacy outcomes in robot programming (Slangen 2016). Some pupils may learn best when they perform all actions and thinking processes themselves with minimal coaching from the teacher, while other pupils may learn most when the teacher explains everything fully (Fanchamps 2016).

Direct instruction can be defined as targeted actions of the teacher with the aim of supporting pupils' learning activities to structure them in a desired direction (Veenman 2001). The starting point for direct instruction is that there are moments in an educational learning process when knowledge, insights, and skills that are considered meaningful and functional within a context can be taught to pupils most effectively, purposefully, and directly (Kirschner, Sweller, and Clark 2006). Direct instruction is particularly appropriate when a well-structured set of knowledge, insights, and skills must be mastered by pupils (Leenders, Naafs, and van den Oord 2010).

Indirect instruction can be defined as an approach that allows pupils to learn more autonomously—where the teacher's help is temporarily adapted to the needs of pupils' learning. It is a method to acquire the desired prior knowledge and to encourage the use of strategic approaches (Kawalkar and Vijapurkar 2011). In case of indirect instruction, the teacher coaches pupils if they are unable to continue independently or when the teacher notices that pupils are heading in a direction that would result in them becoming stuck. In principle, the open problem is structured in such a way that it is expected that pupils will be able to carry out most of the learning activities independently (Hmelo-Silver, Duncan, and Chinn 2007). The teacher must resist direct instruction but can apply verbal guidance techniques that ensure that the thinking process mainly remains with pupils (Hogan and Pressley 1997).

Building on the theoretical exploration mentioned previously, we presume a correlation between the environment, the task design, and the type of instructional method used will have an impact on the level of self-efficacy and on the evocation of SRA thinking specifically and CT more generally. Our conceptual model in figure 11.1 gives an overview of supposed relationships between independent and dependent variables that must be investigated further. Based on this conceptual model and our preliminary research, a number of research questions arise that are elaborated in the following research agenda.

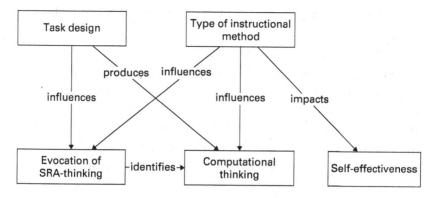

11.1   Schematic representation of the conceptual model.

TOWARD A SENSE-REASON-ACT RESEARCH AGENDA

In our previous research (Fanchamps et al. 2019), we investigated the relationship between the pedagogical environment and the development of algorithmic thinking and SRA programming skills. We found some indications that it doesn't matter which type of teacher guidance is used for pupils to apply SRA programming. But we do have some indications that pupils with experience in SRA programming are better capable of solving mathematical problems based on algorithms. It also seems that the level of self-efficacy is not influenced by the type of research design. Elaborating on these findings and our conceptual model, we want to investigate which aspects can be decisive for better solving programming tasks and an improvement of CT skills. In a broad sense, we assume that it is important to look at the nature of the task design, such as a static/dynamic programming environment and a visual/tangible programming environment.

This brings us to a first research direction of examining whether and how the nature of the programming task and the programming environment affect what pupils can learn from it. From our research and further theoretical exploration we know that pupils, when programming robots, tend to look for solutions based on linear thinking and sequential programming, even though they have been instructed how to use SRA programming (Fanchamps et al. 2019; Slangen 2016). This is striking, because these pupils have an earlier experience that showed that SRA programming is more efficient in certain programming situations. Instead, when children program robots, they predominantly choose the most obvious way that leads to an apparent good solution. Although pupils are not inclined to use SRA programming, we assume that the problem situation and task design are of significant relevance. To find out whether pupils are indeed able to apply SRA programming when they find themselves in a situation where a linear solution is no longer possible, we plan to develop an experimental setting in which a dynamic task design will be used. The assumption is that when the task is dynamic in nature, and the use of linear commands is no longer possible/sufficient, pupils have to apply SRA programming. We expect this can be achieved by designing a dynamic task environment (in opposite to a static task environment) in which the programming task is unpredictable.

Our second direction of research is distilled from theoretical exploration and practical experience, from which we know that pupils seek support by immediately reflecting the outcome of their programming assignment as feedback to the task at hand. Classroom programming can be characterized in three ways: unplugged programming, textual programming, and visual programming. Unplugged programming introduces pupils to how computers and related technology works without the concrete use of this technology (Brackmann et al. 2017). Textual programming refers to the use of a programming language by the application of written commands, specific syntax, and abstract variables (Maloney et al. 2010). Visual programming involves combining icon-based command blocks with predefined parameters, variables, and syntax that can be manipulated on the screen (Korkmaz 2018; Sapounidis, Demetriadis, and Stamelos 2015; Weintrop and Wilensky 2015). Each of these different programming environments can have either a visual and/or a tangible output. Programming robots can be defined as tangible output, while a representation of a tangible world on a screen display can be seen as visual output. It seems enlightening to investigate whether the type of programming paradigm and the output of a programming environment influence the development of aspects of CT and the use of SRA approaches. Korkmaz (2018) compares the use of Scratch and LEGO Mindstorms robots and describes a more positive contribution to thinking skills with the latter. Sapounidis, Demetriadis, and Stamelos (2015) claim that in a tangible programming environment, children were more involved, created more complicated programs, and investigated different commands and parameters more actively. We therefore expect that a more tangible output will lower the degree of abstraction and lead to more understanding about programming. We propose to investigate if there is a difference in the increase of CT skills when pupils apply SRA programming with a visual output compared to a physically perceivable output.

A third research direction should identify whether there is a difference in yield in the development of CT skills when pupils program in a visual, screen-oriented programming environment either with an SRA approach or with an linear approach, respectively with or without the use of sensor-based information, loops, conditionals, functions, and routines (Korkmaz 2018; Sapounidis, Demetriadis, and Stamelos 2015). We expect that pupils who work with the visual SRA approach will show a greater development of CT skills in comparison with pupils who work with the visual linear approach. In a visually oriented programming environment, pupils compose and construct functioning programs by merging programming commands in the correct order, and they receive only visual feedback to inform them whether a particular constructed program is valid (Weintrop and Wilensky 2015).

A fourth direction for research concerns the relationship of pedagogical aspects, such as teacher interventions and self-efficacy, and the use of SRA programming and its effect on the development of CT skills. It is reasonable that teachers will need to guide and supervise pupils while programming (Hogan and Pressley 1997) and that the teacher has influence (directly/indirectly) on the pupils' learning processes in acquiring CT skills (Buitrago Flórez et al. 2017; Lye and Koh 2014). The type of teacher support and number of teacher interventions also have a direct influence on the level of self-efficacy of the learner (Liu, Lin, and Chang 2010; Ramalingam, LaBelle, and Wiedenbeck 2004). We assume that if pupils have to find a solution to a particular programming problem by themselves, this will lead to more in-depth learning than if the teacher presents everything and pupils simply follow along (Igbaria and Iivari 1995; McWhorter 2008). Therefore it is relevant to investigate to what extent the constructed SRA solutions are related to the type and number of interventions of the teacher. The instructional needs of respondents should also determine, to a large extent, which form of guidance the teacher can best use to enable growth in CT skills through the use of SRA programming. This paves the way to create a pedagogical programming environment in which the teacher, through a joint understanding with pupils, does not always provide direction but is available for help, support, and guidance. The teacher, as a reflective practitioner, can have an indispensable role in creating meaningful learning experiences and in extending their pupils' computational skills and practical knowledge.

RECONSIDERING COMPUTATIONAL THINKING

With these directions for future research, we want to contribute to a further development of the construct of CT. Our perspective is that SRA thinking is an underexposed characteristic of CT. We propose that studying SRA programming can provide fruitful directions for a more generic development of CT.

REFERENCES

Alfieri, Louis, Patricia J. Brooks, and Naomi J. Aldrich. 2011. "Does Discovery-Based Instruction Enhance Learning?" *Journal of Educational Psychology* 103: 1–18. https://doi.org/10.1037/a0021017.

Baard, Paul P., Edward L. Deci, and Richard M. Ryan. 2004. "Intrinsic Need Satisfaction: A Motivational Basis of Performance and Well-Being in Two Work Settings." *Journal of Applied Social Psychology* 34 (10): 2045–2068. https://doi.org/10.1111/j.1559-1816.2004.tb02690.x.

Barr, David, John Harrison, and Leslie Conery. 2011. "Computational Thinking: A Digital Age Skill for Everyone." *Learning and Leading with Technology* 38 (6): 20–23.

Brackmann, Christian P., Marcos Román-González, Gregorio Robles, Jesús Moreno-León, Ana Casali, and Dante Barone. 2017. "Development of Computational Thinking Skills through Unplugged Activities in Primary School." In *Proceedings of the 12th Workshop on Primary and Secondary Computing Education*. Nijmegen, Netherlands, 65–72.

Broeck, Anja Van den, Maarten Vansteenkiste, Hans De Witte, Bart Soenens, and Willy Lens. 2010. "Capturing Autonomy, Competence, and Relatedness at Work: Construction and Initial Validation of the Work-related Basic Need Satisfaction Scale." *Journal of Occupational and Organizational Psychology* 83 (4): 981–1002. https://doi.org/10.1348/096317909X481382.

Buitrago Flórez, Francisco, Rubby Casallas, Marcela Hernández, Alejandro Reyes, Silvia Restrepo, and Giovanna Danies. 2017. "Changing a Generation's Way of Thinking: Teaching Computational Thinking through Programming." *Review of Educational Research* 87 (4): 834–860. https://doi.org/10.3102/0034654317710096.

Caci, Barbara, and Antonella D'Amico. 2002. "Children's Cognitive Abilities in Construction and Programming Robots." In *Proceedings. 11th IEEE International Workshop on Robot and Human Interactive Communication*. Berlin, 189–191.

Catlin, Dave, and John Woollard. 2014. "Educational Robots and Computational Thinking." In *Proceedings of 4th International Workshop Teaching Robotics, Teaching with Robotics & 5th International Conference Robotics in Education*. Padova, Italy, 144–151.

Dekker, Rijkje, and Marianne Elshout-Mohr. 2004. "Teacher Interventions Aimed at Mathematical Level Raising During Collaborative Learning." *Educational Studies in Mathematics* 56 (1): 39–65. https://doi.org/10.1023/B:EDUC.0000028402.10122.ff.

Demetriou, Georgios A. 2011. "Mobile Robotics in Education and Research." In *Mobile Robots-Current Trends*, edited by Zoran Gacovski, 27–48. Rijeka, Croatia: IntechOpen.

Dignath, Charlotte, and Gerhard Büttner. 2008. "Components of Fostering Self-Regulated Learning among Students. A Meta-Analysis on Intervention Studies at Primary and Secondary School Level." *Metacognition Learning* 3: 231–264. https://doi.org/10.1007/s11409-008-9029-x.

Dignath-van Ewijk, Charlotte, and Greetje Van der Werf. 2012. "What Teachers Think about Self-Regulated Learning: Investigating Teacher Beliefs and Teacher

Behavior of Enhancing Students' Self-Regulation." *Education Research Journal*: 1–10. https://doi.org/10.1155/2012/741713.

Dragone, Mauro, Ruadhan O'Donoghue, John J. Leonard, Gregory O'Hare, Brian Duffy, Andrew Patrikalakis, and Jacques Leederkerken. 2005. "Robot Soccer Anywhere: Achieving Persistent Autonomous Navigation, Mapping, and Object Vision Tracking in Dynamic Environments." In *Proceedings SPIE 5827, Opto-Ireland 2005: Photonic Engineering*. Dublin, Ireland.

Fanchamps, Nardie. 2016. "De Invloed van SRA Programmeren op Mathematisch Redeneren en Zelfeffectiviteit met Lego Robotica in Twee Instructievarianten [The Influence of SRA Programming on Mathematical Reasoning and Self-Efficacy Using LEGO Robotics in Two Types of Instruction]." Master's thesis, Open Universiteit Heerlen, Netherlands.

Fanchamps, Nardie, Lou Slangen, Paul Hennissen, and Marcus Specht. 2019. "The Influence of SRA Programming on Algorithmic Thinking and Self-Efficacy Using LEGO Robotics in Two Types of Instruction." *International Journal of Technology and Design Education*: 1–20. https://doi.org/10.1007/s10798-019-09559-9.

Gregg, Chris, Luther Tychonievich, James Cohoon, and Kim Hazelwood. 2012. "EcoSim: A Language and Experience Teaching Parallel Programming in Elementary School." In *Proceedings of the 43rd ACM Technical Symposium on Computer Science Education*. Raleigh, NC, 51–56.

Hmelo-Silver, Cindy E., Ravit Golan Duncan, and Clark A. Chinn. 2007. "Scaffolding and Achievement in Problem-Based and Inquiry Learning: A Response to Kirschner, Sweller, and Clark (2006)." *Educational Psychologist* 42 (2): 99–107.

Hogan, Kathleen, and Michael Pressley. 1997. *Scaffolding Student Learning*. Cambridge, MA: Brookline Books.

Igbaria, Magid, and Juhani Iivari. 1995. "The Effects of Self-Efficacy on Computer Usage." *OMEGA International Journal of Management Science* 23 (6): 587–605.

Jonassen, David H. 2000. *Computers as Mindtools for Schools: Engaging Critical Thinking*. Columbus, OH: Pearson Prentice Hall.

Jonassen, David H. 2006. *Modeling with Technology: Mindtools for Conceptual Change*. Upper Saddle River, NJ: Pearson Merrill Prentice Hall.

Kawalkar, Aisha, and Jyotsna Vijapurkar. 2011. "Scaffolding Science Talk: The Role of Teachers' Questions in the Inquiry Classroom." *International Journal of Science Education* 35 (12): 1–43. https://doi.org/10.1080/09500693.2011.604684.

Kennisnet [Knowledge Net]. 2016. "Computational thinking in het Nederlandse onderwijs [Dutch Education]." Zoetermeer, Netherlands.

Kirschner, Paul A., John Sweller, and Richard E. Clark. 2006. "Why Minimal Guidance During Instruction Does Not Work: An Analysis of the Failure of Constructivist, Discovery, Problem-Based, Experiential, and Inquiry-Based Teaching." *Educational Psychologist* 41 (2): 75–86. https://doi.org/10.1207/s15326985ep4102_1.

Korkmaz, Özgen. 2018. "The Effect of Scratch-And Lego Mindstorms Ev3-Based Pro-gramming Activities on Academic Achievement, Problem-Solving Skills and Logical-Mathematical Thinking Skills of Students." *Malaysian Online Journal of Educational Sciences* 4 (3): 73–88.

Leenders, Yvonne, Ferdy Naafs, and Ingrid van den Oord. 2010. *Effectieve instructie. Leren lesgeven met het activerende, directe instructiemodel [Effective instruction. Learn to teach with the activating, direct instruction model]*. Amersfoort, Netherlands: CPS.

Liu, Eric Zhi Feng, Chun Hung Lin, and Chiung Sui Chang. 2010. "Student Satisfac-tion and Self-Efficacy in a Cooperative Robotics Course." *Social Behavior and Person-ality* 38 (8): 1135–1146. https://doi.org/10.2224/sbp.2010.38.8.1135.

Lye, Sze Yee, and Joyce Hwee Ling Koh. 2014. "Review on Teaching and Learning of Computational Thinking through Programming: What Is Next for K–12?" *Computers in Human Behavior* 41: 51–61. https://doi.org/10.1016/j.chb.2014.09.012.

Maloney, John, Mitchel Resnick, Natalie Rusk, Brian Silverman, and Evelyn Eastmond. 2010. "The Scratch Programming Language and Environment." *ACM Transactions on Computing Education (TOCE)*, 10 (4): 1–15. https://doi.org/10.1145/1868358.1868363.

McWhorter, William Isaac. 2008. *The Effectiveness of Using LEGO Mindstorms Robot-ics Activities to Influence Self-Regulated Learning in a University Introductory Computer Programming Course*. Citeseer.

Pea, Roy D., and Midian Kurland. 2007. "On the Cognitive Effects Learning Com-puter Programming." *New Ideas in Psychology* 2 (2): 31.

Petrou, Argyroula, and Angelique Dimitrakopoulou. 2003. "Is Synchronous Com-puter Mediated Collaborative Problem-Solving 'Justified' Only When by Distance? Teachers' Point of Views and Interventions with Co-located Groups, During Every Day Class Activities." In *Designing for Change in Networked Learning Environments, Pro-ceedings of the International Conference on Computer Support for Collaborative Learning 2003*, edited by Barbara Wasson, Sten Ludvigsen, and Ulrich Hoppe, 1–10.

Ramalingam, Vennila, Deborah LaBelle, and Susan Wiedenbeck. 2004. "Self-Efficacy and Mental Models in Learning to Program." In *Proceedings of the 9th Annual SIGCSE Confer-ence on Innovation and Technology in Computer Science Education*. Leeds, UK, 171–175.

Rekimoto, Jun. 2000. "Multiple-Computer User Interfaces: Beyond the Desktop Direct Manipulation Environments." In *CHI EA '00: CHI '00 Extended Abstracts on Human Factors in Computing Systems*. The Hague, Netherlands, 6–7.

Rovai, Alfred P., Mervyn J. Wighting, and Robert Lucking. 2004. "The Classroom and School Community Inventory: Development, Refinement, and Validation of a Self-Report Measure for Educational Research." *Internet and Higher Education* 7 (4): 263–280. https://doi.org/10.1016/j.iheduc.2004.09.001.

Sapounidis, Theodosios, Stavros Demetriadis, and Ioannis Stamelos. 2015. "Evaluat-ing Children Performance with Graphical and Tangible Robot Programming Tools."

Personal and Ubiquitous Computing 19 (1): 225–237. https://doi.org/10.1007/s00779 -014-0774-3.

Sentance, Sue, and Andrew Csizmadia. 2017. "Computing in the Curriculum: Challenges and Strategies from a Teacher's Perspective." *Education and Information Technologies* 22 (2): 469–495. https://doi.org/10.1007/s10639-016-9482-0.

Serafini, G. 2011. "Teaching Programming at Primary Schools: Visions, Experiences, and Long-Term Research Prospects." In *Informatics in Schools. Contributing to 21st Century Education. ISSEP 2011. Lecture Notes in Computer Science (vol 7013).* Berlin, Heidelberg: Springer, 143–154.

Silk, Eli, Christian Schunn, and Robin Shoop. 2009. "Synchronized Robot Dancing: Motivating Efficiency & Meaning in Problem-solving with Robotics." *Robot Magazine Carnegie Mellon Robotics Academy* 17: 74–77.

Slangen, Lou. 2016. "Teaching Robotics in Primary School." PhD, Eindhoven University of Technology. https://pure.tue.nl/ws/files/25754482/20160630_CO_Slangen.pdf.

Slangen, Lou, Nardie Fanchamps, and Piet Kommers. 2008. "A Case Study about Supporting the Development of Thinking by Means of ICT and Concretisation Tools." *International Journal of Continuing Engineering Education and Life-Long Learning* 18 (3): 305–322.

Slangen, Lou, Hanno van Keulen, and Koeno Gravemeijer. 2011. "What Pupils Can Learn from Working with Robotic Direct Manipulation Environments." *International Journal of Technology and Design Education* 21 (4): 449–469. https://doi.org/10.1007 /s10798-010-9130-8.

Slangen, Lou, Hanno van Keulen, and Wim Jochems. 2009. "De bijdrage van Direct Manipulation Environments aan de ontwikkeling van technische geletterdheid in de basisschool [The contribution of Direct Manipulation Environments to the development of technical literacy in primary school]." *HBO-Kennisbank.*

Slangen, Lou, and Ellen Rohaan. 2018. "Programmeren en robotica [Programming and robotics]." In *Onderzoekend en ontwerpend de wereld ontdekken,* edited by Tycho Malmberg, Ellen Rohaan, Sara Van Duijn and Remke Klapwijk, 18. Groningen, Netherlands: Noordhoff Uitgevers bv.

Slangen, Lou, and Peter Sloep. 2005. "Mind Tools Contributing to an ICT-rich Learning Environment for Technology Education in Primary Schools." *International Journal of Continuing Engineering Education and Life Long Learning* 15 (3–6): 225–239.

SLO. 2017. "Curriculum van de toekomst [Curriculum of the future]." SLO: Nationaal Expertisecentrum Leerplanontwikkeling. Accessed June 17, 2019. http://curriculumvandetoekomst.slo.nl/21e-eeuwse-vaardigheden.

Spin, Linda. 2015. "Zelfsturing door leerlingen in het basisonderwijs [Self-management by pupils in primary education]." *DaltonVisie, 4* (1): 18–21. Zwolle, Netherlands: KPZ.

Stevens, Luc. 2004. *Zin in School*. Amersfoort, Netherlands: CPS.

Toh, Lai Poh Emily, Albert Causo, Pei-Wen Tzuo, I-Ming Chen, and Song Huat Yeo. 2016. "A Review on the Use of Robots in Education and Young Children." *Educational Technology & Society* 19 (2): 148–163.

Valcke, Martin. 1985. "Praktische ervaringen met het leren programmeren in de klas—Karakteristieken van de leerkrachtinterventie [Practical experiences in learning to code in the classroom—Characteristics of teacher intervention]." In *Programmeertalen en courseware-aanmaak*, edited by W Decoo, J Heyvaert and R Jansen, 61–90. Gent, Belgium.

Veenman, Simon. 2001. *Directe Instructie [Direct Instruction]*. Nijmegen, Netherlands: Katholieke Universiteit Nijmegen.

Voogt, Joke, and Natalie Pareja Roblin. 2010. *21st Century Skills*. Enschede, Netherlands: University of Twente, Department of Curriculum Design and Educational Innovation.

Vosniadou, Stella, Christos Ioannides, Aggeliki Dimitrakopoulou, and Efi Papademetriou. 2001. "Designing Learning Environments to Promote Conceptual Change in Science." *Learning and Instruction* 11 (4–5): 381–419. https://doi.org/10.1016/S0959 -4752(00)00038-4.

Wang, Danli, Tingting Wang, and Zhen Liu. 2014. "A Tangible Programming Tool for Children to Cultivate Computational Thinking." *The Scientific World Journal* 2014: 1–10. https://doi.org/10.1155/2014/428080.

Weintrop, David, and Uri Wilensky. 2015. "To Block or Not to Block, That is the Question: Students' Perceptions of Blocks-Based Programming." In *Proceedings of the 14th International Conference on Interaction Design and Children*. Medford, MA, 199–208.

Wing, Jeannette M. 2006. "Computational Thinking." *Communications of the ACM* 49 (3): 33–35. https://doi.org/10.1145/1118178.1118215.

Wong, Lawson L. S. 2014. "Rethinking the Sense-Plan-Act Abstraction: A Model Attention and Selection Framework for Task-Relevant Estimation." In *Workshops at the Twenty-Eighth AAAI Conference on Artificial Intelligence*. Quebec, Canada, 71–72.

Wyeth, Peta, Mark Venz, and Gordon Wyeth. 2003. "Scaffolding Children's Robot Building and Programming Activities." In *RoboCup 2003: Robot Soccer World Cup VII. RoboCup 2003. Lecture Notes in Computer Science, vol 3020*, edited by Daniel Polani, Brett Browning, Andrea Bonarini, and Kazuo Yoshida, 308–319. Berlin: Springer.

Yadav, Aman, Sarah Gretter, Jon Good, and Tamika McLean. 2017. "Computational Thinking in Teacher Education." In *Emerging Research, Practice, and Policy on Computational Thinking*, edited by Peter J. Rich and Charles B. Hodges, 205–220. Cham, Switzerland: Springer.

Yadav, Aman, Hai Hong, and Chris Stephenson. 2016. "Computational Thinking for All: Pedagogical Approaches to Embedding 21st Century Problem Solving in K–12 Classrooms." *TechTrends* 60 (6): 565–568. https://doi.org/10.1007/s11528-016-0087-7.

12

COMPUTATIONAL THINKING IN THE INTERDISCIPLINARY ROBOTIC GAME
THE CHARM OF STEAM

Ju-Ling Shih

INTRODUCTION

Computational thinking (CT) allows students to think critically, systematically, and algorithmically to solve problems that are either ordinary or intricate. Hence, it is important to integrate computational ideas into other subjects in school so that students can comprehend, define, and seek appropriate solutions with a wider array of knowledge from various disciplines. This interdisciplinary instructional approach has been widely practiced with science, technology, engineering, arts, and mathematics (STEAM), robots, and maker education.

The key educational matters are the principles and strategies to design a well-rounded curriculum, to conduct dynamic learning activities, and to evaluate students' performance in the physically and socially active learning scenario. This chapter attempts to tackle these issues by presenting a purpose-built robotic game, <STEMport>, along with a conceptual framework that illustrates the following four components:

1. The synergic relationship between CT and interdisciplinary activity. In the section "Computational Thinking with Interdisciplinary Learning," we posit the existence of situative CT that links specific CT and generic CT to contextual interdisciplinary domain learning.

2. The innovative design of the instructional paradigm. In the section "Computational Thinking with Robotic Games," we provide justifications

for the innovation of the particular instructional paradigm using visual programing to perform agent-based computation to facilitate game-based learning.

3. The creation of an interdisciplinary robotic game. In the sections "Educational Implementation" and "Pedagogical Benefits of the CHARM of STEAM," we outline the rationale of the learning game <STEMport>" and the pedagogical underpinning of the extended curriculum in which modules are amenable to users' needs, but at the same time illustrate the core value, the breadth, and the generality of our approach. The <STEMport> learning environment: (a) supports students regardless of their levels of competences; (b) initiates and motivates students to engage with programming; (c) intrigues students to pursue further domain learning; and (d) elevates students' strategic thinking in a constructive fashion.

4. The development of various means of student evaluations. In the section "Evaluations of Students' Computational Thinking Performances," we elaborate the possibilities of multiple assessments that encompass cognitions, affects, and skills of CT, and present preliminary research results.

Finally, in the section "Discussion and Conclusion," we use empirical evidence to sustain the effectiveness of our proposed conceptual framework and the creation of a student-centered learning environment.

This game encompasses more than simple programming skills and is intended to strengthen knowledge of multiple disciplines as well as to promote social interactions that are central to the twenty-first-century 5C skills—communication, collaboration, critical thinking, creativity, and complex problem-solving. <STEMport> can be used as a targeted course with specific purposes or as a mixed-age group activity that serves as an extracurricular event. It can be an activity at the beginning of a curriculum to spark students' learning motivation; a central unit of learning that guides students to construct knowledge; or be the concluding activity of a curriculum that demonstrates students' learning outcomes. The following sections will set forth a general practice of the CT-based robotic game <STEMport> followed by the demonstrations of the extended use of the course to serve diverse needs of age, goals, proficiency level, personality traits, or various instructional conditions.

CONCEPTUAL FRAMEWORK

COMPUTATIONAL THINKING WITH INTERDISCIPLINARY LEARNING

CT is a concept originating from computer science in which computer language is used to manipulate computers to solve daily life problems (Wing 2006). CT can be divided into specific CT—the composition of computer programming language (e.g., loop, if-else)—and generic CT—the cognitive abilities to apply problem-solving methods in ways that a computer could execute (Wing 2014). These can be understood as "CT as programming" and "CT as problem-solving," respectively.

Specific CT is more widely practiced in education, with such examples as code.org, or Scratch. The goal is to learn the principles of programming and to use programming to execute the functions of computers or robots. The use of generic CT in education is a bit more complex and abstract to design for, since it involves the problem-solving process that requires thinking abilities other than programming skills. In generic CT, computers may not be needed because the computation process happens within human brains rather than in the computers. Wing (2008) said that humans process information; humans compute. Generic CT is an approach to designing systems and understanding human behavior that draws on concepts fundamental to computing. It is a model and a process of thinking that uses the basic concepts of computer science to solve problems (Wing 2006). CT is a type of analytical thinking that employs mathematical and engineering thinking to understand and solve complex problems within the constraints of the real world (Voskoglou and Buckley 2012). Therefore, the practice of CT combines logical, arithmetic, efficiency, scientific, and innovative thinking together with qualities such as creativity and intuition (Curzon et al. 2009). Generic CT can be applied to the use of information technology, coding, and robotics (Rogers and Portsmore 2004). For example, Atmatzidou and Demetriadis (2016) showed their educational results in teaching kids programming to mobilize LEGO NXT robots for specific functions or to carry out tasks. Other schools may teach robots to move, line trace, carry balls to certain points, or place bump sensors.

The benefits of using STEM and robotics for generic CT education are manifold. A guided instruction approach using robots facilitates teamwork

(Chambers, Carbonaro, and Rex 2007), develops conceptual understanding, enhances critical thinking (Blanchard, Freiman, and Lirrete-Pitre 2010), promotes higher-order learning in the domains of mathematics and science (Petre and Price 2004), allows the students to develop procedural thinking through programming (Nourbakhsh et al. 2005), and encourages ways of algorithmically solving problems and the acquisition of technological fluency (Papert 1980). Related research (e.g., Bers et al. 2014) obtaining positive research outcomes on CT and STEM demonstrates that children between four and six years old can build simple robotics projects. STEM is a cohesive learning paradigm that is not limited to certain subjects but includes other domains such as social studies, English language arts, visual art, and more (Breiner et al. 2012). It uses an interdisciplinary approach (Barak and Assal 2018) by breaking down the discipline-independent teaching and making connections to the context of the real world (Breiner et al. 2012; Honey, Pearson, and Schweingruber 2014).

Nevertheless, Frymier, Shulman, and Houser (1996) explained that, in a classroom context, students usually have little power to determine the activities to be conducted, which teachers typically control. The same is true for many robotics curricula that guide students to code for uniform tasks or simply learn coding functions. For example, in the program by Chen et al. (2017), students were taught to program robots to do actions such as wave and sit down.

We take a step further and have attempted to create a learning environment where CT is applied in conjunction with interdisciplinary learning. When CT thus becomes situative, it has features that are distinct from generic CT: (1) It uses specific CT and generic CT in combination, writing programming and solving problems at the same time. (2) It is practiced in a contextual situation, normally a theme-based scenario that emphasizes domain knowledge correspondence. (3) Problems in the situation are fluid and dynamic; instead of conducting uniformed tasks, students have to respond to spontaneous situations in context. (4) CT is no longer the learning goal but the tool (figure 12.1). In a situative CT learning scenario, students solve contextual problems by accessing the appropriate resources and strategies to be used.

For those CT curricula in which students are encouraged not just to routinely follow instructions but to creatively find novel approaches to

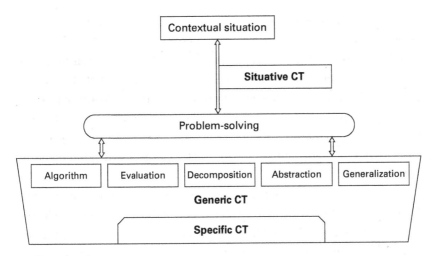

12.1   The conceptual framework of CT with interdisciplinary learning.

the activities (e.g., Brennan and Resnick 2012; Deschryver and Yadav 2015; Voogt et al. 2015), students are more empowered in the learning process. Four empowerment components can increase the likelihood of successful task completion: (1) viewing the purpose of a programming task as meaningful, (2) seeing impact from completing the tasks, (3) believing they can creatively complete them, and (4) perceiving their competence to complete them (Kong, Chiu, and Lai 2018).

COMPUTATIONAL THINKING WITH ROBOTIC GAMES

Robotics provides a very rich and attractive learning environment for STEM education (Barak and Assal 2018) and provides a fun and exciting learning environment because of its hands-on nature and the integration of technology (Afari and Khine 2017). Robotics has the inclusive nature to achieve what situative CT needs, while it creates an environment where children can interact with the context and work with real-world problems.

To activate the curriculum further and enrich the hands-on constructionism of Papert (1980) and Vygotsky's sociocognitive interactions, game-based learning (GBL) is an appropriate means to help students transform from passive to active learners, constructing new knowledge by collaborating with their peers and developing essential mental skills by acting as researchers.

GBL refers to an educational system that implements games or game elements as a motivational driver for students (Park et al. 2019). It is perceived as a potentially engaging form of supplementary learning that could enhance the educational process and has been used at all levels of education, including primary education. Motivation is a learners' willingness to make an extended commitment to engage in a new area of learning (Gee 2003), so many teachers now incorporate GBL to embed learning with carefully designed curriculum so that students learn spontaneously and repeatedly.

The spirit of GBL is not only to allow learning to happen in a fun process (Perrotta et al. 2013) but also to challenge and stimulate higher level learning. Students actively explore the issues assigned by teachers from various perspectives, work with peers to find answers, and then develop the skills to communicate, coordinate, and engage in creative thinking and problem-solving. Within those problem-solving spaces and challenges, students gain the sense of achievement (Qian and Clark 2016). The experiential activities allow students to be more immersed in the learning scenarios, enhancing learning effectiveness and encouraging students to get wider and deeper knowledge and skills. Students learn infinitely more by accessing extended sources, creating strategies for overcoming obstacles, and understanding complex systems through experimentation. GBL also promotes learning in an engaging and entertaining manner to underpin the skills and attitudes of CT (Apostolellis et al. 2014).

EDUCATIONAL IMPLEMENTATION

DESIGN OF THE ROBOTIC GAME <STEMPORT>

<STEMport> was designed by our research team based on the historical context of the Great Voyage (Shih et al. 2017). It is an interdisciplinary game that embeds STEM educational concepts and computational practices. In the game, a large world map (600 by 400 cm) shows the geographical area from Europe eastward to Asia, presenting the territorial scope of the European Age of Discovery in the seventeenth century (figure 12.2). Colonies owned by respective countries are identified by colored symbols on the map, along with specific spices produced in the locations. Students are distributed into five groups, each role-playing one of the European countries—England, the

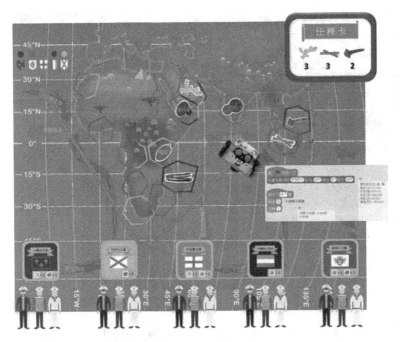

12.2 Game design of <STEMport>.

Netherlands, Portugal, Spain, and France. Robots represent their ships, identified with matching color lights. Since each country has different political and economic status in history, all the ships come with predefined parameters showing discrete strengths and weaknesses. The Dutch ship is faster, the English stronger, the Spanish bigger, and the Portuguese has the most available ports.

Roles in each country group such as navigator, captain, trader, and warrior are decided by the students, so they all have responsibilities in the game. The navigator is the only one who can step onto the large map to physically measure the distance from one point to another; the captain handles the coding job; the trader manages the spice trading processes; the warrior is responsible for robot competitions. The groups take turns to sail their robotic ships by writing block coding, going to designated colonies to perform tasks. The first country to complete its tasks wins the game (figure 12.3).

We initially chose the mBot robotics platform simply out of random convenience. However, we found that its features led to its exclusive use

12.3 Game play of <STEMport>.

with <STEMport>. First, mBot robots are on wheels; unmovable robots are not possible, legged robots inappropriate, and those with sails not convenient. Second, its size is appropriate in comparison with the map, and sailing routes are in a workable range. Third, the robots can be assembled from parts, so an engineering course can be optionally included. Fourth, accessories can be attached to most so that the students can aggregate them as weapons. Fifth, it comes with its own programming software, mBlock, that can easily connect to the robot. Finally, it is in an affordable price range and widely known on the market, so students can extend their learning after class.

COMPUTATIONAL PRACTICES

In the game, the students choose their target destinations, estimate the distances from the starting points to the destinations, use limited game points to move their robots in terms of seconds of moving time, and decide on actions to take, either trading or going into battles to obtain spices. While the students are completing all of these game tasks, they are applying problem-solving CT skills.

Selby, Dorling, and Woollard (2014) defined five core concepts of CT: (1) Algorithm is to the ability to develop rules that can solve similar problems step by step and be implemented repeatedly. (2) Evaluation is the process of ensuring an algorithmic solution is a good one. (3) Decomposition is a way of thinking about problems, algorithms, artifacts, processes, and systems in terms of their parts. The separate parts can then be understood, solved, developed, and evaluated separately. This makes complex problems easier to solve and large systems easier to design. (4) Abstraction is another way to make problems or systems easier to think about. It simply involves hiding details and removing unnecessary complexities. (5) Generalization is a way of quickly solving new problems based on previous problems solved—taking an algorithm that solves specific problems and adapting it to solve a whole class of similar problems.

The problems of the <STEMport> game are situated in the contextual scenario, which are complex and immersive. The students first "decompose" the task requirements with the game rules and try to complete the tasks in predefined parameters and in limited rounds. Then, they apply "algorithm" skills to calculate the distance, angle, speed of the navigations; define the navigation routes; and do "abstraction" to transform the measurements into computer programming codes. After they take actions, the students "evaluate" their programming performances by analyzing the differences between the predicted paths and the actual paths of the robots, and adjust their following actions. As the students solicit the main strategies for the game, they "generalize" the conceptual patterns for the subsequent rounds. The process of game also matches the general problem-solving stages such as defining problems, searching for solutions, implementing solutions, and evaluating results. The students are immersed in the scenario, identifying with their country's strengths and weaknesses, managing the resources around them, including knowledge, peers, and strategies to search for solutions, then reviewing the effects of the strategies after actions. These are the essential logistic and creative skills of CT.

With the instructional design for game-based learning, the game offers coding-based and problem-solving-oriented CT practices at the same time. As Kong, Chiu, and Lai (2018) described for CT education, the programming environment should be created to achieve the instructional goal to cultivate students' CT abilities during programming activities by enabling them to concentrate on the problem-solving process as they learn. The robotics platform also offers a wide range of challenges and opportunities for learners to develop disruptive thinking, innovative ideas, and other learning skills needed both in the classroom and outside the school.

For elementary-level learners, the coding interface is preconfigured, showing only the needed functions while hiding the rest, and making ready needed functions while leaving only the parameters for them to fill in. For higher-level learners, different categories of coding functions and higher levels algorithm can be taught. Coding functions such as motion, sensing, control, event, operators, data chart, and so on would provide students more options to manipulate and create gaming environments.

The game can also be transformed using several levels of difficulties and various forms for different purposes, using game mechanisms. A higher level of programming skills can be reinforced by changing the game rules that require the players to use commands such as loop, if-then, else, and so on. For example, obstacles can be added, such as pirate ships or storms, so that the players would have to code the robots to go around them when encountered. Or, when the ships encounter ocean currents, their ships would be accelerated or decelerated when they are proceeding with or against the flows. Hence, the students have to come up with new strategies to cope with the emergent situations. The process of getting to know the geographic variables and their influences on the ships, and to recognize the patterns of change, is the process of modeling in which relationships between the object, agent, and variables are established.

For increasing game complexities, each country can choose ship parts such as hull, oar, mast, and weapons, which would comprise their total ship parameters, including propulsion power, cargo capacity, deceleration, firing distance, arm force, and sailing duration.

Gaming strategies that link programming with contextual problems that require both generic and specific CT skills are inseparable in this game. The robot is a tool to carry on tasks and solve problems. Robots are the avatars of the students, with which they take actions. In this way, CT skills become explicit actions that are observable and evaluable.

PEDAGOGICAL BENEFITS OF THE CHARM OF STEAM

This robotic game-based activity is unlike others where students code for uniform tasks to compete for higher efficiency, speed, or design of robots. Instead, <STEMport> opens up an exploratory environment in which students start with unequal powers and distinct goals between groups and apply critical thinking skills to find appropriate methods to achieve those goals. In the game, each country has tasks to obtain three spices. The first spice can be accessed by all countries, the second spice can be obtained by single country, and the third spice is owned by the other countries from the single one. With that condition set up, students have to cooperate or compete with each other to obtain the spice from other countries. They can choose to trade, build coalitions, or attack, fight, and battle for the spices. The game encourages the students to have creative solutions in terms of route, communication, negotiation, and competition. In this way, the twenty-first century 5C skills are induced and nurtured.

Coopetition (cooperation and competition) is a common social phenomenon and a rule for achieving success. In the teaching environment, teachers often use competitive psychology to stimulate students' learning motivation to enhance their learning effectiveness (Lin et al. 2017). Thus, <STEMport> has adopted the strategic game mechanism that allows learners to cooperate and compete with other players to successfully carry on their tasks.

Along with the game, we have prepared a curriculum for students' knowledge and skill extensions, such as unplugged coding, coding with a block editor, coding for robots, making and crafting the robotic ships, as well as an advanced issue-based version, the summit game. This is a curriculum of STEAM, the science-oriented disciplines, connected to the humanity-oriented disciplines, CHARM, which includes culture, humanity, adventure education, reading, and maker. The CHARM of STEAM implies that the spirit of interdisciplinary learning is humanity. By providing the geographical context and historical content, the students are also nurtured with the social scientific and humanistic spirit. It is to our understanding and experience that the humanistic context has a large influence on students' attention, extension, and creation in the learning of CT, robotic education, and interdisciplinary contents.

The game transforms the usual lecture-type teaching into an interesting learning scenario. In accord with educational theories such as situated learning, social cognition, and constructivism, we aimed at turning passive classroom learning into one that embraces interaction, participation, exploration, and knowledge construction. The four learning modes—namely, narrative, investigative, strategic, and explorative—are implemented. Interdisciplinary learning is defined in this game to refer to "doing something that requires knowledge and skills from various subjects." Instead of distributing the tasks into classes of different subjects, the students are doing one thing to learn many things.

The game is based on sociocultural constructivism, with which students are situated in contextual learning scenarios. It is different from virtual scenarios such as simulation. The physical world of learning creates a real community of practice, in which collaboration and healthy competition are encouraged. In the gaming process, students work together, play their parts, construct meaning of their own, experience increased motivation, and are stimulated to pursue extended learning that goes beyond the game. They change their habits of treating complex problems and change their way of looking at the world. With the practice of CT and problem-solving, they learn systematic thinking and analytical thinking.

EVALUATIONS OF STUDENTS' COMPUTATIONAL THINKING PERFORMANCES

There are many methods to look at students' CT performances. CT-related evaluations can include knowledge testing, motivation scales, gender differences, group dynamics, and personality traits. In this section, a few tools that we used in previous studies are introduced with brief report of their results followed by extended discussions and implications.

COMPUTATIONAL THINKING QUESTIONNAIRE

A CT questionnaire can be used before and after the game-based learning course as the pre-test and post-test. The results of the questionnaires can be tested through statistical means to evaluate the differences after the instructional intervention. To see whether students' CT skills would influence their gaming results, cross-analyses were done with the students' gaming outcomes.

The CT questionnaire used in our previous studies (Huang, Huang, et al. 2019) was designed based on the relevant literature (e.g., Atmatzidou and Demetriadis 2016; Curzon et al. 2014; Dagiené, Sentence, and Stupuriené 2017; Selby, Dorling, and Woollard 2014) and taking the principles of the Bebras International Challenge on Informatics and Computational Thinking as the main reference. To produce a reliable questionnaire, two academic researchers specializing in education validated the items twice (Chu, Liang, and Tsai 2019). The questionnaire includes the five dimensions of computational thinking: algorithm, evaluation, decomposition, abstraction, and generalization. Each dimension composes five questions with total of twenty-five questions in the questionnaire. Questions include: "I will try to dissect the big problems into small parts" to test the students' perception to the decomposition skills; "I will try to think of the most efficient way to solve the problems" to test their perception to the evaluation skills; "I will figure out the detailed steps for problem-solving" for the algorithm skills; "I will try to find out the key factor of the problem" and "I will try to use previous experience to solve new problems" for the abstraction and generalization skills, respectively. The total correlation analysis showed that the correlation coefficients of the overall divergence ranged from 0.42 to 0.61 and both reached significant ($p < .01$), which was a medium-high correlation, indicating that each dimension has a certain degree of correlation. The reliability Cronbach's alpha of this scale is 0.91. The reliabilities for the five dimensions ranged from 0.74 to 0.83. The pattern coefficient of all dimensions is above 0.4. It shows that the questionnaire has good reliability and validity.

In one of our studies, fifth-grade students in an elementary school in southern Taiwan were invited. There were sixty-five boys and thirty-four girls with a total of ninety-nine students participating in the GBL. It is found that students' algorithmic skills can best predict their learning outcome (Huang, Huang, et al. 2019); therefore algorithmic skill was used as the main predictor to categorize students into high algorithmic (HA) and low algorithmic (LA) groups (tables 12.1 and 12.2).

COMPUTATIONAL THINKING SKILLS

To know what CT skills are important and required in which stage of the game, and how the CT skills influenced the students' gaming outcome, regression analysis was conducted using the five dimensions of the CT skills as predictors in our previous study (Huang et al. 2019; tables 12.1 and 12.2).

The analysis result showed that in the beginning round, decomposition skill was essential because the students need to know how to dissect the navigation routes into small portions for the coding purposes. In the second and third rounds, generalization skill takes effect—students needed to refer to their previous strategies to progress in the game. In the end round of the game, decomposition skill was no longer important because the students were supposed to be very familiar with the game mechanism and programming. On the other hand, evaluation skill showed positive effect, indicating that the students learned the strengths and weakness of various strategies and were able to choose appropriate ones for their victories.

The correlation test results also showed that the students' skills of decomposition and evaluation were closely correlated to their gaming outcomes. Students with high algorithm skill performed better than those with lower algorithm skill. Since algorithmic thinking is the core concept of CT, the fundamental education should place more focus on algorithmic thinking so that students can have stronger problem-solving and strategic-thinking abilities.

STEM ATTITUDE QUESTIONNAIRE

We were curious to see if there were other factors that might influence students' gaming outcome other than CT. We explored students' awareness

Table 12.1 The first-round coefficients of each CT dimension with regression analysis

Model		Unstandardized coefficients		Standardized coefficients	t
		B	Std. error	Beta	
HA	Algorithm	−6.09	4.379	−.21	−1.39
	Evaluation	−3.28	3.377	−.14	−.97
	Decomposition	7.99	2.700	.45	2.96*
	Generalization	−5.81	2.990	−.30	−1.94
	Abstraction	.391	3.572	.02	.11
LA	Algorithm	−9.29	8.34	−.24	−1.11
	Evaluation	.313	6.94	.01	.05
	Decomposition	1.58	4.53	.08	.35
	Generalization	−3.51	4.49	−.18	−.78
	Abstraction	4.29	5.37	.22	.79

*$p < .01$
Source: Huang et al. (2019).

of the importance of STEM learning and attitudes to STEM learning. The STEM attitude questionnaire could be implemented before or after the game. In the study (Huang, Shih, et al. 2019), the STEM questionnaire was distributed with the post-test of CT, and the results of the questionnaires were cross-analyzed with Pearson Correlation Coefficient method.

The STEM attitude questionnaire was designed based on the relevant literature (e.g., Lou et al. 2009; Unfried et al. 2015). The questionnaire includes three dimensions, namely mathematics, science, and ET (engineering and technology). There are nine questions in the mathematics dimension, nine questions in the science dimension, and twelve questions in the ET dimension with total of thirty questions in the questionnaire. The questionnaire includes questions such as, "In the future, I could do harder math problems" to test the students' attitude to mathematics; "Science will be important to me in my future work" to test the students' attitude to science; "I am good at building and fixing things" and "I

Table 12.2 The fourth-round coefficients of each CT dimension with regression analysis

Model		Unstandardized coefficients		Standardized coefficients	
		B	Std. error	Beta	t
HA	Algorithm	3.82	4.39	.14	.87
	Evaluation	7.60	3.39	.35	2.25*
	Decomposition	−9.18	2.65	−.54	−3.46**
	Generalization	3.09	3.19	.17	.97
	Abstraction	−4.12	3.51	−.19	−1.18
LA	Algorithm	−5.15	7.48	−.18	−.69
	Evaluation	−.38	5.99	−.02	−.06
	Decomposition	6.58	4.26	.47	1.54
	Generalization	−5.96	4.63	−.43	−1.29
	Abstraction	3.53	5.21	.28	.68

$*p < .05$, $**p < .01$

Source: Huang et al. (2019).

would like to use creativity and innovation in my future work" to test the students' attitude to ET. The reliability Cronbach's alpha of these three dimensions scale ranged from .568 to .897. The value is above .5.

In the study, a t-test was used to analyze the STEM attitude questionnaire results between high algorithm (HA) and low algorithm (LA) groups. It showed that the students with high algorithmic skills have better STEM attitude than those with lower algorithmic skills. It also showed that the interdisciplinary robotic game is significant for HA students' CT skills in the aspects of decomposition, abstraction, and generalization. Although the LA students' STEM attitudes are not related to CT, the gaming results show that the robotic game could raise their learning motivations. In particular, the LA students were highly motivated in their problem-solving tasks even without extrinsic rewards and scores.

Further exploration into the relationship of students' CT skills and STEM attitudes (table 12.3) has shown that all STEM aspects are correlated

Table 12.3 Correlations between CT and STEM

Fact	N	STEM	Pearson correlation	Sig. (2-tailed)
Abstraction	94	Math	.147	.157
		Science	.165	.111
		ET	.142	.171
Algorithm	94	Math	.148	.154
		Science	.189	.067
		ET	.261*	.011
Evaluation	94	Math	.113	.279
		Science	.082	.431
		ET	.081	.436
Decomposition	94	Math	.356**	.000
		Science	.213*	.039
		ET	.356**	.000
Generalization	94	Math	.319**	.000
		Science	.223*	.031
		ET	.272**	.008

$*p < .05$, $**p < .01$
Source: Huang, Shih et al. (2019).

with decomposition and generalization skills. ET are correlated with only the algorithm skill. It indicates that the interdisciplinary robotic game is significant for students' CT skills in decomposition, abstraction, and generalization. The students were highly motivated in their problem-solving tasks even without extrinsic rewards and scores.

NAVIGATION ROUTE ANALYSIS

The students' CT skills are not only evident from the questionnaires but also demonstrated in their performances in the game. In each round of the game, all the groups have to predict their navigation routes and place markers on the map as the targeted destinations. After they take actions to mobilize the robots, their actual destinations are recorded for comparison. The students' predicted path and actual path of the navigation routes are documented to assess their spatial concepts, judgments of distances and angles, calculation of the robots' speeds, and the students' programming skills (figure 12.4).

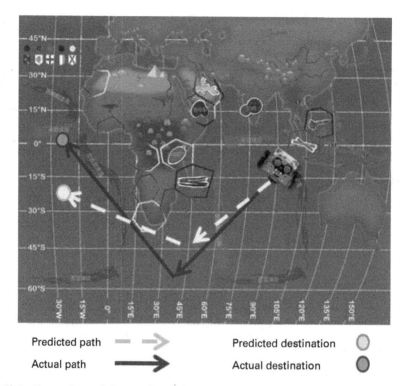

Predicted path   – – ⟹   Predicted destination   ◯

Actual path   ⟹   Actual destination   ●

12.4 Comparison of the predicted destination and actual destination of the mBot navigation.

The formula of the Pythagorean theorem is used to calculate the distance between the student's predicted destination and the actual destination of every navigation. The formula is as in figure 12.5.

In the study (Huang, Huang, et al. 2019), students took four rounds to complete the tasks in the game (figure 12.6). Round 1 involved mostly straight lines to reach the destinations, so the students performed fair and similarly to each other. Round 2 involved making turns, so the measurement and calculation to angles had added complexity. Therefore, the differences between their predicted destinations and actual destinations become larger; the varieties of students' CT abilities were shown. In round 3, students seemed to be more familiar with the measuring and coding processes, and the distances were greatly reduced. Their performances reached peaks at this stage. Thereafter in round 4, their performances remained consistent and stable since the tasks become a routine. From the overall results, it can

The distance between predicted path to actual path:

$$D = \sqrt{|PA^2 - PP^2|}$$

D = Distance, AP = Actual Path, PP = Predicted Path

12.5 The distance between predicted destination to actual destination.

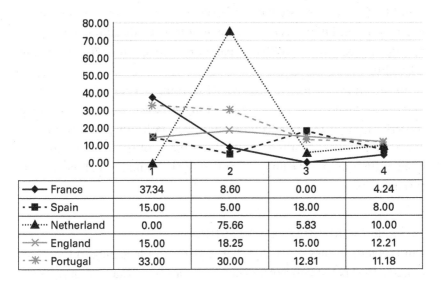

	1	2	3	4
◆ France	37.34	8.60	0.00	4.24
■ Spain	15.00	5.00	18.00	8.00
▲ Netherland	0.00	75.66	5.83	10.00
✳ England	15.00	18.25	15.00	12.21
✱ Portugal	33.00	30.00	12.81	11.18

12.6 The distance between the predicted path and the actual path (Huang, Huang et al. 2019).

be seen that all groups had obvious improvements along the game and they all reached the expected learning outcomes at the end of the game. The students' predicted paths almost match the actual paths of the navigation routes. The game allowed them to continually improve CT skills to the last round.

DISCUSSION AND CONCLUSION

A FRAMEWORK FOR SITUATIVE CT

The game <STEMport> normally runs for sixty to ninety minutes, depending on the level of students' prior knowledge in all aspects. However, the extended curriculum can range from a few hours to a few months. It can be implemented in a short-term student club or camp; it can also be implemented within the structure of formal education as theme-based curriculum or be mentally linked to the curriculum of all subjects. Papert (1980) argued that robotics activities have tremendous potential to improve classroom teaching. Although the classroom teaching he referred to might mean a very different education system from those practiced in Asian countries, what brought us to the same conclusion is that learning is most effective when students are experiencing and discovering things for themselves. Either inside or outside of formal education system, the robotic activities have positive impacts on both specific CT and generic CT abilities.

To construct an effective situative CT learning environment, a few suggestions are given to the instructional designer. One has to set up narrative scenario, provide dynamic context and open tasks for problem-solving, encourage creative solutions, create the demand of negotiations and use of algorithms, and make links to content or skills taught in other domain specific classes.

INTERPRETATION TO PREVIOUS STUDIES

Our previous studies concluded that students in the game can learn and practice the spatial concepts; measure the angles, distances, and speed; as well as solve the navigation problems, all of which increased students' CT skills. However, particular CT dimensions can better predict students' gaming outcomes, especially algorithm. Therefore, it is necessary for us to help the students to increase their algorithm skills so that they can accomplish more in the strategic game and problem-solving tasks and can have better learning performance in general. More dimensions of CT skills should be reinforced in our pre-activity training, such as decomposition of problems, abstraction for concept searching and solutions, and generalization of strategies to other situations. Thus, it is critical to sharing the elements of CT with other disciplines and prepare students for the future.

One of our major contributions is the proposal of an interdisciplinary robotic game-based learning approach that guides students to face dynamic problem situations in an effective and enjoyable manner. From students' feedback, they were generally excited and immersed in playing <STEMport>, which stimulated their interests in related domain learning.

It is a joyful mode of learning that also advances their collaboration, creativity, and self-confidence as they work together in the group for the common goals.

EXTENDING LEARNING INTO THE FUTURE

From other research (e.g., Domínguez et al. 2013), we see that students completed the gamified experience and got better scores in practical assignments and in overall performances. To nurture our next generations with CT competencies, many countries have started spiral interdisciplinary curriculum for students at young ages (e.g., Apostolellis et al. 2014; Bocconi et al. 2016; Shih et al. 2017). Taiwan is no exception and introduced CT in the new curriculum plan to be implemented beginning in August 2019, believing a high-quality computing education can guide the students to understand and change the world just as proposed in the United States (U.S. Office of Educational Technology 2016).

In our study, games helped students to integrate and reinforce existing knowledge and skills in an interdisciplinary way. Just like Barak and Assal (2018) said, this robotic learning environment and the pedagogical approach of involving the students in rich assignments of growing complexity were among the major factors that contributed to students' continuation in learning. Robotics is a learning tool that enhances students' experience through hands-on, mind-on learning that, when combined with project-based and goal-oriented learning experiences, has longlasting impacts on students' learning and motivation for further exploring in STEM-related fields (Eguchi 2010).

Since all the previous studies were short-term activities, it would be meaningful to know whether the students experience better performance in their formal classes after playing the game. Thereafter, linking more content into the regular formal curriculum and doing long-term observation and investigation will be our next step. This game and the related curriculum have successfully been adopted and transformed in several mutations in many elementary schools in Taiwan. We are ready to take the anthropological perspective to look into students' behavioral changes in this innovative and student-centered classroom and to analyze how their personality traits would influence how they take on the role-play and their actions. The humanistic approach for instructional and learning analytics would help us to understand, respect, communicate, and work with others better and to comprehend different individuals and cultures. The understanding of empowered education would sustain students for lifelong learning and would help us to be connected to the "worlds," to adapt to the "differences," and to make positive changes either in education or life.

ACKNOWLEDGMENTS

This study is supported in part by the Ministry of Science and Technology of Taiwan, under MOST 104–2628-S-008–002-MY4. Thanks are due to my research team for contributions to this and several previous studies.

REFERENCES

Afari, Ernest, and Myint Swe Khine. 2017. "Robotics as an Educational Tool: Impact of LEGO Mindstorms." *International Journal of Information and Education Technology* 7 (6): 437–442.

Apostolellis, Panagiotis, Michael Stewart, Chris Frisina, and Dennis Kafura. 2014. "RaBit EscAPE: A Board Game for Computational Thinking." In *Proceeding ICD'14: Proceedings of the 2014 Conference on Interaction Design and Children*. New York, 349–352.

Atmatzidou, Soumela, and Stavros Demetriadis. 2016. "Advancing Students' Computational Thinking Skills through Educational Robotics: A Study on Age and Gender Relevant Differences." *Robotics and Autonomous Systems* 75: 661–670.

Barak, Moshe, and Muhammad Assal. 2018. "Robotics and STEM Learning: Students' Achievements in Assignments according to the P3 Task Taxonomy—Practice, Problem Solving, and Projects." *International Journal of Technology and Design Education*, 28 (1): 121–144.

Bers, Marina Umaschi, Louise Flannery, Elizabeth R. Kazakoff, and Amanda Sullivan. 2014. "Computational Thinking and Tinkering: Exploration of an Early Childhood Robotics Curriculum." *Computers & Education* 72: 145–157.

Blanchard, Samuel, Viktor Freiman, and Nicole Lirrete-Pitre. 2010. "Strategies Used by Elementary Schoolchildren Solving Robotics-Based Complex Tasks: Innovative Potential of Technology." *Procedia Social and Behavioral Science* 2 (2): 2851–2857.

Bocconi, Stefania, Augusto Chioccariello, Giuliana Dettori, Anusca Ferrari, and Katja Engelhardt. 2016. *Developing Computational Thinking in Compulsory Education-Implications for Policy and Practice* (No. JRC104188). Luxembourg: Publications Office of the European Union.

Breiner, Jonathan M., Shelly Sheats Harkness, Carla C. Johnson, and Catherine M. Koehler. 2012. "What Is STEM? A Discussion about Conceptions of STEM in Education and Partnerships." *School Science and Mathematics* 112 (1): 3–11.

Brennan, Karen, and Mitchell Resnick. (2012). "New Frameworks for Studying and Assessing the Development of Computational Thinking." In *Proceedings of 2012 Annual Meeting of the American Educational Research Association (AERA'12)*. Vancouver, BC, 1–25.

Chambers, Joan M., Mike Carbonaro, and Marion Rex. 2007. "Scaffolding Knowledge Construction through Robotic Technology: A Middle School Case Study." *Electronic Journal for the Integration of Technology in Education* 6: 55–70.

Chen, Guanhua, Ji Shen, Lauren Barth-Cohen, Shiyan Jiang, Xiaoting Huang, and Moataz Eltoukhy. 2017. "Assessing Elementary Students' Computational Thinking in Everyday Reasoning and Robotics Programming." *Computers & Education* 109: 162–175.

Chu, Yuan-Kai, Jyh-Chong Liang, and Meng-Jung Tsai. 2019. "Development of a Computational Thinking Scale for Programming." In *Proceedings of the International Conference on Computational Thinking Education 2019*, edited by Siu-Cheung Kong, Diana Andone, Gautam Biswas, Heinz Ulrich Hoppe, Ting-Chia Hsu, Ronghuai Huang, and Bor-Chen Kuo, et al. Hong Kong: The Education University of Hong Kong, 185–189.

Curzon, Paul, Jonathan Black, Laura R. Meagher, and Peter W. McOwan. (2009). "cs4fn.org: Enthusing Students about Computer Science." In *Proceedings of Informatics Education Europe IV*, edited by Christoph Hermann, Tobias Lauer, Thomas Ottmann, and Martina Welte. Freiburg, Germany: Informatics Europe, 73–80.

Curzon, Paul, Mark Dorling, Thomas Ng, Cynthia Selby, and John Woollard. 2014. *Developing Computational Thinking in the Classroom: A Framework*. Swindon, UK: Computing At School.

Dagiené, Valentina, Sue Sentence, and Gabrielė Stupurienė. 2017. "Developing a Two-Dimensional Categorization System for Educational Tasks." *Informatica* 28 (1): 23–44.

Deschryver, Michael, and Aman Yadav. 2015. "Creative and Computational Thinking in the Context of New Literacies: Working with Teachers to Scaffold Complex Technology Mediated Approaches to Teaching and Learning." *Journal of Technology and Teacher Education* 23 (3): 411–431.

Domínguez, Adrián, Joseba Saenz-de-Navarrete, Luis de-Marcos, Luis Fernández-Sanz, Carmen Pagés, and José-Javier Martínez-Herráiz. 2013. "Gamifying Learning Experiences: Practical Implications and Outcomes." *Computers & Education* 63: 380–392.

Eguchi, Amy. 2010. "What Is Educational Robotics? Theories behind It and Practical Implementation." In *Proceedings of Society of Information Technology & Teacher Education International Conference*, edited by David Gibson and Bernie Dodge. Chesapeake, VA: Association for the Advancement of Computing in Education, AACE, 4006–4014.

Frymier, Ann Bainbridge, Gary M. Shulman, and Marian Houser. 1996. "The Development of a Learner Empowerment Measure." *Communication Education* 45 (3): 181–199.

Gee, James P. 2003. "What Video Games Have to Teach Us about Learning and Literacy." *Computers in Entertainment* 1 (1): 20.

Honey, Margaret, Greg Pearson, and Heidi Schweingruber. 2014. *STEM Integration in K–12 Education: Status, Prospects, and an Agenda for Research*. Washington, DC: The National Academies Press.

Huang, Hsin-Yin, Shu-Hsien Huang, Ju-Ling Shih, Meng-Jung Tsai, and Jyh-Chong Liang. 2019. "Exploring the Role of Algorithm in Elementary School Students' Computational Thinking Skills from a Robotic Game." In *Proceedings of the International Conference on Computational Thinking Education 2019*, edited by Siu-Cheung Kong, Diana Andone, Gautam Biswas, Heinz Ulrich Hoppe, Ting-Chia Hsu, Ronghuai Huang, and Bor-Chen Kuo, et al. Hong Kong: The Education University of Hong Kong, 217–222.

Huang, Hsin-Yin, Ju-Ling Shih, Shu-Hsien Huang, and Jyh-Chong Liang. 2019. "Effects of the Interdisciplinary Robotic Game to Elementary School Students' Abilities of Computational Thinking and STEM." In *Proceedings of the 27th International Conference on Computers in Education*, edited by Maiga Chang et al. Taiwan: Asia-Pacific Society for Computers in Education, 95–103.

Kong, Siu Cheung, Ming Chiu, and Ming Lai. (2018). "A Study of Primary School Students' Interest, Collaboration Attitude, and Programming Empowerment in Computational Thinking Education." *Computers & Education* 127: 178–189.

Lin, Chang-Hsin, Shu-Hsien Huang, Ju-Ling Shih, Alexandra Covaci, and Gheorghita Ghinea. 2017. "Game-Based Learning Effectiveness and Motivation Study between Competitive and Cooperative Modes." In *Proceedings of 2017 IEEE 17th International Conference on Advanced Learning Technologies (ICALT)*. Timisoara, Romania, 123–127.

Lou, Shi Jer, C. Ray Diez, Hsi Chi Hsiao, Wen Hsiung Wu, and Shu-Hsuan Chang. 2009. "A Study on the Changes of Attitude toward STEM among Senior High School Girl Students in Taiwan." Paper presented at *2009 ASEE Annual Conference and Exposition*. Austin, TX.

Nourbakhsh, Illah, Kevin Crowley, Ajinkya Bhave, Emily Hamner, Thomas Hsiu, Andres Perez-Bergquist, Steve Richards, and Katie Wilkinson. 2005. "The Robotic Autonomy Mobile Robotics Course: Robot Design, Curriculum Design and Educational Assessment." *Autonomous Robots* 18 (1): 103–127.

Papert, Seymour. (1980). *Mindstorms: Children, Computers, and Powerful Idea*. New York: Basic Books.

Park, Juneyoung, Seunghyun Kim, Auk Kim, and Munyong Yi. 2019. "Learning to Be Better at the Game: Performance vs. Completion Contingent Reward for Game-Based Learning." *Computers & Education*, 139: 1–15.

Perrotta, Carlo, Gill Featherstone, Helen Aston, and Emily Houghton. 2013. *Game-Based Learning: Latest Evidence and Future Directions*. Slough, UK: National Foundation for Educational Research.

Petre, Marian, and Blaine Price. 2004. "Using Robotics to Motivate 'Back Door' Learning." *Education and Information Technologies* 9 (2): 147–158.

Qian, Meihua, and Karen R. Clark. 2016. "Game-Based Learning and 21st Century Skills: A Review of Recent Research." *Computers in Human Behavior* 63: 50–58.

Rogers, Chris, and Portsmore, Merredith. 2004. "Bringing Engineering to Elementary School." *Journal of STEM Education: Innovations and Research* 5 (3–4): 17–28.

Selby, Cynthia, Mark Dorling, and John Woollard. 2014. *Evidence of Assessing Computational Thinking*. https://eprints.soton.ac.uk/372409/1/372409EvidAssessCT.pdf.

Shih, Ju-Ling, Shu-Hsien Huang, Chang-Hsi Lin, and Chia-Chun Tseng. 2017. "STEAMing the Ships for the Great Voyage: Design and Evaluation of a Technology-integrated Maker Game." *Interaction Design and Architectures* 34: 61–87.

Unfried, Alana, Malinda Faber, Daniel S. Stanhope, and Eric Wiebe. 2015. "The Development and Validation of a Measure of Student Attitudes toward Science, Technology, Engineering, And Math (S-STEM)." *Journal of Psychoeducational Assessment* 33 (7): 622–639.

U.S. Office of Educational Technology. 2016. *Future Ready Learning: Reimagining the Role of Technology in Education*. U.S. Department of Education. http://tech.ed.gov.

Voogt, Joke, Petra Fisser, Jon Good, Punya Mishra, and Aman Yadav. 2015. "Computational Thinking in Compulsory Education: Towards an Agenda for Research and Practice." *Education and Information Technologies* 20 (4): 715–728.

Voskoglou, Michael Gr., and Sheryl Buckley. 2012. "Problem Solving and Computers in a Learning Environment." *Egyptian Computer Science Journal, ECS* 36 (4): 28–46.

Wing, Jeannette M. 2006. "Computational Thinking." *Communications of the ACM* 49 (3): 33–35.

Wing, Jeannette M. 2008. "Computational Thinking and Thinking about Computing." *Philosophical Transactions of the Royal Society A: Mathematical, Physical and Engineering Sciences* 366 (1881): 3717–3725.

Wing, Jeannette M. 2014. *Computational Thinking Benefits Society* (blog). http://socialissues.cs.toronto.edu.

ADDITIONAL READINGS ON CT EDUCATION FOR K-12

Angeli, Charoula, Joke Voogt, Andrew Fluck, Mary Webb, Margaret Cox, Joyce Malyn-Smith, and Jason Zagami. 2016. "A K-6 Computational Thinking Curriculum Framework: Implications for Teacher Knowledge." *Educational Technology & Society* 19 (3): 47–57.

Berland, Matthew, and Uri Wilensky. 2015. "Comparing Virtual and Physical Robotics Environments for Supporting Complex Systems and Computational Thinking." *Journal of Science Education and Technology* 24 (5): 628–647.

Buitrago Flórez, Francisco, Rubby Casallas, Marcela Hernández, Alejandro Reyes, Silvia Restrepo, and Giovanna Danies. 2017. "Changing a Generation's Way of Thinking: Teaching Computational Thinking through Programming." *Review of Educational Research* 87 (4): 834–860.

Chen, Guanhua, Ji Shen, Lauren Barth-Cohen, Shiyan Jiang, Xiaoting Huang, and Moataz Eltoukhy. 2017. "Assessing Elementary Students' Computational Thinking in Everyday Reasoning and Robotics Programming." *Computers & Education* 109: 162–175.

Curzon, Paul, Tim Bell, Jane Waite, and Mark Dorling. 2019. "Computational Thinking." In *The Cambridge Handbook of Computing Education Research*, edited by Sally A. Fincher and Anthony V. Robins, 513–546. Cambridge: Cambridge University Press.

Denning, Peter. 2017. "Remaining Trouble Spots with Computational Thinking." *Communications of the ACM* 80 (6): 33–39.

Durak, Hatice Yildiz, and Mustafa Saritepeci. 2018. "Analysis of the Relation between Computational Thinking Skills and Various Variables with the Structural Equation Model." *Computers and Education* 116: 191–202.

Erstad, Ola, Birgit Eickelmann, and Koos Eichhorn. 2015. "Preparing Teachers for Schooling in the Digital Age: A Meta-Perspective on Existing Strategies and Future Challenges." *Education and Information Technologies* 20 (4): 641–654.

Gadanidis, George. 2017. "Five Affordances of Computational Thinking to Support Elementary Mathematics Education." *Journal of Computers in Mathematics and Science Teaching* 36 (2): 143–151.

Grover, Shuchi, and Roy Pea. 2013. "Computational Thinking in K–12: A Review of the State of the Field." *Educational Researcher* 42 (1): 38–43.

Guzdial, Mark. 2019. "Computing for Other Disciplines." In *The Cambridge Handbook of Computing Education Research*, edited by Sally A. Fincher and Anthony V. Robins, 584–605. Cambridge: Cambridge University Press.

Israel, Maya, Jamie N. Pearson, Tanya Tapia, Quentin M. Wherfel, and George Reese. 2015. "Supporting All Learners in School-Wide Computational Thinking: A Cross-Case Qualitative Analysis." *Computers and Education* 82: 263–279.

Kafai, Yasmin B., and Quinn Burke. 2014. *Connected Code: Why Children Need to Learn Programming.* Cambridge, MA: MIT Press.

Kafura, Dennis, Austin Cory Bart, and Bushra Chowdhury. 2018. "A Computational Thinking Course Accessible to Non-STEM Majors." *Journal of Computing Sciences in Colleges* 34 (2): 157–163.

Lévy, Pierre. 1994. *L'intelligence Collective. Pour une Anthropologie du Cyberespace [Collective Intelligence: Mankind's Emerging World in Cyberspace].* Paris: La Découverte.

Lye, Sze Yee, and Joyce Hwee Ling Koh. 2014. "Review on Teaching and Learning of Computational Thinking through Programming: What Is Next for K–12?" *Computers in Human Behavior* 41: 51–61.

Marope, Mmantsetsa. 2017. "Future Competences for Future Generations." *UNESCO International Bureau of Education: In Focus, 2.* Accessed May 11, 2020. http://ibe-infocus.org/wp-content/uploads/2018/03/In-Focus-2017.pdf.

Merkouris, Alexandros, Konstantinos Chorianopoulos, and Achilles Kameas. 2017. "Teaching Programming in Secondary Education through Embodied Computing Platforms: Robotics and Wearables." *ACM Transactions on Computing Education* 17 (2): 9.1–9.22.

Pérez, Arnulfo. 2018. "A Framework for Computational Thinking Dispositions in Mathematics Education." *Journal for Research in Mathematics Education* 49 (4): 424–461.

Porayska-Pomsta, Kaśka. 2016. "AI as a Methodology for Supporting Educational Praxis and Teacher Metacognition." *International Journal of Artificial Intelligence in Education* 26 (2): 679–700.

Przybylla, Mareen, & Ralf Romeike. 2014. "Physical Computing and Its Scope—Towards a Constructionist Computer Science Curriculum with Physical Computing." *Informatics in Education* 13 (2): 225–240.

Román-González, Marcos, Juan-Carlos Pérez-González, and Carmen Jiménez-Fernández. 2017. "Which Cognitive Abilities Underlie Computational Thinking? Criterion Validity of the Computational Thinking Test." *Computers in Human Behavior* 72: 678–691.

Sandoval, William A., and Philip Bell. 2004. "Design-Based Research Methods for Studying Learning in Context: Introduction." *Educational Psychologist* 39 (4): 199–201.

Shute, Valerie J., Chen Sun, and Jodi Asbell-Clarke. 2017. "Demystifying Computational Thinking." *Educational Research Review* 22: 142–158.

Singer-Gabella, Marcy, Barbara Stengel, Emily Shahan, and Min-Joung Kim. 2016. "Learning to Leverage Student Thinking: What Novice Approximations Teach Us about Ambitious Practice." *Elementary School Journal* 116 (3): 411–436.

Sullivan, Florence R., and John Heffernan. 2016. "Robotic Construction Kits as Computational Manipulatives for Learning in the STEM Disciplines." *Journal of Research on Technology in Education* 48 (2): 105–128.

Sung, Woonhee, Junghyun Ahn, and John Black. 2017. "Introducing Computational Thinking to Young Learners: Practicing Computational Perspectives through Embodiment in Mathematics Education." *Technology, Knowledge and Learning* 22 (3): 443–463.

Tan, Jennifer Pei-Ling, Suzanne S. Choo, Trivina Kang, and Gregory Arief D. Liem. 2017. "Educating for Twenty-First Century Competencies and Future-Ready Learners: Research Perspectives from Singapore." *Asia Pacific Journal of Education* 37 (4): 425–436.

Tatar, Deborah. 2007. "The Design-Tension Framework." *Human–Computer Interaction* 22 (4): 413–451.

Taylor, Kellie, and Youngkyun Baek. 2019. "Grouping Matters in Computational Robotic Activities." *Computers in Human Behavior* 93: 99–105.

Tuhkala, Ari, Marie-Louise Wagner, Ole Sejer Iversen, and Tommi Kärkkäinen. 2019. "Technology Comprehension—Combining Computing, Design, and Societal Reflection as a National Subject." *International Journal of Child-Computer Interaction* 20: 54–63.

Turchi, Tommaso, Daniela Fogli, and Alessio Malizia. 2019. "Fostering Computational Thinking through Collaborative Game-Based Learning." *Multimedia Tools and Applications* 78 (10): 13649–13673.

Vahrenhold, Jan, Quintin Cutts, and Katrina Falkner. 2019. "Schools (K–12)." In *The Cambridge Handbook of Computing Education Research*, edited by Sally A. Fincher and Anthony V. Robins, 547–583. Cambridge: Cambridge University Press.

Voogt, Joke, Petra Fisser, Jon Good, Punya Mishra, and Aman Yadav. 2015. "Computational Thinking in Compulsory Education: Towards an Agenda for Research and Practice." *Education and Information Technologies* 20 (4): 715–728.

Walker, Caroline, and Alan Gleaves. 2018. "Teaching Computational Thinking." In *Creating the Coding Generation in Primary Schools: A Practical Guide for Cross-Curricular Teaching*, edited by Steve Humble, 22–35. Abingdon, UK: Routledge.

Wang, Tzu-Hua, Kenneth Y. T. Lim, Jari Lavonen, and Alison Clark-Wilson. 2019. "Maker-Centred Science and Mathematics Education: Lenses, Scales and Contexts." *International Journal of Science and Mathematics Education* 17 (Supplement 1): 1–11.

Webb, Mary, Niki Davis, Tim Bell, Yaacov Katz, Nicholas Reynolds, Dianne Chambers, and Maciej Sysło. 2017. "Computer Science in K–12 School Curricula of the 21st Century: Why, What and When?" *Education and Information Technologies* 22 (2): 445–468.

Weintrop, David, Elham Beheshti, Michael Horn, Kai Orton, Kemi Jona, Laura Trouille, and Uri Wilensky. 2016. "Defining Computational Thinking for Mathematics and Science Classrooms." *Journal of Science Education and Technology* 25 (1): 127–147.

Whitherspoon, Eben, Ross Higashi, Christian Schunn, Emily Baehr, and Robin Shoop. 2018. "Developing Computational Thinking through a Virtual Robotics Programming Curriculum." *ACM Transactions on Computing Education* 18 (1): 4.1–4.20.

CONTRIBUTORS

Harold Abelson Department of Electrical Engineering and Computer Science, Massachusetts Institute of Technology

Cynthia Breazeal MIT Media Lab, Massachusetts Institute of Technology

Karen Brennan Harvard Graduate School of Education, Harvard University

Michael E. Caspersen IT-vest—Networking Universities, Denmark

Christian Dindler Center for Computational Thinking and Design, Aarhus University

Daniella DiPaola MIT Media Lab, Massachusetts Institute of Technology

Nardie Fanchamps Fontys University of Applied Science

Christina Gardner-McCune Computer & Information Science & Engineering Department, University of Florida

Mark Guzdial Computer Science & Engineering Division, University of Michigan

Kai Hakkarainen Department of Education, University of Helsinki

Fredrik Heintz Department of Computer and Information Science, Linköping University

Paul Hennissen Zuyd University of Applied Science

H. Ulrich Hoppe Faculty of Engineering, University of Duisburg-Essen

Ole Sejer Iversen Center for Computational Thinking and Design, Aarhus University

Siu-Cheung Kong Centre for Learning, Teaching and Technology, The Education University of Hong Kong

Wai-Ying Kwok Centre for Learning, Teaching and Technology, The Education University of Hong Kong

Sven Manske Faculty of Engineering, University of Duisburg-Essen

Jesús Moreno-León Programamos.es, Spain

Blakeley H. Payne MIT Media Lab, Massachusetts Institute of Technology

Sini Riikonen Faculty of Educational Sciences, University of Helsinki

Gregorio Robles Universidad Rey Juan Carlos (URJC)

Marcos Román-González Faculty of Education, Universidad Nacional de Educación a Distancia (UNED), Spain

Pirita Seitamaa-Hakkarainen Department of Teacher Education, University of Helsinki

Ju-Ling Shih Graduate Institute of Network Learning Technology, National Central University, Taiwan

Pasi Silander Department of Teacher Education, University of Helsinki

Lou Slangen Fontys University of Applied Science

Rachel Charlotte Smith Center for Computational Thinking and Design, Aarhus University

Marcus Specht Leiden-Delft-Erasmus Center for Education and Learning, Delft University of Technology

Florence R. Sullivan College of Education, University of Massachusetts

David S. Touretzky Computer Science Department, Carnegie Mellon University

INDEX